COUNTRYMAN
TRAVELERS

CUBA
BY BIKE

36 RIDES ACROSS
THE CARIBBEAN'S LARGEST ISLAND

D0950599

COUNTRYMAN
TRAVELERS

CUBA
BY BIKE

36 RIDES ACROSS
THE CARIBBEAN'S LARGEST ISLAND

CASSANDRA BROOKLYN

THE COUNTRYMAN PRESS

A division of W. W. Norton & Company

Independent Publishers Since 1923

Copyright © 2020 by Cassandra Brooklyn

Maps by Michael Borop (sitesatlas.com)
Map data © OpenStreetMap contributors

All rights reserved
Printed in the United States of America

For information about permission to reproduce selections from this book, write to Permissions, The Countryman Press, 500 Fifth Avenue, New York, NY 10110

For information about special discounts for bulk purchases, please contact W. W. Norton Special Sales at specialsales@wwnorton.com or 800-233-4830

Manufacturing by Versa Press

The Countryman Press
www.countrymanpress.com

A division of W. W. Norton & Company, Inc.
500 Fifth Avenue, New York, NY 10110
www.wwnorton.com

978-1-68268-307-1 (pbk.)

10 9 8 7 6 5 4 3 2 1

This book is dedicated to all of my Cuban friends who have helped me—and continue to help me— learn about, appreciate, and navigate their beautiful country. It is also dedicated to every stranger I met along the way who gave me directions, cheered me on, helped me repair my bicycle, gave me a lift during a torrential downpour, or simply shared a story and put a smile on my face. A special thank-you goes out to Jaime, Elizabeth, Felix, Francy, Osmara, Orlando, Didier, Sigfredo, Ermes, Jesus, and Luis. Gracias, amigos, y un abrazo enorme de Nueva York.

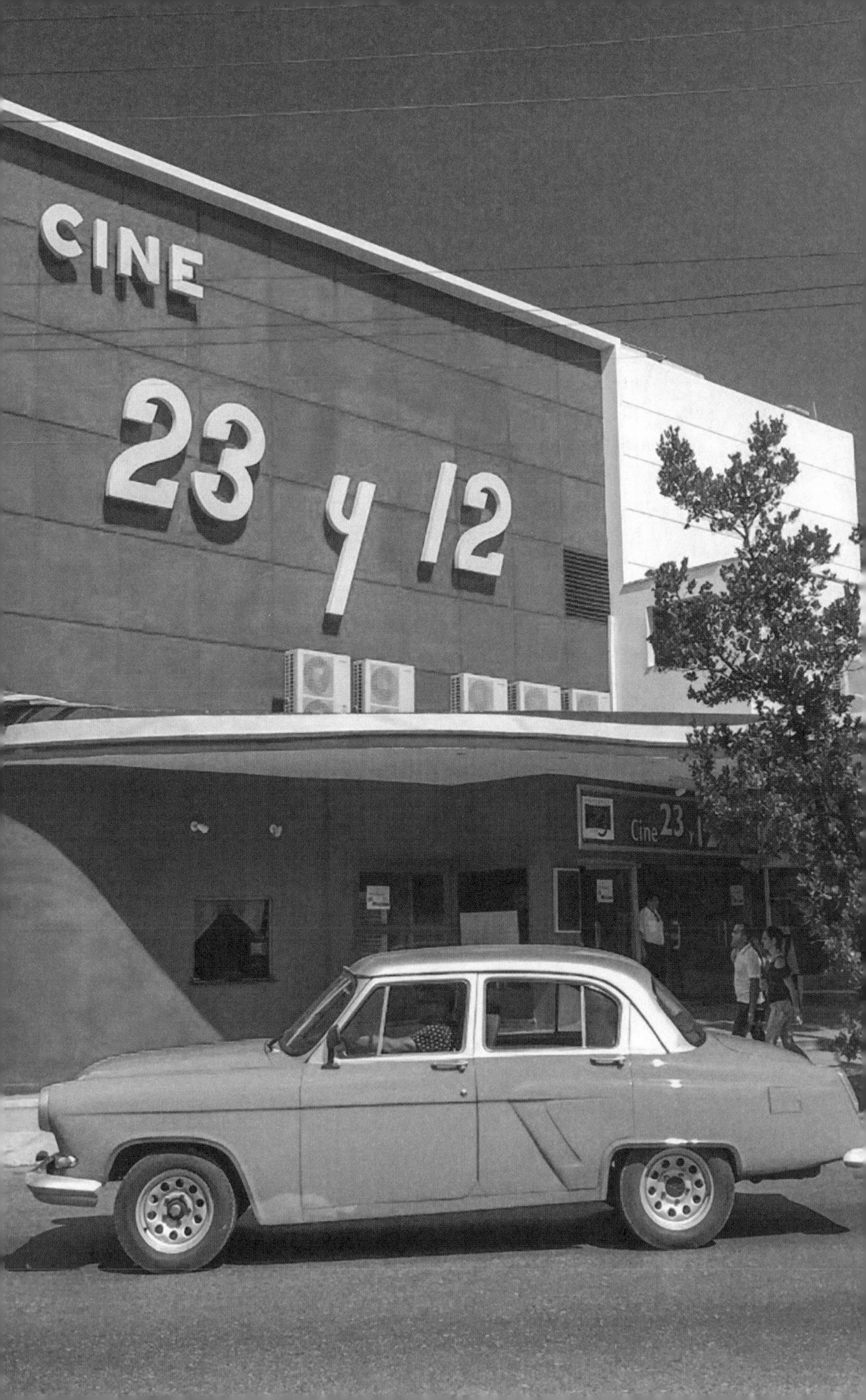
CINE
23 y 12
Cine 23

Contents

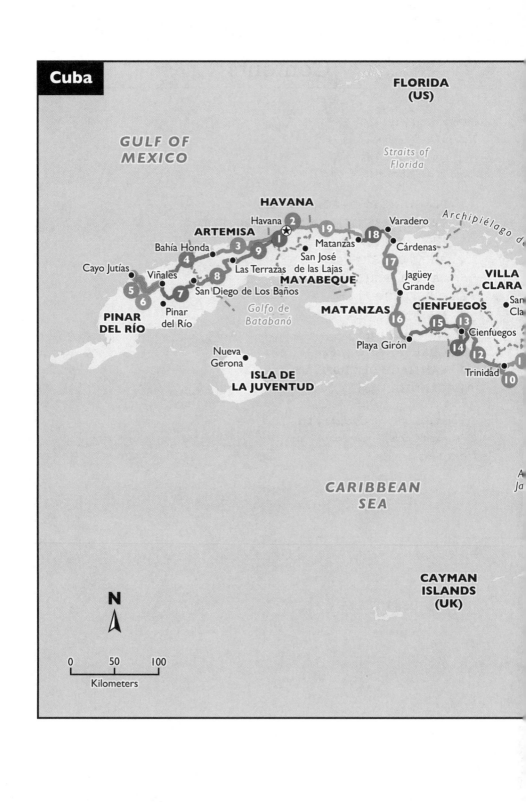

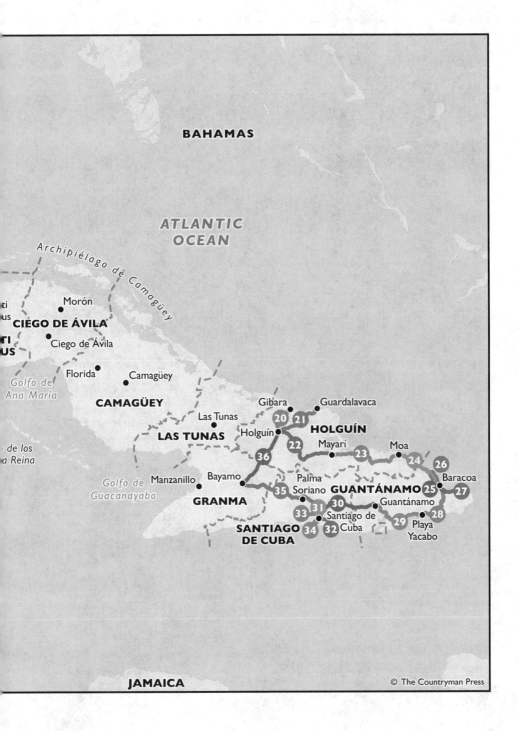

Introduction

Excellent cycling opportunities exist all over Cuba, among various geographical landscapes, and across all different skill levels. No matter your specific cycling preferences or bike-touring experience, it's possible to plan a cycling trip to Cuba that is full of breathtaking landscapes, rich history, and loads of Caribbean culture.

This book details and maps out a selection of the best rides in the country. By no means does it include every single ride in Cuba. The rides range from one-hour city tours to day trips to multiday tours of various levels of difficulty. In addition to suggestions for how to plan your trip and what to pack, this book also provides historical and cultural context and gives recommendations for where to stay and eat, how to transport your bike, and how to stay healthy on your trip.

At 110,860 square kilometers (42,800 square miles), Cuba is the largest country in the Caribbean. Initially home to Taíno indigenous people who came from Puerto Rico and Hispaniola (now Haiti and the Dominican Republic), Cuba was settled in the 1500s by Spanish conquistadors who brought slaves with them from Western Africa. Cuba's strong African roots are most evident in the eastern part of the island, influencing everything from music and dance to religion and language.

Economically, Cuba is a bit of an oddball. One can easily cycle from First to Third World conditions in a few short hours, leaving luxury beachfront hotels behind for modest rural homes that lack indoor plumbing and look as though an afternoon thunderstorm could blow them away. The United States' 57-year ongoing trade embargo against Cuba has crippled the island's ability to develop capitalism and made it difficult for Cubans to access medication, food, and other basic necessities. Low wages across state jobs, ranging from doctors and lawyers to teachers and engineers, are driving professionals to abandon their trade to work in the ever-growing tourist industry.

Many Cuban roads are in good condition, and cyclists are respected and given space. In fact, the rightmost lanes on highways are dedicated to slow vehicles, such as bicycles and horse-drawn carts. Most recreational cyclists can be found in the Havana, Pinar del Río, and Matanzas provinces in the west, and in the Holguín, Santiago de Cuba, and Guantánamo provinces in the east. Single women on touring bikes, young couples on road bikes, older couples on recumbent bikes, groups of friends on mountain bikes, and families towing children behind them in trailers can all be spotted throughout Cuba. Road signage has improved in recent years, but some locations, including some routes in this book, still lack signage at major turnoffs. Lucky for you, there's almost always a friendly Cuban around who would be happy to point you in the right direction.

Three mountain ranges—the Sierra Maestra (eastern), Sierra del Rosario (western), and the Escambray Mountains (south central)—offer challenging and rewarding cycling, while countless semidesert and beachfront coastlines offer flatter pedaling opportunities. It's completely possible to tour Cuba by bike without having to traverse difficult mountain routes. It's also possible to plan a route that avoids completely flat sections. Either way, you are sure to soak in incredible scenery and meet some of the friendliest people in the world.

Cuban tour buses and *colectivos* (shared taxis) are equipped to transport cyclists (with their bikes!) who want to explore multiple provinces but who may not have enough time to do the entire route on two wheels.

Off-bike adventures range from scuba diving and mountain hiking to horseback riding and zip lining. Larger resorts also offer waterskiing, deep-sea fishing, and yachting. If you'd like to explore additional activities beyond cycling (which I strongly recommend doing), be sure to include time for it in your touring schedule.

Cuba is incredibly photogenic. I have thousands of pictures of Cuba that would not fit in this book. Additional pictures I took while bike-touring Cuba (and also while hitchhiking, taking buses/colectivos, and leading group tours there) can be found on my website: www.escapingny.com.

How to Use This Book

There is no single way to use this book. You may follow the routes to the letter, link together portions of several rides, or simply use the book to gather ideas to create your own route. The intention of this book is to detail the best rides in Cuba (in terms of riding and things to do), not *all* rides in Cuba. Should you choose to explore routes not included here, it is highly recommended that you purchase the Cuban highway guide listed in the "What to Bring" section (page 31). This is especially true if you plan to explore rural areas and regions that receive few tourists and thus have less tourism infrastructure.

Conditions are constantly changing, and you may find that prices increase, schedules change, dirt roads become paved, well-paved roads are destroyed by hurricanes, new businesses open, and old ones close. In addition, the Cuban government has been considering combining the country's two currencies into one for several years, which may affect how prices included in this book are understood. If you find conditions different from what's detailed in here, please contact me at cassandra@escapingny.com so that the next edition can be even more useful and accurate.

RIDE DESCRIPTIONS

Each section begins with background information and ride details. The day's ride is summarized and route highlights are detailed in the text as well as being marked on the map and cue sheets. At the end of each day, recommendations are given for where to stay, what to do, and where to eat, along with where to find banks, ATMs, and tourist information. As visitors centers are rare in Cuba, rides typically begin and end at well-known local landmarks such as parks, plazas, and hotels.

Most rides in this book are accompanied by a map that shows the route, indicates amenities provided in towns along the route, and highlights attractions and possible side trips. Each ride also includes an elevation chart that shows steep ascents and descents. These charts are approximate and should be used as guides.

MAP LEGENDS

Route directions are given in a series of brief "cues," which tell you at which kilometer mark to change direction. The cues are also indicated along the route map. Particularly challenging cues may be described in more detail in the ride description. For cue sheets to be as brief and easy to understand as possible, a series of symbols will be used on the cue sheet to help indicate directions.

Once you're following a particular road, stay on that road until the cue sheet tells you differently. Rely on the cues to tell you when to turn. Continue on the road first mentioned in the cue, even though it may narrow, broaden, wind, cross a highway, merge with another road, or change names (name changes are typically also indicated in the cue sheet or ride description).

Distances are approximate and vary across cycling computers and GPS trackers; use them only as guides. To follow the routes as closely as possible, disconnect or pause your cycling computer/GPS tracker whenever you deviate from the main route.

Directions

Start		Capitolio
0 km		Go north on Paseo de Martí
1.1	↰	Malecón
4.3	★	US Embassy
7.4	↱	Tunnel, "PROHIBIDO" sign
7.6	↰	Follow curve left around tunnel
7.7	↑	Continue on Calle 24
8	★	Fábrica de Arte Cubano (FAC)
9	↰	Yellow cemetery wall (at T-junction)
9.8	★	Necrópolis Cristóbal Colón
9.8		Follow curve around cemetery
10.6	↱ ⯃	To "Plaza de la Revolución"
11.6	★	Plaza de la Revolución
11.7	↰	Av. de la Independencia
12.6	↱	Salvador Allende (Carlos III) to "Centro Histórico"
13.8	↘	Merge onto main road
14.6	↰	Águila (unmarked)
14.8	↱	Dragones St. / ETECSA Building
15.1	↰	Capitolio
15.6		Hotel Inglaterra

DIRECTION SYMBOLS

↰	Left turn	↑	Continue straight
↘	Veer left	▲	Steep hill
⟲	Left loop	⚠	Caution / danger
↾	Zigzag left	◉	Traffic circle
↱	Right turn	⯃	Traffic light
↱	Veer right	⚲	Start of route
⟳	Right loop	⚲	End of route
↾	Zigzag right		

Highlighted Rides

TABLE OF RIDES

Cuba offers thousands of kilometers of cycling across mountainous, flat, coastal, semidesert, and other types of terrain. Road quality varies, but most roads are paved. While some road conditions are improving, others have significantly declined after being destroyed by hurricanes or decades of neglect. While this book outlines the condition of roads at the time of research, it's always best to check with locals and other bike tourists you may run into to see if there have been any changes. With few exceptions, such as busy corridors in large cities like Havana and Santiago de Cuba, traffic is very light in Cuba.

BEST MOUNTAIN SCENERY

Viñales's trademark *mogotes* (monolithic limestone mounds) easily make this western region the best place for mountain scenery. Whether you're arriving from the northeast from Havana, riding to stunning Cayo Jutías beach, or heading south toward San Diego de los Baños and Las Terrazas, mogotes are inescapable. To see these mountains from the inside, check out the Gran Caverna de San Tomás (15 kilometers southwest of Viñales).

BEST CITY RIDING

Havana is the most populous and most popular city in Cuba, and with good reason! The Havana City Ride takes you through the city's diverse neighborhoods, including charming Old Havana, a UNESCO World Heritage Site, and to must-see sites such as Revolution Plaza and the Cristóbal Colón cemetery. To get an even better sense of this vibrant and diverse city, tack on the Cristo and Cojímar ride, which takes you to quieter parts of the bustling capital.

BEST COASTAL SCENERY

The Southeastern Circuit offers incredible ocean views from a coastal road so close to the water that the surf splashes onto your legs. At the time of writing, much of this route had been so badly damaged by hurricanes that it was barely doable, even with a mountain bike. As such, it is not included in this book, but an abridged guide is provided (page 201), should road conditions improve in the future. On the opposite end of the country, the short route from Varadero to Matanzas offers excellent ocean views, though

CYCLING THROUGH VALLEYS IN VIÑALES

less dramatic than those found in the east. Cyclists with extremely limited time can enjoy coastal scenery in the Havana city ride and Baracoa city ride, which include long stretches around each city's *malecón* (waterfront boulevard).

BEST DESCENT

The La Farola highway stretch between Baracoa and Yacabo, Guantánamo, is steep and astoundingly beautiful! The winding mountain highway clings to cliffs.

BEST ASCENT

The route from San Diego de los Baños to Las Terrazas, and the stretch from Soroa to Las Terrazas in particular, offers very challenging climbs. The most difficult portions come at the end of the day when you're already tired, but the breathtaking views make it worthwhile.

MOST REMOTE

Though Cienfuegos and the Bahía de Cochinos (Bay of Pigs) are both popular tourist destinations (the Bay of Pigs a bit less so), the road connecting the two cities feels completely separated from tourism. Much of the landscape is made up of agricultural fields, dotted with tiny villages where it's almost certain you won't run into a single tourist.

BEST WILDLIFE SPOTTING

Both the Ciénaga Swamp in the Bahía de Cochinos and the Guanaroca Nature Reserve in Cienfuegos are great for wildlife spotting. The Ciénaga Swamp also offers an opportunity to see crocodiles in the wild, while Guanaroca is home to a large flamingo population. In both cases, the best way to see the wildlife is to get up early and tour the area with local guides, on foot. Wildlife viewing is typically best in the morning, so it requires staying in the city for an additional night.

Rides at a Glance

Ride	Distance (kilometers)	Elevation (meters)
1. Havana City Ride	15.6	87
2. Cristo and Cojímar	18.2	232
3. Havana to Bahía Honda	105.4	661
4. Bahía Honda to Viñales	81.8	784
5. Cayo Jutías	58.7	493
6. Cayo Jutías to Viñales	58.7	638
7. Viñales to San Diego de los Baños	65.5	480
8. San Diego de los Baños to Las Terrazas	73.7	787
9. Las Terrazas to Havana	76.1	576
10. Playa Ancón	29.1	139
11. Manaca Iznaga	39.9	376
12. Trinidad to Cienfuegos	82.6	563
13. Cienfuegos City Ride	10.5	87
14. Rancho Luna Beach Ride	24.5	226
15. Cienfuegos to Playa Girón	80	231
16. Playa Girón to Jagüey Grande	63.4	147
17. Jagüey Grande to Varadero	84.7	297
18. Varadero to Matanzas	37	166
19. Matanzas to Havana	94.6	610
20. Holguín to Gibara	34.3	418
21. Holguín to Guardalavaca	58	385
22. Holguín to Mayarí	88.5	676
23. Mayarí to Moa	96.7	1,158
24. Moa to Baracoa	45.6	879
25. Baracoa City Ride	10.5	116
26. Playa Maguana	39.4	267
27. Boca de Yumurí	56	610
28. Baracoa to Imías/Playa Imías	76.4	1,012
29. Imías/Playa Yacabo to Guantánamo	76.4	515
30. Guantánamo to Santiago de Cuba	82.6	735
31. Santiago de Cuba City Ride	10.4	111
32. Playa Siboney	33.5	354
33. Caridad del Cobre	42.2	518
34. El Morro	23	540
35. Santiago de Cuba to Bayamo	128.9	1,207
36. Bayamo to Holguín	73.2	544

Difficulty	Duration	Page #
Easy	1–2 hours	89
Easy to Moderate	2 hours	90
Very Difficult	7–10 hours	92
Very Difficult	7–10 hours	97
Very Difficult	6–8 hours	103
Very Difficult	6–8 hours	104
Difficult	5–7 hours	107
Very Difficult	7–9 hours	109
Moderate	5–7 hours	113
Easy	2 hours	121
Moderate	3–4 hours	123
Difficult	6–8 hours	125
Easy	1–2 hours	130
Moderate	2–3 hours	132
Difficult	5–6 hours	135
Moderate	4–5 hours	137
Difficult	6–8 hours	141
Easy	2–3 hours	145
Difficult	6–8 hours	148
Moderate	3–4 hours	154
Moderate	4–6 hours	157
Difficult	6–9 hours	160
Very Difficult	7–9 hours	162
Very Difficult	7–10 hours	164
Easy	1–2 hours	173
Moderate	2 days	175
Difficult	3–5 hours	177
Very Difficult	7–10 hours	179
Moderate to Difficult	5–7 hours	183
Difficult	7–9 hours	185
Easy	1 hour	195
Moderate	3–4 hours	196
Moderate to Difficult	3–4 hours	199
Moderate	2 hours	200
Very Difficult	8–10 hours	207
Moderate to Difficult	5–7 hours	209

ONE OF MY BIKE TOURS THROUGH HAVANA

1

PLANNING AND PACKING

GETTING TO CUBA BY AIR

The vast majority of tourists arrive in Cuba by flying into José Martí International Airport, 25 kilometers southwest of Havana, or to Juan Gualberto Gómez Airport, 20 kilometers east of Varadero's resorts. A few international carriers also fly to Holguín and Santiago in the east. Cuba's national airline, Cubana, offers cross-country flights between major cities but has a poor record in terms of reliability and service. They've been known to sometimes leave bikes behind, so the most reliable way to cross the country if cycling isn't an option would be by bus or car.

Large international carriers such as Delta, JetBlue, British Airways, Avianca, and Aeromexico are accustomed to transporting boxed bicycles, but smaller airlines using smaller planes may not be able to accommodate bicycles. Confirm before purchasing your ticket—and again with the gate agent—that your bicycle will go on the same plane as you.

Your bike is likely to be inspected before it gets to the baggage conveyor, but you may also be asked to open the bicycle box to show customs inspectors that there is no contraband inside. Cuban airports do not have facilities to store bicycle boxes, and it will be nearly impossible to find another bicycle box on the ground, so you'll want to confirm with your hotel or *casa particular* (Cuban homestay) in advance that you can store your box/suitcase until your return flight.

WHEN TO RIDE

Cuba is hot year-round, but December through March are slightly cooler and receive the least amount of rain, making them the best months to cycle. Noncycling tourists are also drawn to Cuba during these months, making hotel and casa prices higher and the streets more crowded.

April is also a good month but can be less pleasant than December through March. Much of the landscape is still brown in April and spring break typically falls this month, resulting in higher prices and crowded *campismos* (bungalow campgrounds). I've seen several campismos booked to capacity for weeks at a time in April, which can prove problematic for cyclists too tired to make it all the way to casas in larger cities.

Temperatures really start rising in May and June, but bike touring is still possible then. I've cycled through Cuba during these months and met several other cyclists, most of whom who had wished they planned their trip earlier in the year. June is hot but dry (not counting the humidity), while May is prone to rain and flooding. Rain may only last for a few hours, but it can be quite heavy at times and many routes offer no shelter from the rain.

July and August are the hottest months in Cuba, making cycling much less pleasant. Most days are sunny, but rain often falls in short, hard bursts in the afternoon. Weather is of course unpredictable, and cyclists planning to ride during these months should pack appropriate rain gear. Cubans flock to beaches and surrounding campismos in July and August, making it difficult to find accommodations, but you can experience an authentic alternative to the mostly tourist-filled beaches during the cooler months.

Hurricanes are most common in September and October, and the rain can last for several days at a time. November is at the tail end of hurricane season, so cycling is possible, but tours early in the month run the risk of heavy wind and rains.

Holidays, Festivals, and Special Events

Most offices, shops, and museums are closed on the following holidays:

Liberation Day: January 1
Labor Day/Worker's Day: May 1
National Rebellion Day: July 26 (celebrated July 25–27)
Independence Day: October 10
Christmas: December 25

Festivals and special events can help you determine when to visit certain regions. If you know you want to visit Cuba during a specific month but are unsure where to go, the list below can help you choose special events you'd like to attend or avoid. Note that while large events such as music festivals or carnivals provide an opportunity to observe or participate in a uniquely Cuban experience, they are typically also associated with larger crowds and higher prices.

Some of the largest and most popular festivals and special events are detailed below, along with a brief description of each month's typical highlights and drawbacks.

January
Tourist season is in full swing and can lead to higher prices and overbookings. Cold fronts make for occasionally chilly evenings, but days are still warm and sunny and the weather is perfect for cycling.

- Dia de la Liberación, celebrating Fidel Castro's revolutionary triumph in 1959: January 1
- Incendio de Bayamo, where residents remember the 1869 burning of their city with music, theater, and fireworks: January 12 in Bayamo
- Culture Week: early January in Trinidad
- Festival Internacional de Jazz in Havana draws Cuba's top talent from around the world

February
Peak tourist season is still in effect, so expect larger crowds and higher prices. Calm seas and clear water make this month especially good for diving and snorkeling. The weather is relatively cool and dry and makes for great cycling.
- Habanos Festival, an annual cigar festival in Havana
- Feria de Libros, a massive international book festival in Havana's Fortaleza de San Carlos de la Cabaña: late February

March
Bird-watching is especially good this month, as migrant birds from South and North America cross over en route to cooler and warmer climates. Dry weather makes it a good time for cycling.
- International Women's Day: March 8
- Festival Internacional de Trova, a trova music festival in Santiago de Cuba

April
Expect a bump in prices and in the number of tourists visiting around Easter and spring break, which can span several weeks. The weather begins warming up then, but it is still relatively dry and good for cycling.
- Antonio Maceo Carnival in Baracoa: early April
- Children's Day brings parades and ceremonies across the country: April 4
- Day of the Militias includes nationwide parades and ceremonies: April 15
- Cine Pobre, an international film festival for low-budget films in Gibara, Holguín: mid-April.

May
A low tourist point in between the busy winter and summer seasons, May offers lower prices but is often prone to frequent and sometimes lengthy rainstorms.

FLOODED STREETS IN MAY IN JAGÜEY GRANDE

- Primer de Mayo, known as International Workers' Day (or May Day), is one of the largest celebrations of the year, including massive parades and celebrations in every capital city across the country: May 1
- Romerías de Mayo features music, parades, and pilgrimages to and in Holguín, culminating with a procession to a small shrine at the top of Loma de la Cruz, a 275-meter-high hill: first week of May

CUBA WEATHER IN MAY—I ARRIVED IN HAVANA (FROM MATANZAS) AS SOON AS THE RAIN STOPPED

- Dia Internacional Contra Homofobia y Transfobia is a celebration of gay and transgender rights in Havana. Several weeks of workshops and art exhibitions culminate in a parade down 23rd Street: May 17

June

Heat and humidity begin rising but hurricane season hasn't yet reached its peak, so prices are lower and conditions are still reasonable for cycling.
- Festival Nacional de Changüí, celebrating changüí music, which originated in Guantánamo. The festival is held sometime in May or June.
- Festival Internacional Boleros de Oro is a celebration of the distinctively Cuban bolero style of music. The largest events are held in Havana and Santiago de Cuba.
- Fiestas Sanjuaneras, a festival in Trinidad where local *vaqueros* (cowboys) gallop their horses through cobblestoned streets: last weekend in June.

July

Many tourists are discouraged by the sweltering heat, but those who can stand it are treated to some of the country's best carnivals. July is also peak travel season for Cubans, so expect beaches, campismos, and budget hotels to be crowded.
- Dia de la Rebeldía Nacional commemorates Fidel Castro's failed 1953 attack on the Moncada Barracks in Santiago de Cuba. Expect lots of drinking, music, and lively political speeches on this national holiday: July 26
- Carnaval de Santiago de Cuba is the biggest in the country and arguably the largest in the Caribbean. Rum flows freely and streets are full of colorful floats, dancing, and music: mid-July.

August

Summer heat and humidity continue, but August remains a popular month for tourism as locals and foreigners crowd beaches across the country.

- Carnaval de La Habana fills streets with colorful costumes, live music, dancing, and parades along the capital city's famous Malecón.

September
Peak hurricane season may bring lower prices and near-empty beaches, but storms can be fierce and some facilities close completely, regardless of the weather.
- Fiesta de Nuestra Señora de la Caridad features religious devotees from across the country embarking on a pilgrimage to Santiago de Cuba's Basílica de Nuestra Señora del Cobre: September 8

October
Consistent rain and strong storms ensure that streets and beaches are quiet and resorts are semi-empty until the end of the month.
- Ten Days of Culture (nationwide music and cultural events): October 10–20
- Festival de Bailador Rumbero features local musicians performing at Matanzas's Sauto Theater for 10 days: mid-October
- Festival Internacional de Ballet de La Habana: even-numbered years in Havana
- Festival de Cultura Iberoamericana finds artists from dozens of countries coming to Holguín to perform dances such as salsa, merengue, mambo, changüí, flamenco, and tango: late October
- International Chorus Festival in Santiago de Cuba: every other October

November
As Caribbean storms calm and North American and European temperatures plummet, tourism jumps in November.
- Benny Moré International Music Festival pays tribute to one of the country's most famous singers, in his hometown of Santa Isabel de las Lajas in Cienfuegos.
- Marabana is Havana's famous marathon, drawing thousands of competitors from around the globe.
- Ciudad Metal is an edgy music festival in Santa Clara where Cuban bands play hardcore and punk music.

December
The busiest and most expensive time to visit Cuba is between Christmas and New Year's, when hotels and casas sometimes double their prices and rooms sell out quickly. Booking ahead is essential. The weather is perfect for cycling.
- Festival Internacional de Nuevo Cine Latinoamericano is a Havana-based film festival showcasing films from across Cuba and Latin America.
- Las Parrandas is the largest Christmas Eve celebration in the country,

held in Remedios in the Villa Clara Province. The town divides into two teams which compete against each other to see who can create the most colorful floats and the loudest frenzy of fireworks: December 24.

WHERE TO RIDE

Cuba is a large country, and unless you have several months to explore it, you may want to choose which regions you explore based on the type of riding environment you enjoy most (coastal, mountain, flat plains), particular cities you want to visit, or location-specific activities you want to experience, such as scuba diving or visiting a tobacco plantation.

Provincial capitals and larger cities tend to have live music and special events on the weekends, whereas smaller cities may be quiet the entire week. Mondays are the quietest in virtually every city, and museums are often closed that day. As such, I typically try to visit larger cities Thursday through Sunday to enjoy the most activities possible, and then I ride to smaller, quieter cities midweek to rest those evenings.

Cycling from east to west is generally recommended in Cuba for numerous reasons: the sun will be behind you; the wind typically blows east to west; there is a slight downhill slope from east to west; the weather is generally hotter in eastern Cuba, meaning you'll ride to progressively cooler weather; and mango and avocado season start first in the east, so you'll enjoy more varying scenery.

CYCLING ROUTES

Though freeways such as the Carretera Central are safe for cyclists and are surprisingly uncrowded, they also tend to offer unimpressive scenery. The right lane is reserved for slow-moving traffic such as bicycles and horse-drawn carts, so highways are often the most direct route between major cities.

Multiday rides are divided into daylong stages. When possible, rides are divided into approximately equal days, in terms of time and difficulty. Given the absence of accommodations in more remote areas, some ride days are longer or more difficult than others. Especially strong riders should feel free to condense two ride days into one. In some cases, additional stopover cities and accommodations are included for riders who want to break up rides even further.

RIDE DIFFICULTY

Every ride is graded according to its difficulty in terms of distance, terrain, and road surface. The duration and difficulty of each ride appears in the ride's description and in the Rides at a Glance (page 18). Grading is intended as a guide—it's inherently subjective. Cyclists accustomed to long, flat rides may find a "moderate" ride quite difficult if they are not used to riding hills.

A ride's difficulty and the time it takes to complete it can also vary based on the weight of your panniers, how hungry or tired you are, and the weather—extreme heat makes everything more difficult! The suggested riding times given reflect the actual time it takes to complete the ride and do not include breaks for resting, eating, or sightseeing. Several city rides in this book could be completed in an hour but are likely to stretch out three to four hours if all the sites are visited.

PEAK TOBACCO HARVESTING SEASON IS FROM JANUARY TO APRIL

Easy: These rides are short and/or ride along mostly flat roads in good condition.

Moderate: These rides are moderately challenging to someone of average fitness. The rides can be long or short and are likely to include some hills. They may involve riding on roads with gravel and potholes.

Difficult: These rides are geared toward fit riders who enjoy a challenge. They tend to be long rides that include steep climbs and may contain rough roads and a few navigational challenges.

Very Difficult: These rides should only be attempted by experienced cyclists accustomed to riding long distances with significant elevation. Less experienced cyclists may want to break them into smaller sections.

BUDGETING TIME

Even during the driest months, rain is possible, as are leg cramps, stomach indigestion, and other unanticipated delays, so it's wise to schedule in an extra day or two for the unexpected. Also remember to schedule in days for rest and exploration! Cycling 50 miles per day in a hot, humid, and sometimes hilly environment requires a lot of energy, and you may arrive in a city too tired—or too late—to visit its attractions that same day.

Unless you're visiting during extremely busy weeks, such as spring break or the week between Christmas and New Year's, you will likely be able to find accommodations in virtually any Cuban city (though beach resort areas like Varadero offer fewer affordable options for day-of arrivals). Many cyclists enjoy staying flexible with their schedules and do not book casas more than a few days in advance. The exception, of course, would be confirming the first and last couple days of a trip, when you know you'll be in a specific city to catch your flight. Countless travelers have rushed through cities or skipped them entirely simply because they had made a reservation elsewhere, several months previously, and didn't want to lose the money.

Flexibility is often the key to happiness when traveling, particularly for cyclists who run into unexpected delays or opportunities. I've met quite a few bike tourists who completely changed their intended route based on a beach

A CYCLIST IN VARADERO CARRYING DOZENS OF CRABS ON HIS BIKE

they couldn't resist camping on, a family they wanted to spend more time with, a city they wanted to get to know better, another cyclist they met along the way, unexpected weather, or construction and road condition reports they heard from cyclists riding in the opposite direction. If you are completely committed to a specific route and unwilling to consider route alterations, you may endure unnecessary hardship and miss out on wonderful experiences.

Taking buses and colectivos or *maquinas* (ride shares in classic cars) is a great way to save time for bike tourists who are not too proud to be caught riding in a four-wheeled vehicle. Various transportation options are detailed in the "Nonbicycle Transportation" section (page 76). Many bike tourists in Cuba either plan to take buses across long, less-interesting stretches from the outset, or they update their route to include a bus so they can spend more time exploring a city they really enjoyed. Don't feel bad about taking your bike on a bus.

Casa owners can also let you know where you can catch a bus at an unofficial bus stop or midway point to save time. More details are provided on how to catch buses midroute in the "Nonbicycle Transportation" section.

CYCLING INDEPENDENTLY VERSUS ORGANIZED GROUPS

Any reasonably fit cyclist with bike-touring and basic bike maintenance experience should be able to ride any route in this book. However, if you've never ridden a loaded bike or don't know how to fix a flat, then you should consider riding with an organized cycling group. On a typical organized cycling tour, experienced guides will lead the ride and help with basic bike repairs, and a van or truck will carry the gear. A list of bike-touring organizations is included on page 212.

Though commercial cargo vans can be hard to come by and bike racks are nonexistent in Cuba, it's possible to put together your own supported bike tour by hiring a driver to haul your gear in a van or large classic car. A group of friends could easily organize its own bike tour, hire a driver to haul luggage, and use this guide to aid route planning.

Cuban drivers tend to be honest and professional, but you don't want just anybody carrying all of your belongings, particularly if every person in your

During April and May, many roads along Cuba's southern coast are plastered with the bodies of dead crabs. They begin in Guantánamo and stretch west to Matanzas, but the absolute worst stretch is the coastal road between Playa Girón and Playa Larga in the Bay of Pigs. Crabs are most likely to scurry about in the early evening but can be seen any time of day. I've been able to avoid them fairly easily at the end of crab season, but I have heard from other cyclists that it is much harder during peak crab season, when they like to puncture bicycle and car tires. In fact, many taxi drivers avoid driving the route in the evening precisely because doing so results in so many flat tires.

group is on a bicycle and no one is in the car with the driver. It would be wise to use a driver who has been recommended by one of the trusted organizations listed in the appendix, or to work with an established bike shop in Cuba (mostly in Havana) to put together a self-organized, supported bike tour.

BRINGING YOUR BIKE TO CUBA

Bringing a bicycle to Cuba works exactly as it would bringing a bicycle to any other overseas destination. Airline fees vary but generally charge US$50–$75 per bicycle. My Bike Friday New World Tourist folding bicycle fits into a normal Samsonite suitcase, allowing me to avoid additional bicycle fees. Note that if you have a folding bike or decoupling bike that can be broken down, you can avoid the bike fees, but you still may incur overweight luggage fees if your suitcase exceeds the weight limit.

Chosing Which Bike to Bring

Road bikes, touring bikes, folding bikes, hybrid bikes, mountain bikes, and recumbent bikes can comfortably ride just about any route in this book. The bikes that should be avoided are ultralight road bikes with very thin tires and cheap "department store" bicycles. The former would be difficult to use on many of the rides (which have bumps, gravel, and potholes), and the latter would be heavy and unreliable.

More important than the type of bicycle you ride is how you set it up. Sturdy wheels and good tires are essential, as many of the most beautiful routes are along roads that are perpetually under construction. All of the routes in this book are paved, but the quality of the pavement varies dramatically. A comfortable saddle is essential for any bike tour, and a shock-absorbing seat post is a good idea for those of us with sensitive backsides.

If you choose to ride a mountain bike, tires with aggressive tread are

RIDING THROUGH VIÑALES ON MY FOLDING BICYCLE

not required for routes in this book. Do yourself a favor and save weight by choosing tires with a higher air pressure and a smoother tread.

RENTAL BIKES

Bicycles are available for rent all over Cuba, but very few are suitable for bike touring. Tourist resorts tend to rent better quality bikes than private homes, but even the best bikes are typically heavy, poorly maintained, and lacking essential touring accessories such as water bottle cages and racks. Cyclists interested in biking in Cuba but not actually bike touring could get by with a rental bike to complete day trips. This is especially true in Havana, Trinidad, Santiago de Cuba, and Cienfuegos, where bicycles are plentiful and the routes are relatively short.

I lead "bike-themed" trips to Cuba where cars transport the group between cities and rental bikes are used to explore cities and nearby attractions. This setup works well for cyclists who want to maximize a short trip or who travel with a noncyclist who can do walking tours while they ride. Note that the quality and availability of rental bikes across Cuba varies dramatically, so if you'd like to do something similar, contact one of the bike shops in Havana (page 86) or organized cycle tour operators (page 212), as they are the most likely to have high-quality bikes.

If you plan to rent a bicycle in Cuba, it's a good idea to bring your own wrench, multitool, and lube. Bike shops and bike rental companies may have a hard time finding the most basic tools, making something as simple as adjusting the height of your saddle impossible. Note that while some of the bicycle companies listed in the "Bicycle Shops" section and appendix do rent (or sell) bicycles that could work for bike touring, the selection may be limited, so it's *very* important to confirm the exact bike you would rent and its condition, along with crucial parts, like racks and bottle cages. The last thing you want is to arrive in Cuba to find that the shop rented your bike to someone else, that it isn't the size you anticipated, or that it is rusty or missing essential parts.

ME WITH ONE OF HAVANA'S NEW STATE-SPONSORED HABICI RENTAL BIKES

WHAT TO BRING

The only items consistently available across Cuba are cigarettes, rum, and pork. Aside from that, there are no guarantees, making bike equipment and first aid supplies absolutely essential. See the "First Aid Kit" (page 39) and "Bike Spares and Parts" (page 37) for a guide of absolute necessities. Nobody wants heavy panniers, but be sure to pack any consumer item—from skin cream to energy bars—you think you can't live without. Anything you don't fully use on the trip can be left behind and will be very much appreciated.

Sunblock is absolutely essential year-round, and while it can sometimes (but not always!) be found in Cuba, the SPF is often impractically low. Bug

PONCHERAS

Though proper bike shops are few and far between and are very poorly stocked, *poncheras* (tire repair shops) are everywhere. Even the smallest village has at least one ponchera, where skilled mechanics make do with what they have, which is often not very much. Don't count on them having specialized tools, or even basic tools, lube, tubes, or patches, for that matter. They definitely won't have the parts required to fix a high-tech bike. See the "Bike Spares and Parts" section (page 37) for a list of what to bring. You may even consider leaving your tools or parts behind with a ponchera in a small town, where the supplies will surely go to good use for the entire community.

DUE TO LACK OF ACCESS TO PLASTIC BAGS, CARDBOARD BOXES, AND REUSABLE CONTAINERS, MANY PEOPLE CARRY CAKES WITH NO CONTAINER

repellant is also occasionally available but often of inferior quality.

Women should bring whatever feminine care products they prefer, as tampons can be hard to find. I recommend the Diva Cup or another reusable menstrual cup that is easy to use, takes up minimal space, and is environmentally friendly.

A powerful, easily detachable front bike light doubles as a flashlight, but if you plan to do a lot of camping, consider bringing a good headlamp.

Batteries can be hard to find, and those available in stores may be expired. Electronics that are charged by USB cable are best, but if your electronics require batteries, be sure to bring extra.

Many casas have a washing machine and are happy to wash clothing for you, but commercial dryers are virtually nonexistent. Most Cuban homes have an outdoor area where clothing can hang-dry in the sun. On rainy or especially humid days, clothing must be dried indoors. In this case, a travel clothesline can come in very handy. Alternatively, a piece of twine or thin rope can also work. Be sure to bring laundry soap and a sink plug so you can wash small amounts of clothes in your bedroom when a proper washing machine isn't available.

Snorkeling is great along the coast of Cuba (mostly in the north, south, and east), so a snorkel and mask would be handy if you enjoy snorkeling and have extra room. Snorkels are available for rent at many larger beaches (Playa Ancón in Trinidad, Guardalavaca in Holguín, Varadero in Matanzas), but smaller beaches often won't have facilities or will only have broken, useless equipment available.

Despite the lack of consumer products in Cuba, don't go overboard when packing, and pay close attention to the weight of your luggage. Save space and weight by using a backpack pannier that doubles as a day pack (one of my Arkel panniers is a backpack).

For more tips on what to pack for Cuba, see www.escapingny.com/home/packingforcuba.

Clothing

Pack clothes that are light, dry quickly, and can be worn both on and off the bicycle. Synthetic fibers, wool, and silk are best. Avoid cotton, which retains water and dries slowly. Do not pack brand-new clothing that you have never worn before. Even if it's a brand and style you normally wear, you'll want to test it out before your trip. In the event that the clothing doesn't fit right, you will not be able to find anything remotely equivalent in Cuba.

On the Bicycle

Padded bicycle shorts are designed to be worn without underwear to provide additional support and prevent chafing. They can either be worn on their own or underneath "ordinary" shorts. Two pairs of bicycle shorts should be enough, even for a long trip. I prefer one pair of padded shorts and one pair of padded three-quarter length tights to shield more skin from Cuba's fierce sun.

Cycling jerseys made from synthetic fabrics keep you cool and dry quickly. Long sleeves provide the best sun protection, and removable arm sleeves achieve this and prevent overheating. Long sleeves keep you cool and protected in the sun, but once you're in the shade or inside, sleeves make you warmer, so it's preferable to have the option to remove them. Be sure to purchase light sleeves intended for warm weather, not the more common winter sleeves, which provide additional warmth—something you will absolutely *not* need in Cuba.

Underwear and socks should be made of quick-dry materials, but remember to *not* wear underwear if you are wearing padded shorts. Otherwise, you risk chafing and saddle sores.

It's unlikely you'll encounter cold weather in Cuba. Anytime it's cool outside it's usually raining, so instead of bringing a light sweater, save space by bringing a lightweight, waterproof jacket. If you will be biking in July through October, packing a jacket that can withstand heavy downpours will be especially important.

Cycling shoes are ideal because the stiff soles transfer power from your pedal stroke directly to the pedal. That said, cycling shoes are not at all practical for walking around town and are impossible for hiking and dancing. Unless you want to pack an extra pair of walking shoes (or will be satisfied only wearing sandals off the bike), consider stiff-soled shoes that either don't clip into pedals or are specifically designed for walking. I opt for Chrome stiff-soled sneakers, as they make better walking shoes than sandals on muddy, rainy days.

Sunglasses are absolutely essential to minimize UV radiation exposure and to protect eyes from insects and wind. Cheap sunglasses will do, but professional cycling sunglasses are more comfortable, block more light, and are less likely to fog up in heat and humidity. Helmets are also necessary and are extremely difficult to find in Cuba. It is very likely a Cuban will ask to buy your helmet from you. Considering bicycle helmets are the only option many motorcycle drivers can find, helmets make great gifts when you leave.

Fingerless cycling gloves with padded palms help to reduce impact on bumpy roads, protect hands in a fall, and prevent sunburn. Don't forget to put sunblock on your fingers, especially your thumbs!

Off the Bicycle

Even if you don't plan on eating in fancy restaurants, you will likely want to bring at least one "regular" outfit. Lycra is fine for the museum, but many nightclubs, jazz clubs, and nice restaurants demand more "standard"

NOTHING GOES TO WASTE IN CUBA—EVEN "DISPOSABLE" DIAPERS ARE WASHED AND REUSED

clothing, and some clubs prohibit men from wearing shorts altogether. Given that mosquitoes and sand flies are prevalent throughout Cuba, it's wise to pack a pair of lightweight pants and a long-sleeved shirt. Save even more space by choosing a long-sleeved outfit that doubles as "nice" clothing.

A thin scarf (made of silk or polyester) makes a handy travel item, providing warmth as a shawl or neck scarf on an airplane, serving as an eye mask while sleeping, converting into a sarong on the beach, and doubling as a towel in a pinch. I opt for a scarf with a fun, colorful print that turns simple black leggings and a tank top into a semifashionable outfit for a night out.

In addition to a swimsuit, a microfiber, quick-dry towel is also a good idea, especially for camping. Cheap rubber sandals make handy house shoes and are necessary to walk along beaches, many of which are lined with sharp, jagged rocks or broken glass and garbage.

If your cycling shoes are not comfortable to walk in, consider bringing a pair of running shoes or sturdy sandals that are rugged enough for a long day of walking or hiking.

A wide-brimmed hat is a good idea to shield you from the sun. Straw and synthetic hats are sold as souvenirs across Cuba, but I prefer a foldable, polyester hat that provides better sun protection.

Maps

The most thorough map available in Cuba is the Guía de Carreteras/Road Guide, available at auto rental agencies and Infotur offices. Some hotels, bookstores, and hotel gift shops also sell them.

A phone app that allows you to access digital maps offline is an extremely valuable tool. Be sure to download the map before you get to Cuba, as some apps cannot be downloaded there, even though they will work if they've already been downloaded. Maps.me and OsmAnd are popular navigation/map apps that allow you to search and save hotels, casas, restaurants, beaches, and other attractions and refer to them even without an Internet connection. After downloading the app to your phone, be sure to download the map for Cuba, as maps are not preloaded in the app.

Ride With GPS and Strava are apps (and full websites) that allow users to not only track their ride but also search by city or location for routes that other riders have uploaded. You can see various routes that other riders have used (including elevation and distance), and in some cases download the route right to your phone to follow the GPS navigation.

Given how difficult it is to acquire everyday items in Cuba, many travelers enjoy bringing gifts and donations. Here are some suggestions for highly useful items that won't take up a lot of room in your luggage.

- Clothing: Pack clothing to wear that you'll leave behind
- Any toiletries (leave whatever is leftover)
- Old cell phones and chargers (yes, even flip phones!)
- Batteries (reusable or single-use)
- Sturdy plastic food containers
- Zip-lock storage bags
- USB drives and micro SD cards
- Sewing kits
- Headphones
- Multivitamins/pain killers
- Neosporin, Bengay, Tiger Balm, other ointments
- School supplies (pens, highlighters, notebooks, crayons)
- Wristwatches

The poorest people in Cuba live in small towns across the country that rarely or never receive tourists. With no tourist dollars flowing in and no donations left behind, "everyday items" are even more scarce. Bicycle tourists are in a unique position to leave donations in these "middle of nowhere" towns as they ride between larger cities. I like to leave donations with men and women selling fruit along the side of the road, but if it would make you more comfortable, swing by a school to leave a bag of donations with a teacher, who will distribute them according to need.

Don't worry about offending anyone by offering donations; it's very common and always appreciated. No words are needed, but even the most Spanish-challenged traveler could muster up a simple "*Quieres?*" ("Do you want this?") while handing off a bag of donations.

Camping Equipment

Camping equipment doesn't exist in Cuba. Any tents or equipment you come across were probably left behind by tourists. Because Cuba's version of camping is *campismo* (campgrounds with bungalows and cottages), tents are not available to rent, and some campismos won't even allow you to set up your

MY ATTEMPT TO MAKE MY OWN TUPPERWARE BEFORE CAMPING IN GUARDALAVACA, HOLGUÍN

own tent on their grounds. If you plan on tent camping in Cuba, it is essential that you bring your own tent. Given the large numbers of mosquitoes and sand flies, particularly at night, make sure the tent seals completely and is fully waterproof.

Light sheets can be used for bedding, but a sleeping pad or inflatable mattress and pillow will make the night far more comfortable. Considering the weather, a sleeping bag will likely be too hot, though I've enjoyed sleeping on top of a sleeping bag on multiple camping trips in Cuba. The most attractive campsites are on beaches, which get quite windy at night, so be sure to bring a lot of tie-down twine.

Know that it's unlikely you'll find campsites with groceries and a water supply, so allow for enough room in your luggage to pack extra water and food. Also keep in mind that it's very unlikely that toilets will be available near your campsite.

Fuel cannot be carried on planes, and butane gas (which is used in many camping stoves) is not available in Cuba. If you're going to bring a stove, consider a universal stove that can run on gasoline, which can be purchased from gas stations in Cuba. Another option would be a small burner stove (such as those made by Trangia) that can run off rubbing alcohol. Also, be sure to have a wind shield so it doesn't take an hour to boil water on windy beaches.

Keep in mind that Cuban grocery stores do not specialize in foods that are easily prepared on camp stoves. Locals are always happy to prepare a cheap, tasty, hassle-free meal, so consider leaving the stove at home altogether.

Equipment Checklist

Bike Clothing
- Padded shorts
- Cycling tights
- Short-sleeved cycling jersey
- Detachable SPF sun sleeves
- Helmet with visor
- Sunglasses
- Lightweight waterproof/windproof jacket
- Cycling shoes and socks
- Padded cycling gloves

Off-the-Bike Clothing
- Change of clothing
- Semi-dressy outfit for nice restaurants/clubs

- Sandals or flip-flops
- Swimwear
- Wide-brim sunhat or baseball cap
- Underwear and spare socks
- Light sweater or long-sleeved shirt for cool evenings

Equipment
- Rear and front bike lights (front bike light that doubles as a flashlight)
- Daypack or fanny pack
- First aid kit (see "First Aid Kit" box, page 39)
- Toiletries
- Bungee cord
- Sewing/mending kit
- Sink plug for washing clothes
- Panniers with waterproof liners and/or covers
- Handlebar bag, ideally with map case
- Microfiber towel
- Pocketknife
- Multiple water bottles
- Water filter and/or purification tablets
- Spare batteries for any device that requires batteries
- Tool kit, tire pump, and spare parts (see "Bike Spares and Parts" below)

Camping Equipment
- Cooking, drinking, and eating utensils
- Clothesline and dishwashing items
- Sleeping pad or inflatable mat
- Very lightweight sleeping bag
- Matches and lighter
- Tent with rain cover
- Extra toilet paper

Bike Spares and Parts

Bike tourists often find themselves riding alone for long stretches, so they must be self-sufficient. At minimum, you'll want to carry some spare parts and a basic toolkit. Multitools, which combine Allen keys, screwdrivers, and wrenches of different sizes into the same tool, are small, lightweight, and very handy. If your bike requires any custom or hard-to-find parts, you'll want to bring spares.

Bare Minimum Gear
- Pump (be sure the valve matches your tires)
- Water bottles (at least two or three)
- Water bottle holders
- Spare tubes (two to four)
- Tire levers (two)

- Chain lube and a rag or small towel
- Patch kit/puncture repair kit (check that the glue hasn't dried out)
- Small Phillips screwdriver
- Small flathead screwdriver
- Allen keys to fit your bike
- Spare screws and bolts (for pannier racks, seat post, etc.)
- Spare chain links (two)
- Spare brake pads

For Experienced Bike Tourists
- Chain breaker
- Pliers
- Spare spokes and nipples
- Spoke key
- Tools to remove the freewheel
- Spare rear brake and cables

Other Handy Items
- Electrical tape
- Zip ties of various lengths/sizes
- Nylon ties of various lengths/sizes
- Carabiners
- Hand cleaner (store it in a pill jar)

HEALTH INSURANCE

Proof of health insurance is required to visit Cuba. I recommend purchasing more comprehensive travel insurance instead, which includes health insurance and also protects you against theft, flight delays and cancellations, missing luggage, and emergency-related trip interruptions.

At the time of research, all US-based airlines include basic health insurance within the price of the ticket. Note that this health insurance only covers the first 30 days of the trip. Travelers who extend their visas will be required to prove that they have purchased another form of insurance that will cover them for the remaining portion of their trip. If a traveler cannot provide this documentation, he or she will be required to purchase health insurance on the spot.

Travelers must save their boarding pass, as hospitals will request it as proof of insurance.

While major international hospitals, such as the one in Havana, are known to happily process airline-issued health insurance, I've seen smaller hospitals in rural areas claim an airline has denied coverage and then request cash payment by the patient. This happened to a client on one of my group trips to Cuba who injured herself and was told that her airline refused the claim. When she returned to the United States and contacted the airline, they said that no claim had been made on her behalf. Fortunately, she had purchased travel insurance, which covered her costs.

First Aid Supplies

- Band-Aids/bandages
- Cloth bandages and safety pins
- Butterfly closure strips
- Nonadhesive dressings
- Elastic support bandages for sprained ankles/sore knees
- Gauze
- Sterile alcohol wipes
- Small pair of scissors
- Latex gloves
- Tweezers

Medications

- Antidiarrhea, antinausea drugs
- Antifungal cream or powder for thrush/yeast infections/candida
- Antihistamines for allergies, insect bites, and stings
- Antiseptic wipes and solution for cuts
- Aloe vera or calamine lotion to ease sunburn and insect bites
- Cold and flu tablets
- Throat lozenges and nasal decongestants
- Painkillers such as aspirin, ibuprofen, or acetaminophen

Miscellaneous

- Sunscreen and SPF lip balm
- Insect repellent
- Eye drops
- Oral rehydration salts or electrolyte tablets

VISAS, DOCUMENTS, AND CUSTOMS

Passport and Tourist Visa

Every visitor to Cuba, including babies, needs a passport that is valid for at least six months ahead and a *tarjeta del turista* (tourist visa), which typically allows a 30-day stay.

Travelers booking their trip to Cuba through a tour operator may receive their tourist visa through the tour operator. Those planning their own trip will purchase their tourist visa at the airport, either at the check-in counter or boarding area.

A BICYCLE TAXI READY FOR BUSINESS IN TRINIDAD

The price of the tourist visa varies from country to country. I traveled to Cuba (with an American passport) three times through Mexico and was charged the same for the visa as Mexicans traveling to Cuba, roughly $25. The current price of a tourist visa to Cuba in the United States is $50, though some airlines may charge an additional "visa processing fee."

The passport number on the tourist visa must correspond with the passport you use to travel. If you get a new passport, you'll also need to get a new tourist visa.

Within Cuba you will seldom, if ever, need to show your tourist visa, but it is required to leave the country, so store it safely. If your visa is lost within Cuba, you will not be allowed to leave the country until you purchase a new visa (often through a highly bureaucratic process).

You will constantly be asked to show your passport in Cuba—when checking into a hotel or casa particular, purchasing an Internet card, exchanging money, or cashing bills over $50. I recommend showing your actual passport when checking into hotels and casas, and leaving the passport in the room while exploring the city. Carry a copy of your passport instead; a photocopy is sufficient for purchasing an Internet card or exchanging money.

If you choose to carry your passport with you everywhere, be sure to check that the visa is still inside of it when a hotel clerk or bank teller returns your passport to you. Better yet, leave the visa at home or in a safe space within your luggage, as it is not required for daily transactions.

Visa Extensions

A 30-day visa extension can be arranged by visiting an immigration office in any capital city (and some noncapital cities) in Cuba a few days before your visa expires. Travelers from most countries are allowed to renew their visa once or twice while in Cuba. After that, they must leave the country, even for just one day, before they can return and apply for another visa.

Though Americans are currently only allowed to renew their visa once (for a total stay of 60 days in Cuba), this American author was able to extend her visa twice when the visa was issued in Mexico. That said, Americans should plan to either stay in Cuba for less than 60 days or leave the country for a day and return.

Immigration offices are closed on Sundays and typically open only a few hours on Saturday and the last day of the month. You can find the business hours posted outside the office. Note that even if the office displays hours from 8 a.m. to 5 p.m., the office typically only admits travelers until about 1 p.m., as office staff leave the afternoon free to process paperwork. Also keep in mind whether there are any holidays when the office may be closed, such as Workers' Day on May 1.

The following items are required to extend your visa:

- Passport
- Current visa or tourist card
- Bank stamps worth CUC$25 (must be purchased from the bank before you apply for the visa extension)
- Receipt of payment for bank stamps
- A business card or receipt from your current casa particular
- Proof of health insurance (see "Health Insurance," page 38)
- Proof of return ticket out of Cuba

Travelers are typically only allowed to extend the visa within "a few" days of its expiration. If you try to extend it a week before it expires, you will likely be told to come back closer to the date. I have renewed my visa three times within two to three days of the expiration but have heard of others turned away within that same window, being told to return the day the visa actually expires. I've even been told by immigration officials that I could extend the visa "a couple days" after the visa expired, but I didn't want to take that risk.

As with many things in Cuba, it's impossible to give a black-and-white answer when it comes to visa extension procedures. In some cases a visa may be extended 30 days from the day the visa is being renewed and not 30 days from the day the initial visa expires, essentially losing two to three days. I have successfully extended my visa 30 days from the initial visa expiration date despite making the request several days before the initial visa expiration. On another occasion, my visa was extended less than 30 days, only to the date of my departure flight back to the United States. The immigration official assured me there would be no problems, even if my flight was delayed beyond the visa expiration date.

Though the visa extension process may be a bit confusing, and you may be asked to return to the office with more information, know that Cuban immigration officials are typically very happy to help you through the process. If you know you will need to renew your visa, start the process two to three days in advance and request to have the visa extended 30 days from the initial visa's expiration date, so you don't lose days on the original visa. Know that if you cannot stand to lose a couple of days and the official says you will only be able to receive the full 30 days if you renew the visa on the actual day it expires (which is not true), you may simply have to return to the immigration office another day. If you will not be in a major city (such as Havana or Holguín) at the time you renew your visa, check with your host or local information center to determine where you can renew your visa.

There are immigration offices in the capital city of every province and also in some noncapital cities across the country that receive a lot of tourists (such as Baracoa, Guantánamo).

Expect to spend at least a few hours at the immigration office and have *all* documentation with you. The immigration office does not sell stamps, so you *must* bring these with you. It's possible you may spend most of the day at the office, so do not plan any significant riding for that day.

US Visitors to Cuba

As of this writing, the US Department of State has declared, "Tourist travel to Cuba remains prohibited. You must obtain a license from the Department of Treasury or your travel must fall into one of 12 categories of authorized travel."

These 12 categories of authorized travel to Cuba are:

- Family visits
- Official business of the US government, foreign governments, and certain intergovernmental organizations
- Journalistic activity
- Professional research and professional meetings
- Educational activities
- Religious activities
- Public performances, clinics, workshops, athletic and other competitions, and exhibitions
- Support for the Cuban people
- Humanitarian projects
- Activities of private foundations or research or educational institutes
- Exportation, importation, or transmission of information or informational materials
- Certain authorized export transactions

Most US travelers to Cuba choose the "support for the Cuban people" category and demonstrate this "support" by spending the majority of their time doing activities that support the livelihood of the Cuban people. This might include:

- Staying at a casa particular
- Eating at *paladares* (privately owned restaurants)
- Attending salsa lessons, cooking classes, walking tours, etc., hosted by locals
- Shopping at independently run businesses

The intention behind these restrictions is to limit support of the Cuban military, which controls many hotels, tour buses, and other travel-related entities across the country. In fact, the US government has declared it illegal to stay in any hotel that is partially or entirely owned by the Cuban military (such as the Gaviota chain).

Travelers are required to put together a detailed itinerary before traveling to Cuba and to keep this itinerary on record for up to five years should the United States choose to verify that the visit met the requirements. Americans caught traveling to Cuba without permission could be subject to a fine. Under the Bush administration, some Americans were fined up to $10,000 for visiting Cuba without permission, but the Obama administration relaxed travel restrictions to Cuba. Donald Trump reinstated some travel restrictions in 2017 and added additional restrictions in 2019, though they are not as harsh as they once were. American diplomats and staff have also been pulled out of the US Embassy in Havana, so American travelers who encounter legal troubles in Cuba will find less support at the embassy.

FOCFORERAS REFILL AND REPAIR BROKEN AND EMPTY CIGARETTE LIGHTERS

Cuban immigration officials know that a Cuban stamp in a US passport can create problems and are happy to avoid putting the stamp directly in the passport. Travelers who do not wish to receive a stamp in their passport can inform the immigration official, who will instead stamp the tourist visa or a separate piece of paper.

Travel restrictions for US citizens have changed so much in the past few years that it's best to check the State Department's website for recent updates before planning your trip. The Fund for Reconciliation and Development (www.ffrd.org) is a good resource for the state of US-Cuba relations. I've also published a blog post on the topic with updated information on travel policy for Americans. Find it here: www.escapingny.com/home/legalcuba.

Embassies

US Embassy
Calzada between L and M Streets, Vedado, Havana
+(53) 7-8394100 / +(53) 7-8333543
acshavana@state.gov
cu.usembassy.gov/embassy/havana

Canadian Embassy
Calle 30 #518, Playa, Havana
+(53) 7-2042516

UK Embassy
Calle 34 #702, Miramar, Havana
+(53) 7-2142200

TYPICAL CUBAN PROPAGANDA IN BARACOA, GUANTANAMO

Onward Tickets

Every person entering Cuba must have a return or onward plane ticket, which is sometimes checked by immigration. This onward ticket is also important for travelers who wish to renew their visa. Those who arrive without an onward ticket risk being granted only a week-long stay. It is best not to arrive in Cuba without an onward plane ticket.

Other Documents

A regular driver's license or an international driving permit should be sufficient to rent a car in Cuba. Hostel, student, senior, or AAA discount cards will give you no advantage in Cuba.

Customs

Entering Cuba

Visitors are allowed to bring personal belongings into Cuba, including cameras, laptops, camping equipment, bicycles, and other sports equipment. Your bicycle will be inspected, either before or after you retrieve it from the luggage carousel. If you are asked if you will leave the bike in Cuba, say no.

Avoid bringing in any materials, such as books or magazines, that are critical of the Cuban government.

Travelers who try to bring in any item (USBs, bike tools, clothing, etc.) in a large quantity may be questioned by customs officials and risk having the items confiscated. I attempted to bring a $10 hot plate (mini electric stove) as a donation, only to spend three hours waiting for customs officials, who then confiscated the item. The officials said that some electrical items are not allowed because they conflict with Cuba's current and could cause electrical problems. After much back-and-forth, officials revealed that the potentially dangerous product would be "distributed" at a shopping mall. Go figure! During this same visit, two men were held by customs officials for bringing in a backpack full of dozens of tennis balls they planned to donate to a charity. If you plan to bring donations, avoid electronics and don't bring a quantity that will draw attention. If you say it's for charity, you may be asked to provide documentation about the charity. If you can't provide this, the items may be confiscated.

Leaving Cuba

It is prohibited to leave Cuba with any Cuban money. Many travelers save some Cuban pesos (CUCs) to spend on rum, cigars, and other souvenirs at the airport, but some travelers have been apprehended (and have nearly missed their flight!) for attempting to leave the country with CUCs.

Leaving Cuba with more than US$5,000 is also prohibited. If you arrive in Cuba with such a large amount of cash, it's important that you record the cash on a customs declaration form when you arrive in Cuba. You will then be able to leave Cuba with as much cash as you declared upon entry.

Though travelers are allowed to purchase artwork in Cuba—and many, many travelers do—avoid anything that looks even remotely antique. Customs officials do not care if a shopkeeper assured you that an item could be exported. Stick to purchasing artwork from reputable galleries, who will issue you an official document proving the origin of the piece. I have bought artwork on several occasions, as have dozens of travelers on my group tours, and none of us has ever been questioned by customs, but know that it is possible.

2

TRAVEL ESSENTIALS WITHIN CUBA

COMMUNICATIONS

Mail

Most post offices in Cuba are open 8 a.m.–6 p.m. Monday–Friday and 8 a.m.–noon Saturday. Postcards are sold in many shops and outdoor markets, but it may be easiest to purchase prepaid postcards from post offices and hotels. Letters and postcards may be sent from blue mailboxes or directly from the post office, but parcels must be sent from international post offices.

DHL has offices in Cuba where you can mail packages back to the United States. However, there is only one DHL office in the United States (in Miami) where parcels can be shipped to Cuba. Parcels must be dropped off in person at the Miami office and cannot be mailed there from elsewhere.

DHL's Cuban office can be contacted at the following telephone numbers:

- Within Cuba: 7204-1876
- Outside Cuba: +53-7204-1876

The United States Postal Service (USPS) can also mail packages directly to Cuba, but many items are prohibited, including money, jewelry, or anything valued at over $200. Check the USPS website, www.usps.com, for details.

Mobile Phones

Voice and data charges vary across providers and individual plans, so contact your phone carrier prior to your trip. Most carriers do offer service in Cuba, but calls may be prohibitively expensive. To avoid incurring fees, keep your phone on airplane mode the entire time. Even while in airplane mode, you can connect to the Internet at WiFi hotspots.

For everyday communication abroad, a phone application such as WhatsApp (download prior to trip) is simpler, easier, and cheaper than calling from a Cuban phone or your own mobile. WhatsApp allows text, recorded audio, and video communications via WiFi.

Telephone

Most casas particulares have a landline they will be happy to let you use to make calls within Cuba. I've used the phone at restaurants and other small businesses in a pinch.

Cuba's telecommunications company, ETECSA, has installed public phones around the country where local calls can be made using a calling card. Calling cards are sold at hotels, post offices, and telephone centers. After making a call, the remaining card balance is displayed on the phone.

International calls can be made from ETECSA communications centers. US citizens needing to make a collect call should do so with a calling card (CUC$1/minute).

Local numbers in this book are given as they should be dialed from that area. Note that cell phone numbers have eight digits and always begin with a 5.

Calling a mobile phone (from either another mobile or a landline): Dial the eight-digit number, which always begins with a 5.

Calling a landline (from either another landline or a mobile): Dial the provincial code + the local number.

International calls: Dial 119 + the international number.

Making a collect call: Dial 180 + the phone number.

Calling Cuba from abroad: Dial the country code 53 + the area code (minus the zero, which is used domestically when calling between provinces) + the local number.

Internet Access

Internet access in Cuba has increased dramatically in recent years and continues to expand to small towns across the country. Most hotels and some casas particulares have a private WiFi connection, though most Cubans and tourists rely on public WiFi hotspots. Public WiFi hotspots are typically

---

IMPORTANT PHONE NUMBERS

Remember that when calling the following numbers, the operators will probably only speak Spanish, so have a dictionary or translation app handy.

International Operator	180
Direct International Line	119
Local Operator	110
Information	113
Police	116
Ambulance	185
Fire Department	115

located in the central park or main plaza of small towns. Large cities have multiple WiFi hotspots, located in parks, plazas, and public squares across the city.

Regardless of where you connect to the Internet, a scratch-off WiFi card is required to gain access. WiFi scratch-off cards cost CUC$1 per hour and are available in 1-, 5-, and 10-hour blocks. At the time of research, unlimited WiFi, as it's known in much of the world, had not yet arrived in Cuba. Mobile data plans only launched in Cuba in late 2018 and are restricted to Cuban-issued mobile phones. Perhaps in the future it may be possible to purchase a SIM card and a short-term data plan in Cuba.

When purchasing a scratch-off WiFi card from ETECSA, photo identification is required (a copy of a passport is sufficient). Many hotels and some independent businesses also sell WiFi cards and do not typically require identification. Cuba's famous *jineteros* (street hustlers) often attempt to purchase all the WiFi cards from the ETECSA office and sell them to tourists on the street at a premium. They typically charge an extra 50 cents to CUC$1 per card and are often the only option to secure an Internet card after business hours. When purchasing a WiFi card on the street, be sure to confirm that the password has not been scratched off.

Most tourists get by with just their phones, but if an actual computer is needed, larger hotels (and some casas) have desktop computers available for their guests. Hotels can sometimes be persuaded to allow nonguests access. Note that some websites are blocked in Cuba, and Americans, in particular, may have difficulty accessing finance-related websites and apps, including bank websites, PayPal, and Venmo. iPhones tend to have more difficulty connecting to the Internet than do other phones but usually connect eventually if you keep logging out of WiFi. For more information on how the Internet works in Cuba and potential challenges to be aware of, see www.escapingny .com/home/wifi-internet-in-cuba.

CENSORSHIP, SAFETY, AND SECURITY

Freedom
While it is true that Cuba doesn't have a completely free press and there are restrictions on freedom of expression, you can still have frank discussions with Cuban people, who are becoming increasingly comfortable speaking openly about (and sometimes against!) the government. It would be considered rude and inappropriate to ask a stranger about their political views, but as you make friends with locals, you can certainly express interest in learning about their lives and political beliefs.

Even if you disagree with Cuba's political system, it's important to show respect for it. Though the Cuban government may go a bit overboard in the way it depicts the treatment of Cuba by other countries (the US "Yankee imperialists," in particular), it is true that much of Cuban politics remains misunderstood by much of the world. Chatting with locals you meet is a great way to learn about Cuban culture, history, life, and politics firsthand.

PROPAGANDA IS EVERYWHERE IN CUBA, INCLUDING THIS PIECE IN TRINIDAD

It is also wise to refrain from openly criticizing the government if you want to avoid unwanted attention from the authorities.

Safety and Security

In terms of physical safety, Cuba is one of the safest countries in the world. Most streets can be walked or biked alone at night, violent crime is extremely rare, and Cubans are friendly and quick to offer helpful advice and directions to befuddled-looking travelers.

Theft is another matter. Just as in virtually any other country you travel to (and likely within your home country as well), it's just not a good idea to leave valuables in plain sight. The same goes for leaving valuables displayed in your hotel room. Many Cubans earn less than CUC$25 per month, so they may define "valuables" differently than you do, though I have found Cubans to be some of the most honest people in the world. Any time you stop somewhere with your bike, you will surely be warned to keep an eye on it, often by someone pointing to their eye and then to your bike. In many cases, someone will volunteer to watch your bike for you as you quickly run an errand.

I've trusted someone (usually an old woman) to watch my bike while I ran in to purchase a WiFi card, ask a question in a bank, and buy a bus ticket. That said, any time you leave your bicycle with someone, you are taking a risk. The safest option is to bring a good lock or find one of many, many *parqueos* (bicycle parking stations) located in just about every city in the country. Note that locking a bike to a gate or post will not stop someone from stealing lights, pumps, mirrors, saddle bags, or other detachable accessories. If you must leave a loaded bike unattended, it should be at a parqueo.

Cuban bike thieves don't typically walk around with strong bolt cutters, so a good-quality cable lock should do. However, if you plan to camp and leave your bike outside overnight, you'll want to bring a stronger lock. Most casas particulares will let you store your bike inside overnight. Hotel policies vary widely; some hotels will allow you to bring the bike into your room, others will offer to keep it in a locked storage room, and some won't allow the bike inside at all. Confirm the hotel's bicycle storage policy before booking your room.

UTILITIES

Electricity

The power supply in Cuba is mainly 110 volts, though most modern hotels have both 110- and 220-volt outlets in the rooms. The voltage of an outlet is typically displayed on a sticker, but ask your host if you're unsure. Air conditioners are typically plugged into the 220-volt socket, and 110-volt sockets are used for charging phones and other small batteries. Do not attempt to charge your phone on the 220-volt socket unless you want to burn out the battery.

HOW TO ASK DIRECTIONS

Need to ask directions but don't speak Spanish? First, check the Spanish dictionary you should have downloaded prior to your trip (tons are available in online app stores), then get ready to gesture!

When asking for directions, complex sentences are less important than knowing which direction you should be heading. If you attempt to ask a full question such as "How do I get to Havana?" you may receive a long-winded answer that's difficult to interpret. Instead, point in the direction that you believe to be correct and ask, "Havana?" Your interlocutor is likely to nod in reassurance or, if you were wrong, point you in the correct direction.

If it seems that your interlocutor is confused, you may just be mispronouncing the name of the city, and showing them the name of the city in this book or on your map could solve the problem. If they still seem confused, look for someone else or flag down a taxi driver for directions—they're always the best source of information.

North American–style plugs (two flat, parallel prongs) are the norm, so if your devices don't fall into that category, you should bring an adapter with you. You may be able to find an adapter in Cuba, but it may be of questionable quality and safety, so bringing your own is best.

LAUNDRY IS TYPICALLY HUNG TO DRY OUTSIDE, AS IT IS HERE IN BARACOA, GUANTANAMO

Laundry

Public laundromats are not common in Cuba, so you'll either be washing your clothing by hand in your room or paying the hotel or casa particular to wash it for you. Each establishment has its own price, some charging per piece, others by vague categories such as "large bag" and "small bag" of laundry. If a home is not accustomed to washing laundry and they leave it up to you to come up with a price, offer about CUC$5 for a small load.

Note that while most casas particulares have washing machines, it is highly unlikely the home will have a dryer. If it does, it is probably a no-heat "spin dryer" that spins out more water than the washer can but still leaves clothes a bit damp. If you arrive at a *casa* in the afternoon and wash your clothing immediately, the hot afternoon sun should be able to dry it in time to wear the next day. Be sure to only hang clothing outdoors if it's within the host's enclosed property or if someone is keeping an eye on it.

Functioning washing machines are never guaranteed, so pack quick-drying clothing and bring a sink plug to wash clothing in your room as needed.

Toilets

Public toilets can be found in bus and train stations and near the town plaza or main park in most small towns. Large hotels also have public toilets, typically somewhere near the check-in counter, and are your best bet for modern washrooms.

Many Cuban toilets do not have toilet paper, soap, or running water, so carrying toilet paper and hand sanitizer is essential. Also carry small change (25 cents and under) to tip bathroom attendants.

Most Cuban toilets cannot accommodate toilet paper, which can clog the sewage pipe. If you see a small basket next to the toilet, deposit your toilet paper in there. Some travelers are uncomfortable doing this, but a bit of discomfort is better than clogging someone else's toilet, particularly if that person lacks a plunger!

In some cases, the toilet is flushed by dumping a bucket of water down the toilet. This task is usually done by a bathroom attendant, who should receive an additional tip.

Thanks to the 1993 film *Fresa y Chocolate* (*Strawberry and Chocolate*) that sparked a national conversation about homosexuality, and the efforts of gay rights activist Mariela Castro (daughter of former president Raul Castro), Cuba is one of the most progressive countries in Latin America when it comes to LGBTQ+ rights. In fact, Cuba began providing state-sponsored gender reassignment operations in 2010 and is considering legalizing same-sex marriage.

Most casas particulares won't take issue with hosting an LGBTQ+ person or couple, but if you'd like to specifically be hosted by a gay couple, check out Casa Roberto Carlos in Cienfuegos, Casa Flamboyan in Havana, and Villa Paradiso in Baracoa.

The largest gay rights celebration in the country is the International Day Against Homophobia and Transphobia on May 17. Several weeks of workshops and art exhibitions culminate in a parade down 23rd Street in Vedado, Havana.

WHERE TO STAY

Though it's possible to arrive in Cuba without having booked any accommodations in advance, it's wise to book at least the first night. Cuban customs and immigration officials sometimes ask tourists where they are staying and become skeptical of travelers who arrive without a plan. After your first night, it's easy to keep a flexible schedule. Regardless of where you'll stay (hotel, private home, campismo), you'll need to show the host/staff your passport so they can record your information in their log. Photocopies of passports are often accepted, but it's wise to keep your actual passport with you for safety reasons.

When possible, this guide lists high-season prices, which can be 20 percent to 30 percent higher than low-season prices. All accommodations listed here offer some form of bike storage (indoor patio, garage, locked shed), or allow bicycles right in the rooms, but it's always best to confirm with the host when making your reservation.

This book includes contact information for several casas particulares and hotels in each city. Unless it's very high season (Christmas through New Year's, Easter, or spring break week), you can likely get away with making reservations a few days in advance should you wish to remain flexible. If the casas listed don't have room, they can help you find lodging at another *casa*, though the accommodations may be a bit different. The easiest way to book hotels on semi-short notice is to do so directly from tourism offices in major cities across the island (Baracoa, Guantánamo, Santiago, Havana, etc.).

Casas Particulares

Casas particulares are private homes where families rent individual rooms or entire apartments as bed & breakfast–style accommodations. The quality and price of casas vary widely, and some even include beachfront balconies, pools, and on-site restaurants. Homeowners are taxed heavily, including a monthly fixed fee and a variable fee based on the total income from bookings.

Casas particulares offer the absolute best value in terms of quality and service. The food served in casas is nearly always better than local restaurants and hotels, making staying in casas easy and affordable. The average price of a standard casa is US$25–$35 for either single or double occupancy, though you will pay more in especially popular locations such as Old Havana. Some rooms are single rooms rented within the family's own home, while others are self-contained apartments on the same property or near the owner's home. Renting a room within a family's own home is the best way to interact with Cubans and learn about local life and culture, but there will be less privacy, as you may hear the kids getting ready for school in the morning or watching TV at night. While many rooms have their own bathroom, it is very common for two guest rooms to share the same bathroom.

Most families will go all out to accommodate their guests, helping them wash laundry, sewing on a button that has fallen off, or calling homes in the next town to check weather and road conditions for your ride. Few casa owners will try to take advantage of you, but it's important to confirm when you check in what will be included. Some homes may offer a fresh juice when you arrive, but any additional drinks or services are likely to be charged to the bill, which is paid at checkout.

Licensed casas particulares will display a blue anchorlike symbol outside their home that may say DIVISA, which refers to the CUC (Cuban peso). Red anchors indicate that the home is only licensed to host Cubans, who will pay in CUP (moneda nacional).

Someone may try to take you to another house that will have a legitimate-looking RENT ROOM sign. The room may be unlicensed and may be offered for a cheaper price than casas listed in this book. Staying in one of these homes is only recommended if there is no other option. These homes are usually clean and safe, but there is always a possibility that Immigration may throw you out in the middle of the night.

Note that when asking for directions to a casa particular, instead of asking about a specific address or intersection, it's often better to ask for the name of the casa or simply say "casa particular"? In small towns, even if someone doesn't know exact street names, they will know where the casas are and can direct you there. Some will even take you there to ensure you arrive safely. Some may expect a tip (or will later request a commission from the homeowner), but most people just want to be helpful.

Cubans, and children in particular, have long enjoyed having their pictures taken. However, as tourism increases and social media–crazed travelers flood the island and take pictures of people without asking, it's becoming even more important to ask permission. I have encountered far more fruit vendors and artists in recent years who do not want to be photographed. In 2019 I encountered several Cubans yelling at tourists, angry to have been photographed without their permission. If someone declines to be photographed, it is very important to respect their decision. No person wants to feel on display, and a person's dignity should not be compromised simply for a souvenir.

As most Cubans do not have cameras or easy access to pictures, they would greatly appreciate if you would send a copy of the picture you take of them. If you plan a return trip, bringing a printed copy of the picture would be much appreciated. Otherwise, you can ask if the person has an email account—or knows someone who does—where you could send the picture.

Note that taking photos of soldiers, military facilities, and factories is prohibited, though I've managed a few shots with soldiers (with permission, of course). Photography is allowed inside most museums for an additional fee (typically an extra CUC$1–$3). Museums that do not allow photography will display the policy in the museum and have staff on hand to stop anyone who attempts to take pictures.

BE SURE TO ASK PERMISSION BEFORE TAKING PHOTOS OF PEOPLE. THIS TRAVELER BROUGHT A POLAROID CAMERA TO TAKE PICTURES OF PEOPLE IN SMALL TOWNS TO LEAVE BEHIND WITH THEM.

HAVANA'S FIRST INFINITY POOL, ON TOP OF THE GRAN MANZANA HOTEL

Hotels

All Cuban hotels are operated by the state, often as joint ventures with foreign companies. Some of these hotels are owned by the Cuban military (such as the Gaviota chain) and recently became off-limits to American travelers, though that could change under future presidential administrations. Hotels range from budget to luxury, including five-star hotels, though one or two stars should be deducted from the rating to approximate international standards.

Cubanacán, Iberostar, Meliá, and Gran Caribe operate some of the most expensive hotels (CUC$150–$400/night), which often include amenities such as swimming pools, organized group activities, higher-end restaurants, and massage therapists. Midrange hotels such as those operated by Gaviota and Horizontes run CUC$75–$200/night, with comfortable rooms and third-rate restaurants.

Most of the least expensive hotels (CUC$30–$50/night) are operated by state-run Islazul, but the rooms, service, and food are nothing to brag about and pale in comparison with private casas that cost the same price. Rooms in this category can be comfortable, but there is always a risk that the AC is broken or the water isn't running properly. You'll also want to check that there are sheets, towels, and toilet paper, which are not always considered standard. If something is missing, let the front desk know immediately so you are not charged when you check out.

School teachers, economists, janitors, engineers, and other hardworking Cubans in state jobs are paid in pesos, roughly about $15–$25 per month, far less than is needed to get by. Though every Cuban receives a ration book that allows them to purchase coffee, cooking oil, rice, and other provisions for next to nothing, the portions are small and most Cubans must dig into their pocketbooks to purchase additional food on the "free market."

To make ends meet, many Cubans are taking on side jobs or leaving their state jobs entirely to open private businesses. I have a friend in Havana who adored being an elementary school teacher but had to abandon the CUC$15/month job in exchange for a construction job at a private company that paid him double (still not enough to get by). In the long run, Cuba can't stand to lose all of its professionals to the tourism industry, but in the short run, switching career paths has been the only option many Cubans see to provide for their families.

Cubans who are able to tap into the tourist industry have the best opportunity to earn higher incomes. Since 1993, Cubans have been allowed to engage in private enterprise, such as opening a restaurant or casa particular. Many doctors, lawyers, psychologists, and other professionals who earn state income in pesos also run a casa particular (operating in CUCs), where earnings from a single evening can exceed their entire monthly peso salary. Staying in a casa particular supports not just the homeowner, but also the people the homeowner hires to help cook, clean, and do the laundry. However, the owners of casas particulares are already relatively well-off Cubans who have nicer homes with additional rooms to rent. Most Cubans do not live in a home that is fit to receive tourists, so they are left behind as the disparity between well-off and less fortunate Cubans grows. Cubans who are able to tap into the tourism trade, particularly those who are receiving money from abroad, are able to do quite well. Those who do not have access to tourist dollars struggle to get by.

An unfortunate symptom of this dual economy is the presence of *jineteros*, street hustlers or touts who collect commissions from "helping" tourists find taxis, casas, restaurants, and more. Those who speak English sometimes offer themselves as city guides even if they have no formal experience. I've seen English-speaking "guides" charging some tourists up to $100 per day simply to walk around with them and take them to restaurants and nightclubs,

HIGH-END CASA PARTICULARES RESEMBLE BOUTIQUE HOTELS, SUCH AS THIS WATERFRONT CASA IN HAVANA

where they collect an additional commission off everything the tourists consume. Some jineteros provide a genuine service—if you arrive in a city and have no idea where to find a casa particular, the hour they save you biking from house to house in the hot sun is worth the extra $5 that may be added to your bill. However, jineteros can be extremely pushy and annoying, particularly for solo female tourists, who tend to attract scores of them every day. See the "Cycling as a Woman in Cuba" section (page 74) for more on this.

Airbnb has been operating in Cuba since 2016, and for many travelers it's an easy way to find accommodations. Airbnb allows users to search hundreds of listings across Cuba, including everything from $10/night apartments in Guantánamo to $500/night waterfront villas in Havana. Users can scroll through pictures and read reviews from past guests and, best of all, they can pay in advance using a credit card, eliminating the need to bring extra cash to Cuba.

As of this writing, several significant challenges exist with the Airbnb platform in Cuba that travelers should be aware of:

- The Airbnb app doesn't work properly in Cuba, and you *cannot* make new reservations on the app within Cuba, though you can do so through an Internet browser.
- Slow technology results in double bookings. Many casa owners list their homes on multiple websites, and Cuba's slow technology makes it difficult to impossible to update multiple listings in real time.
- Cuban *casa* owners have long operated their own reservation and referral system where hosts switch reservations based on demand. Unfortunately, some Airbnb users book a *casa* because they want that specific casa, so it can be frustrating to be moved to a home other than the one you reserved online.
- Many of the Airbnb accounts for Cuban homes are managed by people who do not actually live in Cuba, resulting in disappointment and miscommunication.
- The map function doesn't always work properly and sometimes displays a home's location as more than a kilometer from where it actually is.

If you choose to book an Airbnb in Cuba, always read the comments (and look at the comment date), confirm amenities that are important to you, and bring extra cash.

To learn more about how Airbnb works in Cuba and to increase your chance of having a good Airbnb experience, see www.escapingny.com/home/airbnbcuba.

Islazul used to be the only option in many remote areas of Cuba, but now casas particulares are available in virtually every town in this book. Cubans are most likely to stay at Islazul due to its affordability. While this allows for a more authentic feel and an opportunity to engage with locals, it almost guarantees that loud music will be blaring late into the evening.

In general, casas particulares offer better value, and the hosts are better able to accommodate special needs, diets, and requests, such as very early breakfasts and on-the-spot laundry. Higher-end hotels offer a level of luxury that most casas can't provide, so some cyclists enjoy staying in five-star (really three- or four-star) resorts at the end of a bike tour to relax and unwind before heading home.

Campismos

Camping is not part of Cuban culture, so while the word "campismo" sounds like "camping," it's not quite the same thing. Campismos provide inexpensive accommodations for Cubans on holiday, who pour into clusters of basic bungalows and cottages scattered along beaches and forested areas across Cuba. Many of the cottages cost CUC$10–$15 per night, can sleep three to six people, and include on-site restaurants, so they can be a good option for groups. That said, the food is usually awful and sometimes nonexistent.

Many campismos will have room for walk-in guests during off-peak season, but reservations are absolutely necessary during high season (particularly during Christmas, New Year's, and spring break/Easter). To book accommodations, stop into a campismo office anywhere in the country, and be sure to bring your passport. The offices have helpful signs with the prices of various campismo sites, but unfortunately there is no single brochure with all the info you may need. It's also possible the office will be out of some or all brochures, so staff may have to verbally explain (in Spanish) where the sites are.

As many Cubans bring their own food and drinks with them to campismos, the on-site canteens and restaurants don't expect to do much business. As a result, they offer minimal options. This can prove especially problematic for cyclists with dietary restrictions. This (vegetarian) author arrived at a campismo outside Baracoa, Guantánamo, on a weekday afternoon and found nothing more than ham sandwiches and coffee. The following morning, the only offerings were hot dogs and watery soy yogurt. Reggaeton music blared from 10 a.m. until after midnight as Cubans sang, danced, and ate the food they brought from home while their kids enjoyed donkey rides on the campgrounds.

Quality varies dramatically across campismos, so if possible, have a look around the site before making a reservation. Some windows do not have screens or have holes in the screen, inviting mosquitoes in overnight. While many cottages have their own bathroom and shower, some only offer a shared outdoor shower. Hot water is usually not an option. In addition, many of the cottages in coastal areas have been destroyed by hurricanes. Some sites have yet to be repaired, while others have been newly renovated and offer comfortable accommodations only steps from the water. In many cases, campismos are located only 5 to 15 kilometers from a town with a casa particular, so if you're not happy with the quality, pedal on for better accommodations.

Camping

Proper campgrounds with facilities for tent campers do not exist in Cuba, so the rides in this book have been designed for camping gear to be optional. You may be able to offer a campismo manager a few CUCs in exchange for pitching your tent on the ground, but given that toilets and running water are typically only available within the cottages, it's usually worth paying $5 or $10 more for the cabin.

Cuba has no shortage of beaches that make for lovely campsites, but remember that they will have no tourist facilities. Beaches and forested areas in more remote areas pose the largest challenge, so be sure to bring extra food and water. Camping along beaches in tourist areas such as Guardalavaca, Holguín, means you can purchase food and water at the hotel and restaurants, but don't expect to find showers, sinks, toilets, or amenities found at traditional campgrounds.

Beaches can be extremely windy at night, so look for trees and shelter and be sure to tie down your tent. Sleeping without a tent is strongly discouraged, as your sleep would be constantly interrupted by mosquitoes, crabs, and invitations to sleep in someone's home.

If there is someone nearby, be it a guard, police officer, homeowner, or any random person, ask permission to set up your tent. You will likely be told that you are free to camp (at your own risk), but in rare cases you will be told camping is not allowed. Be mindful of your guest status, remain polite, and if the officials insist that camping is not allowed, ask them what your options are. When there truly are no casas, hotels, or campismos around, you may be granted special permission, but it's not guaranteed.

MONEY MATTERS

Currencies

There are currently two types of currency in Cuba, the Convertible Peso (CUC) and the Cuban Peso (CUP), though the government has vowed to unify the two currencies in the future. The colorful CUC, also known as *divisa*, is roughly pegged to the US dollar and is what most tourists use in Cuba to pay for hotels, casas particulares, taxis, and restaurant meals. The CUP, also known as *moneda nacional*, is worth just 1/24th of the CUC and is what Cubans use in their everyday lives to pay their utility bills and buy produce at markets. Many restaurants and shared colectivo taxis operate primarily with CUP but will happily accept CUC. Note that change may be given in CUP and it's unlikely there will be enough to break a large bill.

I have camped at half a dozen sites in Holguín, Guantánamo, Santiago, Matanzas, and Granma provinces and interviewed several other bike tourist campers in Cuba. As enjoyable as bike camping can be, it's often worth it to pay a few bucks to stay in a casa particular in Cuba. Hot and humid nights, mosquitoes, nonstop reggaeton music, and lack of access to food and water make touring dramatically more difficult here than in other countries. Many bike tourists who brought a tent to Cuba wound up only using it once or twice, so if you're on the fence about camping, consider what you could bring if you left the tent at home.

No recounting of my experience camping in Cuba would be complete without a mention of the time I got locked in the toilet overnight at a scuba diving center in Guardalavaca in 2016. I set up my tent in front of the dive center, and a friendly security guard kept an eye on it while I used the outdoor shower. During a quick bathroom run before turning in for the night, the lock in the single-stall bathroom malfunctioned and the bolt got jammed in the door. The security guard spent five hours trying to unjam the door as I hovered over the toilet, counting spiders. The dive instructors had a good laugh the next morning. When I returned to the dive shop in 2018 and mentioned having camped on the beach a couple years previously, they jumped up and said, "Did you get stuck in the toilet?" They had another good laugh and assured me that the bathroom door had since been fixed. Should you find yourself at the dive shop, tell them Cassandra sent you!

The best way to distinguish between the two currencies is to look at the main marking on the bill. CUCs (divisa) display monuments and statues while CUPs (moneda nacional) display the faces of revolutionary heroes like Camilo Cienfuegos and Che Guevara.

Divisa are multicolored notes of 1, 3, 5, 10, 20, 50, and 100, and coins of 5, 10, 25, and 50 cents, along with a 1-peso (CUC) coin.

The Cuban peso comes in notes of 1, 3, 5, 10, 20, 50, 100, 200, and 500, and coins of 1, 2, 5, 20, and 40 *centavo* (cents), and one of 3 pesos. The 5-centavo coin is called a *medio* and the 20-centavo coin is a *peseta*.

Most travelers visiting Cuba get by just fine without ever seeing or handling moneda nacional, but that is because they tend to stick to major tourist destinations. Cyclists riding through more remote areas and to smaller towns will find themselves at restaurants and shops that may *only* accept CUP. Travelers who plan to stray outside of the main cities should exchange

CUC$20 for CUP, which is especially handy for buying street food like pizza and sandwiches.

US Dollars in Cuba

While US dollars can be exchanged for CUC in financial institutions (banks, money exchanges, and at some hotels), there is an additional 10 percent penalty on top of the usual banking exchange rate. To avoid the penalty, many Americans exchange US dollars for another internationally accepted currency, such as Canadian dollars or euros, prior to arrival in Cuba.

Exchanging Money

Only exchange money at reputable banks and money exchanges, called *CaDeCas* (short for *casas de cambio*). Do NOT exchange money on the street. Taxi drivers, hosts, tour guides, and random people on the street will likely offer to exchange money for you (particularly if it's US dollars or euros), offering a better exchange rate than banks and CaDeCas. The person exchanging the money for you would likely take it to an "official" black market money exchanger who offers a favorable enough exchange rate that, even after the handler's transactional commission has been subtracted, you would still fare better than at the bank. While many of these money exchangers only deal with legitimate bills, it is possible that you'll be given counterfeit bills. You may also be given legitimate bills, but of the wrong currency.

Tourists who have not familiarized themselves with the difference between CUC and CUP notes may trade a US$100 bill and hope to get back CUC$92, a much more favorable rate than the CUC$86 offered at the CaDeCa. Instead, they may be given moneda nacional, or CUP$96, valued at 1/24th of the CUC, roughly $4. The same can happen at restaurants and

CUC DIVISA (WITH MONUMENTS) VS. CUP PESO/MONEDA NACIONAL (WITH FACES)

shops. Look very carefully at the change you are given, and if you paid in CUC, make sure that the bills you receive have monuments on them and not faces.

When making everyday purchases, small bills are best, because most businesses won't be able to make change for large bills. Many shops will even struggle making change for a $20, so be sure to always have singles, fives, and tens with you. The only businesses that accept $50 and $100 bills are typically hotels or restaurants that deal with a large number of tourists. In these cases, you may also be asked to show ID. If your bill at a casa particular approaches CUC$50 or CUC$100, the homeowner should be able to make change, but don't expect to pay for a single night with a CUC$100 if your bill is only CUC$25.

Purchasing WiFi cards from ETECSA is a great way to break large bills. Even though the card may only cost a dollar, ETECSA handles so much cash that they are usually able to break a CUC$50 note. Be sure to bring your ID!

Credit Cards and ATMs

Though some establishments do accept credit cards, the practice is still very uncommon, and there is always the possibility that the credit card machine is broken. Credit cards can be used to pay for plane tickets and book rooms in large hotels but are often not accepted outside large resorts. Also note that even if credit cards are generally accepted, US-issued cards will not be accepted.

ATMs are few and far between and are most likely to be found at banks in large cities. They do not yet accept US-based credit cards.

Going to the Bank in Cuba

Going to the bank in Cuba can prove to be quite an adventure. The guidelines below will save you time and frustration.

- **Get there early:** Most banks have long lines even before they open. If you arrive after the bank opens, you could be waiting over an hour. Note the hours before arriving; some banks close early on some days of the week or on the last day of the month.
- **Bring an ID:** Identification is required for just about any transaction at the bank. A photocopy of your passport may sometimes be sufficient, but bring your passport just in case.
- **Determine which line you need:** Most banks have separate lines for social security checks, transactions involving CUCs, transactions involving CUPs, and a host of other reasons that may not be evident to tourists. Be sure to ask the security officer and people in line what each line is for so you don't spend an hour waiting in the line to receive a social security payment.
- **Establish your place in the queue:** See "Who's Last?" (page 64) for more information on how to do this.
- **Keep your eye on the monitor:** Some banks have monitors that display the number of the person being served. Since banks may issue numbers to clients in multiple types of lines, the numbers displayed typically don't go in chronological order. If you're not paying attention, you may miss your number.

Costs

Cuba is certainly a much more affordable country to visit than the US, Australia, or Japan, but it is by no means "cheap." The cheapest rooms will likely run about US$15/night and you could fill your belly with peso food for roughly

Seemingly disordered masses of Cubans huddle in front of banks, stores, bakeries, and ETECSA offices, somehow maintaining order without actually being in line. These masses are, in fact, waiting in a queue; it's just invisible to most foreign onlookers. Instead of standing in an actual line, Cubans simply ask for *el último* (the last person) who is waiting. They take note of the person they are behind "in line" and then announce themselves to the next person asking for el último. With this system, people often come and go from the line, keeping an eye on the person they're behind as they grab a snack or make a phone call from across the street.

US$5/day. Nicer casas will average around US$25–$35/night, and will serve considerably higher quality breakfast for US$5–$6 and dinner for US$8–$15.

Cuban resorts tend to be less expensive than others in the Caribbean, but they also tend to be of a lower quality and offer fewer amenities. Basic rooms in three- to four-star resorts will cost about US$75–$150, depending on whether meals and drinks are included. Higher-end resorts charge US$300–$500/night.

Since many casas particulares charge the same per night for one to two people, traveling in pairs and groups makes travel much more affordable. Some casas will offer a discount to single travelers, and some casas even let three to four people stay in the same room without charging extra. I typically travel alone and stay in casas particulares, having breakfast at the *casa* and rotating dinners between peso and CUC restaurants—averaging about US$30–$50/day, which includes the occasional museum, nightclub, or national park admission fee.

Tipping

Most Cubans will tell you that they do not tip in restaurants, but do not take that to mean that *you* shouldn't tip. Cubans working in service jobs (guides, restaurants, taxi drivers, etc.) are accustomed to receiving tips from tourists, and it helps to supplement state wages that may average between US$15 and US$25 a month. That said, the service in some state-run restaurants is abysmal. If you receive bad service, tip as you would in your own country.

Just about anyone who does a service for you, be it carrying your luggage or watching your bike in a parking lot, deserves a tip. Usually CUC$1 is adequate, though if you don't have any singles and don't want to leave a larger tip, leaving another currency is acceptable. As an American, I've received requests from bathroom and bicycle parking attendants across the island to exchange CUCs for the US dollars that other American tourists had left behind as tips. It's often not worth their time to stand in line at a CaDeCa to exchange a few dollars, so try your best to leave tips in the local currency.

Staff at low-end facilities such as cafeterias and campismos may not expect a tip, but they subsist on extremely low wages and are very hopeful (and grateful) to receive them. It is not necessary to leave a tip at a casa particular unless your host does something special, such as launder your clothes or wash your bike. If you see that a maid is the one actually preparing your meals, cleaning your room, or washing your clothes, give the tip directly to her. In some cases a maid may ask that you inform the homeowner that the money, clothing, or donation you leave them is, in fact, for them, so they won't be accused of stealing.

IF NOBODY IS STAFFING THE FRUIT STAND, LEAVE A FEW CUCS IN EXCHANGE FOR FRUIT

FOOD AND DRINK

Where to Find Food

Cuba is not known for particularly creative or flavorful food, but you shouldn't have any difficulty finding enough to eat. You'll be able to eat fairly cheaply though not very well. Fine dining is rare, but very good food can be found in high-end paladares in cities frequented by lots of tourists (Havana, Trinidad, Varadero, etc.). Large cities and provincial capitals have the widest selection of restaurants, supermarkets, and food stalls, but even the smallest towns have roadside stalls selling ham sandwiches and pizza.

Self-Catering

Two things you absolutely will not find in Cuba are energy bars and protein powders. Compact, high-energy foods aren't popular in Cuba, so bring your own supply. You may also consider bringing trail mix, dried fruit, and mixed nuts. While it's possible to find nuts in Cuba, you'll mostly find peanuts sold in small paper tubes for one Cuban peso or hyper-sugary peanut bars sold for a few Cuban pesos at street carts and food stalls. For tours to more remote areas, you may want to bring a couple jars of peanut butter or cans of tuna fish for easy protein. This is especially true if you plan to camp. Both can be found in large supermarkets (and some gas stations) in main cities, but neither are guaranteed. If you have room in your luggage, considering bringing these supplies with you to Cuba.

Cookies, candy bars, chips, and junk food are readily available at street carts, food stalls, hotels, and supermarkets around the country. Bread is also readily available, though usually limited to highly refined white loaves. You can follow your nose to the bakery or purchase bread from a street vendor, typically a man carrying a large tray of loaves on his shoulder or in a basket on the back of his bicycle. The previously mentioned super-sweet peanut bars can stand in for peanut butter to make a sandwich, or you can ask your *casa* owner to boil a few eggs for you to pair with the bread.

Fresh fruit and vegetables are sold at mercados in just about every town in Cuba. The best selection is available first thing in the morning (usually around 8 a.m.), and many mercados are closed or out of food by early afternoon. For a slightly higher price, you can purchase produce from street carts or vendors, who are usually out after the markets have closed.

Cooking equipment adds a lot of weight to luggage, and camp stove fuel is not readily available, so travelers planning to camp should consider bringing some dehydrated food, which is also not available in Cuba. If you have difficulty starting a fire to boil water, there's almost always a home nearby that will happily give you some boiled water, in which case you should leave a tip.

STREET STALLS ARE EVERYWHERE, SELLING FRESH FRUITS AND VEGETABLES

Street Food and Cafeterias

Street vendors typically set up around 8 a.m. to sell to locals on their way to work and school, offering a good place to stock up on snacks for the day's ride. Some only sell crackers, candies, and chips, while others display *boca-dillos*, meat-stuffed sandwiches, behind a glass case. Note that most home-made sodas, juices, and drinks are made with unfiltered water, so coffee (made with boiled water) is the safest bet.

The challenge with finding food along many routes is that there isn't consistency. Many entrepreneurs set up stalls selling drinks and snacks outside their home, but there are no set business hours or menus. Perhaps one day they open at 8 a.m. but they do not open until 1 p.m. the next day because they had an appointment in the morning. Perhaps they won't open at all, because they weren't able to source any merchandise.

Restaurants and markets run out of food on a regular basis, so it's always best to find snacks when you arrive in a city and bring them with you when you go out the next day. Bananas, peanut bars, and rolls are compact, high-energy, and relatively easy to find and carry.

The most popular street food is pizza, usually a tasteless crust smeared with red sauce and a sprinkling of cheese. Various meats and sometimes vegetables (usually limited to onions and bell peppers) can be added for variety. The most interesting part of ordering street pizza is noticing the type of homemade oven it is cooked in, typically an old oil drum converted into an oven. Spaghetti is another popular street food, and is just as bland as the pizza, with tasteless, watery red sauce poured over mushy noodles. Cuban pizza and spaghetti are consistently disappointing, but they are cheap and filling (less than CUC$1 each) and are often the only option.

Cafeterias are state-run lunch counters that offer little more than coffee and sandwiches. The offerings are displayed on a board that usually includes ham sandwich, cheese sandwich, ham and cheese sandwich, chorizo sand-wich, chorizo and cheese sandwich . . . you get the point. The options are bland and repetitive and run out quickly, but they are cheap and filling. Cigarettes and rum are also usually on the menu and seem to never run out. None of the food is ideal for cycling, but cafeterias are sometimes the only option. The healthiest option would be the yogurt, a watery, bland concoction served in a glass that can be improved if you slice your own fruit into it. If you've brought nuts or trail mix from home, you can even make yourself a parfait! Some cafeterias will sell you a large container of yogurt to take with you. Without commercial packaging, most liquids are sold in repurposed water and rum bottles.

Casas Particulares

Dining at your casa particular is often the most convenient—and most delicious—option. Some casas operate a small restaurant at their home, while others simply prepare meals for guests in their own kitchen (off the books). Licensing is quite strict, so many hosts are eager to earn a few extra bucks by preparing meals that they may not pay a commission to the government

THE BEST MEALS ARE OFTEN FOUND IN CASAS PARTICULARES

for. You may notice that some hosts will negotiate a lower price for the room if you agree to eat all your meals in the home.

Breakfast is almost always CUC$5, and dinners range from CUC$6–$8 for rice, beans, salad, plantains, and pork to CUC$12–$20 for shrimp, lobster, crab, and even more exotic items like crocodile and octopus. Avoid ordering crocodile in homes, as most of it will come from illegal sources that thwart local conservation efforts. Drinks are extra, and most homes keep bottled water, soda, and beer on hand. Some have rum and most offer fresh juice.

Casa owners are very happy to accommodate and are the best option for anyone with an allergy or dietary restriction. If you arrive at a casa late in the day and request a meal, the host may be limited to what is available at the markets since Cubans don't keep a lot of food on hand in their homes. However, if you place your order a day in advance, they will arrive early at the market to ensure they get the best pickings. You can even call ahead before arriving in the city to let them know you'd like to have dinner at the house. Hosts are accustomed to waking up early to prepare breakfast, which is usually a bountiful spread consisting of bread, fruit, eggs, cheese, butter, ham, juice, coffee, and milk. There is usually enough left over to pack a few small sandwiches for the road.

Paladares

Paladares are privately run restaurants, sometimes operating out of private homes, that usually provide good food for a good value. The quality of the food is similar to food served in casas particulares. Paladares sometimes offer unique art and decor or enhance the dining experience by hiring local musicians to serenade guests. Some state-owned restaurants call themselves *paradores* (inns) to attract tourists who may confuse the word with paladares.

Hotel Restaurants

The quality of food in hotels varies considerably and most often comes in buffet form. Most all-inclusive hotels serve all-you-can-eat breakfast, lunch, and dinner buffets and allow nonguests to dine for around CUC$10–$20. It's worth inspecting the food before paying, because the food is not cheap and is sometimes disappointing. Hotels that are run as a joint international venture, such as the Meliá, offer better-than-average food, while lower-end hotels like Islazul offer the least appealing food.

Cuba may be known for pork—and lots of it!—but vegetarians won't have much difficulty finding food. Spaghetti and cheese pizza are street food staples, albeit not very healthy or high quality. Nearly every meal is served with rice, salad, and a starchy vegetable such as yucca, potatoes, sweet potatoes, or *malanga*, a root vegetable. Standard Cuban breakfasts include bread, eggs, cheese, fresh fruit, and juice, and are typically large enough that you could make bread and egg sandwiches to eat for lunch. Casa owners who prepare meals tend to be more flexible than restaurants, as they purchase ingredients and prepare meals according to what the guest requests. Be sure to place your dinner order in the morning to ensure your host has enough time to purchase ingredients at the market before they run out.

Vegans are going to have a harder time finding food in Cuba; Cubans don't have a strong tradition of eating vegetables. Salad is very common and usually consists of shredded green cabbage, sliced tomatoes, and cucumbers. Heartier vegetables such as eggplant and squash are available and make occasional appearances as side dishes, but vegans can ask their *casa* host to prepare them as a main dish. Beans are more likely to be found mixed into rice and served as congri or *moros y cristianos* (Moors and Christians). Plant-based diners (or anyone getting sick of the standard large portions of rice and meat) can request beans to be prepared as their own side dish or main dish.

Soups almost always contain meat, but casa owners are able to prepare homemade soups that are delicious and satisfying. Soup is my go-to meal request in Cuba, and homemade soups range from tomato-based spaghetti soups to thick plantain and pumpkin stew to cabbage and potato stew. Carrying a reusable container to refill with leftover soup and rice is a great way to guarantee you have a snack in between cities, where ham sandwiches are the only option.

There is no vegan—or even vegetarian—culture in Cuba, so there's not an understanding of why people abstain from consuming animal products. Restaurants are not used to people asking for menu alterations, and Cubans tend to be extremely easygoing and don't consider it a big deal should they be served something a bit different from what they ordered. Despite being very clear about your diet, it's very possible that you will be served something that you don't eat.

Find more tips on how to find vegetarian or vegan food in Cuba here: www.escapingny.com/home/vegancuba.

State-Owned Restaurants

Some state-run restaurants are surprisingly fashionable and could be mistaken for privately run paladares. However, most offer bland food and bad service. Note that any item that is not specifically listed as being part of the meal will carry an additional cost, which may be absurd (such as CUC$1 for a pat of butter). Items that are sometimes complimentary in other countries, such as a bread basket, may cost several dollars, though the server won't mention the cost when the basket is offered. As in any restaurant in Cuba, if you ask for water, you will be served bottled water and be charged.

Drinks

Water

Avoid drinking tap water when possible, though in a pinch it is better than dehydration. Cubans are accustomed to drinking the tap water in many areas, but it can give tourists an upset stomach. When possible, drink bottled water, or better yet, bring a filter or water purification tablets. Bottled water can be purchased at hotels, supermarkets, gas stations, and casas particulares.

I've met bike tourists who claim to have drunk tap water throughout their entire trip without any problems, while many Cubans distrust their own water and will only drink boiled water. In some cities, such as Holguín, locals rely on purified water delivered to their door for pennies. I drank dozens of liters of purified Holguín tap water without any ill effects but *did* get

OLD WATER BOTTLES ARE REPURPOSED TO SELL TOMATO PUREE, HOMEMADE JUICES, AND PICKLES

sick from drinking homemade juices in Santiago made with tap water. Whatever the kind of water you drink, remember to stay hydrated and drink before you get thirsty—take small sips regularly.

Juice

In Cuba, *jugo* (juice) is not actually the fresh juice extracted from a fruit, as it is in many countries. Rather, jugo is fruit blended with water and sugar and then strained. The result is sweet and tasty but much thicker and *much* sweeter than actual juice. Juice prepared at casas particulares and restaurants catering to tourists will be prepared with bottled or boiled water that is safe to drink. Juice served at street stalls and restaurants catering to Cubans may be made with tap water and should be avoided.

BARTENDER CHINO TOPS OFF DRINKS AND REFILLS BOTTLES WITH RUM IN RECYCLED CONTAINERS IN SANTA LUCIA, CAMAGUEY

Coffee

As Cuba is a proud coffee-producing nation, you are likely to be offered a coffee in just about every home you step into. Coffee is sold for pesos out of the windows of homes in just about every city and is also sold in hotels, in high-end restaurants, and at an ever-growing number of stylish cafés. Cuban coffee tends to be strong, sweet, and served with milk unless you request otherwise.

Refrescos

Refrescos are sodas, but unless they come out of a can, they're typically homemade concoctions made with unfiltered tap water. Street stalls and restaurants catering to Cubans sell various flavors, such as *limonada* (lemonade) or *naranja* (orange), usually poured out of 1.5-liter soda bottles that may give tourists the impression that the drink is a commercially manufactured soda.

Guarapo

Guarapo is fresh sugarcane juice pressed right on the spot and sold for either one CUP or one CUC, depending on whether the stall caters to locals or tourists. The sweet, refreshing drink is especially satisfying on warm days and is often served in an old glass beer bottle that's been sawed off and smoothed along the rim. The ice guarapo is served with is made from tap water, but usually such a small amount that it won't cause stomach problems.

Batidos

Batidos are milkshakes made of ice, fresh fruit, and milk or powdered milk. The most popular flavors are *mamey* and *zapote*, two sweet tropical fruits you can also find in the market. Restaurants catering to mostly Cubans will typically use ice made from tap water.

Rum

Perhaps Cuba's most popular drink, rum has been prepared in Cuba since the 16th century. Made of fermented sugarcane, rum is available at corner shops, street stalls, hotels, restaurants, supermarkets, beach canteen stalls, and just about any outlet imaginable. Havana Club is the most widely available brand, though Santero, Santiago de Cuba, and other popular brands can be purchased at liquor stores and airport shops.

HEALTH AND SAFETY

Cycling Safety

Basic cycling safety tips are the same anywhere you ride in the world, but there are also some cycling tips specific to Cuba.

General Safety Tips

- Ride to the right of traffic, but allow a meter between you and the shoulder.
- When riding in a group, ride single file so that cars can safely pass you.
- Never swerve or turn unpredictably.
- Always maintain a safe speed, particularly when riding downhill.
- When braking, use both front *and* rear brakes simultaneously.
- Ride within cycle lanes when they are available.
- Remain constantly alert and aware of traffic and road conditions.
- Use front and rear lights and wear reflective gear to stay visible.
- Always wear a helmet.

Cuban Cycling Safety Tips

- **Heat:** Cuba can get extremely hot and humid, which makes every ride more difficult. It's important to stay hydrated and take frequent rest stops in the shade. When possible, avoid riding during the hottest time of day, from about 12 to 3 p.m. If you are prone to saddle sores, chafing, or fungal infections, Cuba's heat can make them worse. Shower as soon as you finish your ride, put on clean clothing immediately, and bring your favorite calming creams.

A BICYCLE SHOP IN HOLGUÍN

- **Rain:** During Cuba's rainiest months (May, September, and October), roads can become quite slippery and may even flood. In wet conditions, brakes are less responsive, so allow yourself extra time to brake. If you get caught in a downpour, pull over to the side of the road. Visibility will be extremely poor, and even if you think that you can see clearly enough, the cars behind you, which may not have functioning windshield wipers, may not be able to see you.

- **Road Conditions:** Though the conditions of many roads in Cuba have been improving over the years, many roads remain in disrepair, particularly those that have been battered by hurricanes. Be aware of road surfaces at all times, especially when riding quickly downhill. Potholes can be especially dangerous in the rain, where the depth of the hole cannot be quickly determined.

- **Night Riding:** You will certainly see Cubans riding their bikes late at night, without helmets, without bike lights, and in the absence of street lights. This can be extremely dangerous, but many of them have no choice. If you have a choice and can avoid riding at night, refrain from doing so.

- **Animals:** In rural areas it's possible that cows, pigs, goats, or other animals may stray onto the road. Always keep your eyes open—especially when riding downhill and around curves. Be especially careful not to run over animal poop on the road in the rain, as the brown slurry can spray onto your legs, panniers, or worse—your water bottle!

Health Issues

Knowing basic first aid procedures and carrying a first aid kit are important for cycle touring anywhere in the world. See the "First Aid Kit" (page 39) for a suggested packing list. In Cuba, where it can be impossible to find many medications, it's especially important to bring more than you think you will need and to leave behind whatever you don't use. Even a few painkillers or throat lozenges will be deeply appreciated.

Sunscreen should be worn every single day, even in the early evening, when sunburn is still possible. Mosquito repellent will be needed in some locations, especially at night and in coastal or rural areas. When at the beach, watch out for sea urchins, whose sharp spines love to dig into bare feet, and jellyfish, who enjoy stinging unsuspecting swimmers. Locals can usually tell you when and where jellyfish have been problematic.

Overall, Cuba is a very healthy country with an excellent public health system. Large cities have "international hospitals" fit to cater to tourists, but even small towns and remote areas have clinics staffed with well-trained doctors and nurses. Medical supplies can sometimes be in short supply, but supplies can often be brought from a nearby town if necessary.

Women's Health

Health issues facing women who are cycle touring through Cuba are the same as they would be anywhere else in the world. The main difference is that they can be more difficult to cope with in Cuba. The country's intense

Cuba is an extremely safe country with very low rates of rape, assault, and sexual violence. That said, women are objectified and harassed around the world, and Cuba is no different. While most of this harassment comes in the form of unwanted catcalling, whistling, and kissing noises, women should take the same precautions they do elsewhere:

· Ignore catcalls and keep walking with confidence.
· Keep your belongings close to you.
· Only carry as much cash as needed.
· Take a taxi home if you've had too much to drink.
· Always carry the business card of the establishment where you're staying.

In addition to the usual catcalls, Cuban jineteros are known to bestow grandiose compliments on female travelers, often claiming they're the most beautiful woman in the world. Some of these men are simply trying to find you a casa or restaurant so they can collect commission from the deal, while others are hoping to woo you into buying them Internet cards and putting money on their phones.

Cubans are often kind, generous people, eager to engage and make friends with travelers, but if you hear, "*Linda* (beautiful), where you from?" the caller is almost certainly a jinetero. When catcallers are persistent, try "*No me moleste*" (Don't bother me), pronounced "no may mol-ES-tay."

For more information about traveling alone as a woman in Cuba, including personal (very unpleasant) experiences, see www.escapingny.com/home/tips-for-solo-female-travel-to-cuba.

heat and humidity can make vaginal infections more frequent, while the lack of access to medications makes them harder to treat. If you're especially prone to yeast/candida/thrush, request a prescription from your doctor or bring over-the-counter pills and creams (such as clotrimazole). In a pinch, natural yogurt can be used to treat candida by applying it to a tampon and inserting it into the vagina.

To help prevent candida, shower immediately after a ride, avoid using scented soaps, put on clean clothing, and opt for loose-fitting cotton underwear off the bicycle. Avoid eating yeasty products such as beer and bread, and seek out acidophilus-rich yogurt, which is sold at many breakfast stands.

Urinary tract infections (UTIs) are another condition that many women are prone to. If you think you have a UTI, drink plenty of water and seek out nonprescription medication. It's possible to find medication at pharmacies in large cities, but if you're especially prone to UTIs, bring some medication with you. Cranberry juice is often recommended to prevent/treat UTIs but is not available in Cuba, so consider bringing cranberry pills with you.

GETTING AROUND—ON AND OFF YOUR BIKE

Note that while each city is unique and has its own appeal, most medium and large cities in Cuba have a similar setup, making them easy to navigate. Most important sites and buildings will surround the town park, which is typically called the *parque central* (central park) or named after a revolutionary hero, such as Céspedes, Martí, or Calixto García. In large cities there will be several parks surrounded by important buildings, including museums, art galleries, nightclubs, tourist information centers, banks, money exchanges (known as CaDeCas), and ETECSA communication centers, where WiFi cards can be purchased. Each town typically has (on or near the park), a municipal museum, a movie theater, and a live music venue such as La Casa de la Trova and/or La Casa de la Música. These are typically the best places to go for live music.

Understanding Kilometers

Rides in this book are listed in kilometers because that is the unit of measurement used in Cuba. Cyclists accustomed to using miles (hello, fellow Americans!) should get comfortable using kilometers. Even if you map out your route in miles and use a GPS device that uses miles, you will be thrown off by signage on the ground, which is exclusively in kilometers. Should you need to ask for directions, responses will be given in kilometers. As such, it is recommended you begin thinking about your ride in terms of kilometers. You may also want to consider switching your GPS device, if you're using one, to track in kilometers.

One kilometer = 0.625 miles, not quite two-thirds of a mile, but close enough to make for easier mental calculations. A 100-kilometer ride is the same as a 62-mile ride.

A typical touring cyclist with a lightly loaded bike will average around 15 to 20 kilometers per hour. At this rate, you can ride about 40 to 50 kilometers between breakfast and lunch. If the roads are hilly,

MANY CUBANS TRAVEL IN OPEN-AIR TRUCKS THAT CAN ACCOMMODATE BICYCLES, *IF* THERE'S ROOM

One of my main challenges while solo bike touring is finding a suitable place to use the bathroom, a particularly challenging task for women, who require a bit more privacy. Squatting on the side of the road is often a good option for bike tourists, but many Cuban roads offer no trees or bushes to hide you from trucks, cars, tractors, and horse carriages passing by. Men are often scattered along the side of the road, chopping grass with machetes. Mango, sugarcane, and corn fields are also full of men tending to the crops.

Sometimes I find a small house and ask to use their bathroom. Some very modest homeowners may be embarrassed to show you their bathroom, but if you explain that you can't find anywhere to use the toilet, they will likely let you use theirs. Ask the homeowner to watch your bicycle and tip them for the courtesy.

Some larger restaurants will allow you to use their bathroom even if you don't eat there. Once I was directed to the local funeral home to use the bathroom. In all cases, the only option is to ask an employee or random person nearby to watch your fully loaded bicycle. I've never had anything stolen, but always make sure to detach bike lights and handlebar bags, which are especially easy targets. Be creative, open-minded, and always bring toilet paper and hand sanitizer!

there is a strong headwind, or your bike is particularly heavy, you may only average 12 to 15 kilometers per hour. A moderate riding day will include about 60 to 100 kilometers (37 to 62 miles), which is the approximate range that most rides in this book fall into.

Cycling computers and GPS-tracking mobile phone apps, such as Strava and Ride with GPS, are handy but not necessary. Even the slightest variation, which can easily be caused by making additional bathroom or food stops or through technology malfunctions, can result in significant discrepancies over the course of a day. Focus less on the accumulated miles or kilometers on your computer/app and more on the distances between turns or on the landmarks given to identify turns.

Nonbicycle Transportation

Cuban tour buses and colectivo shared taxis are equipped to transport bicycles and are a great option for cyclists who may not have enough time to ride the entire route.

Viazul operates on a reliable daily schedule that casa particular owners and hotel staff are familiar with. If you would like to catch a bus part of the way, they can direct you to an unofficial bus stop or midway point to save time. For example, the Viazul bus from Baracoa to Guantánamo makes an unofficial stop in Imías and a couple of other small towns every day at the same time. Locals will know what time the bus passes through, so you can catch the bus right from Imías or ride part of the way to Guantánamo and then catch the bus. You could also skip the most difficult part of La Farola and catch the bus from Baracoa to Imías and then ride to Guantánamo.

Because drivers pocket whatever fares they charge at unofficial stops, you could be charged anywhere from a few CUCs to the full fare even if you're only riding for a small portion. Your bike may ride for free or you may be charged an additional fee. If you're too tired to ride or are behind schedule, you may have little choice. Either way, the convenience will likely be worth the cost.

Tour Buses

Cuba's state-owned, air-conditioned tour bus fleet, Viazul, is the most reliable form of transportation in Cuba. It caters mostly to tourists, but locals do ride and many drivers pick up Cubans along the route to fill up empty seats (and to collect a small fare). Many cycle tourists use buses for part of their trip, so office staff and drivers are very accustomed to accommodating cyclists. That said, bicycle pricing is not set in stone, so your bike may ride for free or you may be charged an additional CUC$5–$10 per ride.

Routes popular with bicycle tourists hoping to save time are Viñales to Havana, Viñales to Trinidad, Havana to Trinidad, Holguín to Baracoa, Baracoa to Santiago, Santiago to Bayamo or Holguín, and cross-country from Santiago or Holguín to Cienfuegos, Trinidad, or Havana.

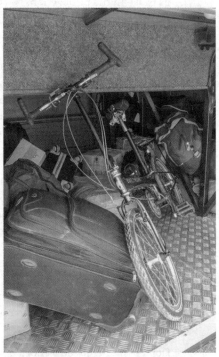

MY BICYCLE WITH OTHER LUGGAGE ON A VIAZUL BUS

MY BICYCLE STRAPPED TO THE TOP OF A CAR IN HOLGUÍN

I've transported my bicycle on Viazul half a dozen times and spoken with at least half a dozen other bike tourists who have done the same. In every instance, drivers were professional and took great care positioning the bicycle among other luggage. Regardless, it's recommended that you watch your bicycle and luggage be stored under the bus to ensure there is minimal risk of damage. Resting your bicycle chain-side up on top of panniers is a good way to minimize damage to the frame and components.

Colectivos

Colectivo shared taxis, also known as *maquinas* (machines) or *almendrones*, are old American classic cars that shuttle people along a set route, both within and between cities. Colectivos run between large and small cities within the same province and also go between provinces. Routes popular with bicycle tourists hoping to save time are the same as those in the bus section.

Prices vary based on the route length and popularity, and tourists are sometimes charged more than Cubans, but the rates are still very affordable. A 150-kilometer ride might cost around CUC$20–$30 and will save several days of riding. Colectivos are parked at virtually all bus stations in Cuba and often at other designated points around a city. For instance, in Holguín, colectivos going to Guardalavaca park in one area of the city, while colectivos going to Gibara park in another area. In Havana, colectivos are parked at the Viazul tourist bus terminal and also at the Ominibus terminal, which caters to Cubans. Colectivo parking locations sometimes change, so it's best to ask your host where to find a car.

Colectivo drivers are very accustomed to strapping everything from bicycles and boxes to sacks of potatoes and washing machines to the tops of their cars, and many drivers have installed proper racks and secure ropes to accommodate passengers with odd luggage. Some drivers will also offer to store your bike in the trunk, which may be a viable option on smooth roads. You don't want your bike crammed into a trunk along a bumpy road, where it's more likely to get damaged. The fare is paid in cash and there is little recourse should your bike fall off or be damaged, so watch closely as the driver secures your bike, and object if he stacks other luggage on top of it.

Trains

Don't do it. I enjoyed a short, bike-free adventure on Cuba's rail system but have heard no positive reviews from cyclists who have brought their bicycles on a train. The trains are crowded, run less frequently, and break down more than buses, and there is a much greater chance that your bicycle will go missing on a train.

In July 2019, Cuba began rolling out modern Chinese-built trains as part of a 10-year effort to modernize train commuting across the country. It's worth researching how reliability may have improved since publication of this book.

3

HAVANA

QUICK LOOK

The city of Havana sprawls 781 square kilometers across the province of Havana and is home to 2.1 million people, making it the largest (by area) and most populous city in the Caribbean. To the west of Havana is Viñales province, known for lush valleys and tobacco plantations; to the east is a long stretch of beaches, known collectively as Playas del Este. Havana's harbor made it a wealthy city during colonial times, and its world-famous Malecón, or sea wall esplanade, continues to be one of the most interesting and lively places to people-watch in the city.

Excellent urban cycling exists within Havana, while more rural landscapes intrigue riders heading in or out of the capital city. Bicycle ferries offer an alternate route to the eastern suburbs of Casablanca (where ancient forts and a massive Cristo statue preside over the Havana harbor) and to Cojímar, the quiet fishing village where Ernest Hemingway famously docked his boat.

Highlights

- A seaside bike-friendly stretch can be found along the **Malecón**, with grandiose and sometimes crumbling buildings on one side and splashing, salty waves on the other.
- Che Guevara and Camilo Cienfuegos murals decorate the **Plaza de Revolución** across from the impressive **José Martí Memorial**.
- **Necropolis Cristóbal Colón** is one of the largest cemeteries in the Americas, famous for its elaborate marble statues, mausoleums, and striking religious iconography and folklore.
- Spectacular views of the city from the historic **El Morro** and **Fortaleza de San Carlos de la Cabaña** can be had across the harbor. La Cabaña hosts a nightly *cañonazo* ceremony at 9 p.m., where actors dressed in 18th-century military regalia reenact the firing of a cannon over Havana harbor—a ritual that used to signify the closing of the city gates.
- The **Fábrica de Arte Cubano** (FAC) nightclub and art gallery could easily be mistaken for a hip Brooklyn art space. Several bars and restaurants cater to a mixed crowd of tourists and locals.

FELIX GUIROLA RIDING HIS "SMALL BIKE" TO REVOLUTION PLAZA

- **Museo de la Revolución,** housed in the former Presidential Palace, chronicles the events leading up to, during, and immediately after the Cuban Revolution.
- **Museo Nacional de Bellas Artes de La Habana** is arguably the finest art gallery in the Caribbean. The museum is spread across two campuses: the Arte Cubano building, which displays purely Cuban art, and the Arte Universal building two blocks away, exhibiting international art. If pressed for time, opt for Arte Cubano.
- Live music can be found around every corner in Havana, but the best salsa bands perform at **La Casa de la Música.** For cabaret, head to **the Tropicana,** which puts on an excellent, albeit expensive, show. For salsa dancing, head to **1830.**

Need-to-Know

- Old Havana may have colonial charm and a very dense concentration of museums, galleries, and attractions, but the dizzying maze of poorly maintained streets and third-floor walk-up casas make it a less than ideal base for cyclists.
- Bikes are not allowed on Fifth Avenue in Havana.
- Traffic moves quickly, with cars dodging around bicycles, bicitaxis, and pedestrians, so full concentration is required to bike in Havana.
- Parqueo bicycle parking stations are located on nearly every block in Old and Central Havana.

Terrain

A few hills exist in the province, but it is generally flat, especially toward the coast and in Havana city proper.

Special Events

- International Jazz Festival: January
- Feria de Libros (International Book Fair): February
- Habanos Cigar Festival: February
- Dia Internacional Contra Homofobia y Transfobia (LGBTQ+ pride events): May 17
- Festival Internacional Boleros de Oro: June
- Carnaval along the Malecón: August
- Festival Internacional de Ballet de La Habana: Even-numbered years in October
- Marabana marathon: November
- Festival Internacional de Nuevo Cine: December

Tourist Information

Most hotels have a state-run tour information desk (such as **Gaviota**) with maps, brochures, and general information. Proper **Infotur** offices are located in Old Havana on the corner of Obispo and San Ignacio and at Obispo #524 between Bernaza and Villegas. **Cubatur** is located on the corner of 23rd and L (Vedado) and also has offices in many large hotels.

Internet access is available at dozens of hotels, plazas, parks, and public areas (such as the corner of 23rd and L in Vedado), as are **ETECSA** WiFi cards. It's best to ask your host for the nearest location.

The **Banco de Crédito y Comercio** is in Vedado on the corner of Línea and Paseo and in Old Havana on Mercedes and Amargura. The **Banco Financiero Internacional** is in Old Havana on Oficios and Brasil. All are open 9 a.m.–3 p.m. Monday–Friday. There are numerous **CaDeCas** around the city, including the corner of Oficios and Lamparilla in Old Havana, the corner of Neptuno and Consulado in Central Havana, and the corner of 23rd and J in Vedado. Hours vary but are typically 7 a.m.–6 p.m. Monday–Saturday and 8 a.m.–1 p.m. Sunday.

ACCOMMODATIONS IN HAVANA

Havana is large, and every neighborhood has its own appeal. One of the most popular neighborhoods is *La Habana Vieja* (Old Havana). It's located smack dab in the middle of the action, but most accommodations are on the second and third floors, complicating bike storage. Vedado has fewer museums and historic plazas but has loads of restaurants, entertainment, and nightlife. Apartments in Vedado are often on the first floor (or at least have first-floor bike storage) and tend to be larger and quieter than other neighborhoods. *Centro Habana* (Central Havana) is located between Old Havana and Vedado, and apartments there tend to be noisy and on upper floors.

Casa Las Bicicletas

(Also known as "La Ventilada")
Amargura #360, between Aguacate and Villegas, Old Havana
7-8635566 or 5-5106443
laventilada360@gmail.com or lasbicicletas260@gmail.com

Vintage bicycle photographs and posters decorate this aptly named four-bedroom casa—two on the ground floor and two upstairs (CUC$30–$40 each). Each room has two beds, and there's a fourth-floor terrace for relaxing.

Casa Jesús y María

Aguacate #518, between Sol and Muralla, Old Havana
7-8611378 or 7-8667765
jesusmaria2003@yahoo.com
www.housejesusymaria.com

A dozen flags from around the world decorate the rooftop of this bright blue home, making it easy to spot from a distance. Take your pick of five bedrooms (one to three beds each, CUC$30–$40 per room) and relax on the sunny, plant-filled patio.

Casa Magda

Calle K #508 Bajos (lower), between 25th and 27th, Vedado
7-8323269 or 5-2732376
milagrotrev@informed.sld.cu

This large, classic house offers two ground-floor rooms in the family's home and another two in a private apartment behind the house. The street is quiet and tree-lined, and the porch has inviting rocking chairs. If Casa Magda is full, the owner's upstairs neighbor, Marina Madan Bugarín, rents a massive room with a private, luxurious, European-style bathroom (7-8321639 or 5-266353). Ground-floor bike parking and comfy porch rocking chairs are also available if you book with Marina.

Casa Flamboyan

Calle 19 #459 Bajos Apt. 1 (lower), between E and F Streets, Vedado
7-8353963 or 5-8457913
reservation@lacasaflamboyan.com

It's no wonder that this modern, elegant, three-bedroom home is one of the top-rated and most sought-after homes in Havana. Alex (Italian) and his husband, Jesús (Cuban), live on the premises and are a friendly, upbeat couple who know absolutely everything about the city. Jesús is also a registered tour guide, and the couple can arrange excursions.

RESTAURANTS IN HAVANA

The Internet and travel guides are full of top restaurants in Havana and typically include La Guardia, where the decapitated statue and grandiose staircase at the entrance are worth a visit in and of themselves; San Cristóbal, where President Obama and other famous world leaders have dined; and Mama Ines, run by Fidel Castro's former chef. Here are a few fun options that, as of publication, were still a bit under the radar. All offer vegetarian options.

Sushi Sayu

Corner of Obrapia and Aguacate, Old Havana
Monday–Saturday 10 a.m.–7 p.m.
Mains $3–$5

This tiny corner joint in Old Havana serves Japanese cuisine that is as authentic as possible while using ingredients available in Cuba. It's run by a Japanese woman who married Cuban painter Nelson Dominguez. The restaurant attracts just about every Japanese tourist in Havana; they crowd around the main six-seat table or perch on one of 10 small stools that border the walls, where bowls of Japanese curry and oyster sushi balance on narrow shelves affixed to the walls. The chirashisushi is an especially refreshing sweet and sour rice dish with a fresh ginger punch.

El Café

Amargura #358, between Aguacate y Villegas, Old Havana
Daily 9 a.m.–6 p.m.
Mains $5–$8

This hip café serves all-day breakfast (eggs, toast, yogurt, pancakes with fresh fruit) and several sandwiches, including hummus and veggies served on the best grilled sourdough in the country. The café is open late on Fridays, when a live DJ spins until midnight. Guests dine on a collection of picnic tables, with light streaming in from front windows and a small patio. You may not see a name outside, so look for the large *Guardia en Alta* mural directly across from the restaurant.

Camino al Sol

Calle 3 #363 at the corner of Paseo (across from the Meliá Cohiba), Vedado
Daily 10 a.m.–10 p.m.
Small plates $2–$4

Havana's first vegetarian restaurant attracts mostly locals who are eager to try the eclectic plant-based dishes that can't be found anywhere else in the city (or country). You'll see them bringing their own plastic containers for takeaway. The menu changes daily, but a typical day may offer a selection of fresh pastas, quinoa-stuffed zucchini and cabbage rolls, vegetable tarts, potato lasagna, millet cakes with stewed okra, and yucca-beet burgers.

CLASSIC CAR IN FRONT OF A CLASSIC OLD HAVANA BACKDROP

Helad'oro
Aguiar #205, between Empredrado & Tejadillo, Old Havana
Daily 11 a.m.–10 p.m.
$2–$4
Far from Havana's most famous ice cream parlor, Coppelia, which serves government-subsidized scoops for pocket change, typically only available in chocolate and strawberry, Helad'oro offers artisan ice cream in over 30 flavors, including mojito, blackberry, mamey, and "tropical breakfast."

BICYCLE SHOPS

Proper bike shops offering rows of shiny new bikes and parts don't exist in Cuba as they do elsewhere, but Havana is the best place in the country to find spare parts. The businesses below rent bicycles (about CUC$15–$20/day) and lead guided city bike tours (about CUC$30 for a three-hour tour). Even solo bike tourists can enjoy one of the guided city rides to engage with local cyclists and see the city through their eyes.

Each business is run by cycling enthusiasts who would be happy to sell you parts (if they're available), and some may be available for hire for custom tours outside Havana. Any of them would be a great place to leave behind whatever spare cycling clothes, bike parts, or entire bicycles you don't need to take with you, though bicycle parts are in much greater need in small towns that don't receive tourists.

Velo Cuba
Montero Sánchez #34 between 21st and 23rd, Vedado
Prado #20, across from Iberostar Grand Packard, near the Malecón, Old Havana
5-2825148 or 7-8368820
veloencuba.com
- Female-run bicycle shop that focuses on teaching women bicycle maintenance and leading cycling-themed youth programs
- Offers discounts to students, children, and retirees
- Daily tours focusing on culture, history, and Afro-Cuban religion in addition to custom guided tours to beaches and nearby provinces
- Full-service bicycle maintenance and repairs at two locations
- Some employees/owners have experience organizing small bike tours to other provinces
- Bicycle rentals
- Velo Cuba oversees a state-sponsored bikeshare program that launched in Havana in late 2018, and they're leading efforts to institute car-free streets in Old Havana

Mountain Bici Cuba
Office/Casa: Calle 27 #51B, between N and O, Vedado
Workshop: Calle 6, between Línea and Calle 11. There is no building number, but the shop is 10 meters from the corner of Línea. Note that they're normally only in the work-

shop from 8:30–9 a.m. and 2:30–3 p.m., before/after their group rides, so phone is the best way to catch them.
5-3877152 or 7-8708690

- A self-described group of "Cuban entrepreneurs dedicated to cycle tourism"
- Offers daily history and culture tours of Havana and the bay
- Every group tour includes multiple guides and a bicycle mechanic for support
- The only bicycle tour company in Havana that specializes in mountain bikes
- Some of the owners are cycle tourists and might be available for hire to lead a small group tour to other provinces
- Bicycle rentals

Ruta Bikes
16th Street #152, on the corner of 13th Street in Vedado
5-2476633
info@rutabikes.com
www.rutabikes.com

- Havana's first bicycle tour and rental company
- Offers daily morning, sunset, and bay tours
- Bicycle rentals

Bike Rental & Tours Havana
Carlos III #1115 between Luaces and Montoro, Plaza, Havana, Cuba
5-4637103
bikerentalhavana@nauta.cu or bikerentalhavana@gmail.com
bikerentalhavana.com

- Offering daily historical and "Real Havana" tours
- Bicycle rentals, including rear bicycle seats for children

CRITICAL MASS IN HAVANA

On the first Sunday of each month, cyclists gather in the Parque de los Mártires Universitarios on the corner of Infanta and San Lazaro, on the border of Central Havana and Vedado. At 5 p.m. they embark on a casual group bike ride modeled after Critical Mass, an informal monthly cycling ride that takes place around the world, aiming to reclaim streets and promote cycling. In Havana, casual cyclists, professional racers, bike tour organizers, families with children, and tourists gather for the ride, which has swelled to over 100 people. If you plan to be in Havana during the first weekend of the month, the event is definitely worth checking out.

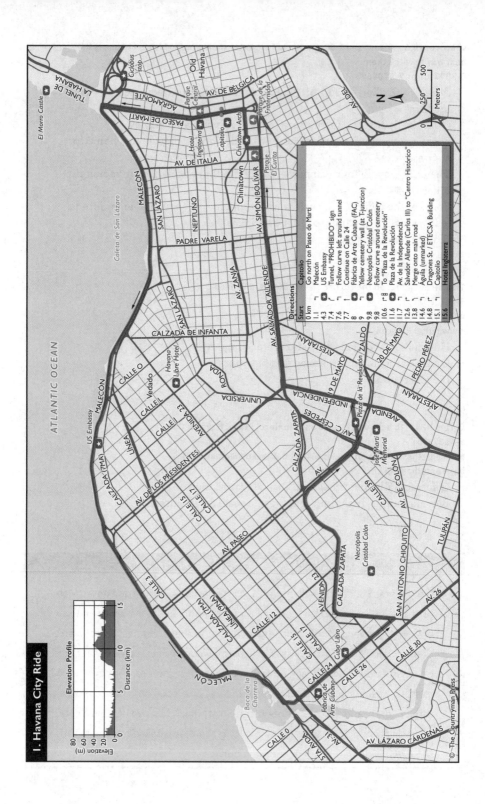

I. Havana City Ride

Elevation Profile

Elevation (m): 80 60 40 20 0
Distance (km): 0 5 10 15

Directions

Start		Capitolio
0 km	↑	Go north on Paseo de Martí
1.1	←	Malecón
4.3	←	US Embassy
7.4	⌒	Tunnel, "PROHIBIDO" sign
7.6	←	Follow curve left around tunnel
7.7	↑	Continue on Calle 24
8	←	Fábrica de Arte Cubano (FAC)
9	←	Yellow cemetery wall (at T-junction)
9.8	←	Necrópolis Cristóbal Colón
9.8	⌒	Follow curve around cemetery
10.6	↑B	To "Plaza de la Revolución"
11.6	←	Plaza de la Revolución
11.7	←	Av. de la Independencia
12.6	←	Salvador Allende (Carlos III) to "Centro Histórico"
13.8	←	Merge onto main road
14.6	←	Águila (unmarked)
14.8	←	Dragones St. / ETECSA Building
15.1	←	Capitolio
15.6		Hotel Inglaterra

© The Countryman Press

CicloCuba
San Pedro #258, between Sol and Muralla, Old Havana
7-8662559
reservas@ciclocuba.com
- Bicycle and bike-touring equipment rental
- Secure luggage storage for clients
- General repairs
- Support planning for a self-guided bicycle tour

RIDE #1. HAVANA CITY RIDE

Distance: 9.7 miles/15.6 kilometers
Elevation: 284 feet/87 meters
Difficulty: Easy
Time: 1–2 hours

This ride can be completed in a couple hours or can stretch across the entire day if you visit all the attractions. You'll pass the **US Embassy** and **Fábrica de Arte Cubano (FAC)**, Havana's best-known art gallery and nightclub (Thursday–Sunday 8 p.m.–3 a.m.). Fresh sugarcane juice, much harder to find in Havana than elsewhere, is available at the **guarapera** on Calle 24 (between 15th and 17th). Two blocks farther (between 19th and 21st) is **Cuba Libro** bookstore, lending library, and café. Bring your bike into the patio, grab an iced coffee or tea, and relax on a hammock under the trees. Check flyers posted on the wall that may announce upcoming film nights, parties, or bike rides. Say hi to the owner, Connor, an American woman who's been living in Cuba since the early 2000s, and let her know you're bike touring the island!

Necropolis Cristóbal Colón is one of the largest cemeteries in the Americas and can be a quick stop or a half-day activity. The marble statues are especially photogenic just before sunset. Should you wish to enter the cemetery, leave your bike with the parking attendant and pay the $5 entrance fee plus tip for parking. Note there are bathrooms inside the cemetery and in the restaurant across the street.

Camilo Cienfuegos and Che Guevara murals decorate the walls surrounding the **Plaza de Revolución,** which is across from the massive **José Martí Memorial.** Bicycle riding is not permitted anywhere on the plaza. Walk your bike to the opposite corner (behind Camilo Cienfuegos's image) and be careful as you turn left onto Avenida de Independencia, a very wide street with fast-moving traffic. Look both ways several times before crossing. Once you're on Salvador Allende (Carlos Tercero), stay in the right-hand buffer road to avoid heavy traffic.

HAVANA'S CHINATOWN

Parque El Curita is one of several city parks where old colectivo cars gather to recruit passengers heading to nearby cities. This is the place to catch a shared taxi to Guanabo or Playas del Este. The signage is poor, so note that you will turn immediately after the park, where there is a four-story building. Just after the 10-story, ornately decorated ETECSA building, you'll ride under the **Chinatown arch** and arrive at **Parque de Fraternidad,** where the busts of historical leaders and personalities are on display, including Abraham Lincoln, Simón Bolivar, and Benito Juárez.

After years of construction, Havana's **Capitolio** reopened in 2018 and now offers tours in English or Spanish. One block farther is the lively **Parque Central,** a great place for people-watching, and where you can frequently catch live music, dance, and theatrical performances. The ride ends across the street from Parque Central at **Hotel Inglaterra,** which opened in 1875 and is Havana's oldest hotel. Famous past guests include José Martí and Anna Pavlova. Even if you don't stay at the hotel, you can enjoy live music on the outdoor patio or the upstairs rooftop, which has a bar and grill and offers astounding views of the city.

RIDE #2. CRISTO AND COJÍMAR

Distance: 11.3 miles/18.2 kilometers
Elevation: 762 feet/232 meters
Difficulty: Easy to Moderate
Time: 2 hours

This ride starts at the dock of the **Casablanca Ferry.** Note that there are two different ferries, Casablanca and Regla, so make sure you take the right one. Both ferries, or *lanchitas,* leave from the ferry terminal on Avenida del Puerto. During the ferry ride, you're likely to see spandex-clad Cubans, as many Habaneros train along the highway and at the velodrome across the water. The ferries operate from 5 a.m. to midnight and cost one Cuban peso. They run approximately every 15 minutes during the day and once an hour in the evening. It's a more reliable and scenic means to cross the water than the Ciclobus, which goes through an underground tunnel, where cycling is prohibited.

A DAY AT HAVANA'S VELODROME

Aside from the steep, winding hill up to the **Cristo statue,** the ride is relatively flat. After passing the Cristo, which presides over the bay, you'll ride through the working-class Casablanca neighborhood and on to Havana's **Velodromo,** which is worth a stop. I have been invited inside several times to meet and take pictures with athletes. Pull up to the entrance and ask if you can go inside to watch the riders!

Next up is **Cojímar,** which sits within the city limits of Havana but feels as though it's worlds away. Hemingway

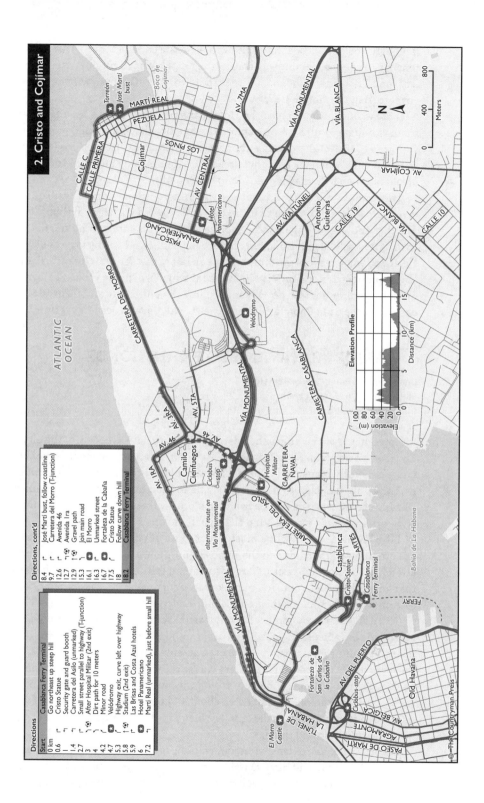

famously docked his boat here, and while classic cars and tour buses bring tourists to see the Hemingway statue, the neighborhood retains a nontouristy feel. This ride is the most direct route through Cojímar and hugs the coast to visit the **Hemingway bust.**

Instead of continuing past the **Hotel Panamericano** at 6.1k, an alternate route would be to turn left to explore the neighborhood a bit and meander your way to the waterfront. In either case, immediately after the José Martí bust and park, you'll take a right to reach the Hemingway bust and **Torreón,** an old Spanish fort, then zigzag along the coastline.

The route detailed in the directions will take you along a gravel route that turns into a rocky dirt path that can get muddy when it's been raining a lot. The dirt and gravel only last for about a kilometer before joining the main road. If it hasn't been raining, this route can be followed on any type of bicycle. If you wish to avoid the dirt path, take a left at marker 12.6 (Ave 46), then a right onto the Autopista/Via Monumental, which will guide you to **El Morro** castle, standing guard over Havana. Follow the curve left to the **Fortaleza de San Carlos de la Cabaña** and then back to the Casablanca ferry terminal.

🚲 RIDE #3. HAVANA TO BAHÍA HONDA

Distance: 65.5 miles/105.4 kilometers
Elevation: 2,170 feet/661 meters
Difficulty: Very Difficult
Time: 7–10 hours

Riding outside of Havana is the best way to appreciate the scale of the city. The ride starts off on Havana's hectic Malecón, where traffic moves quickly but is generally respectful of bikes. The right lane is reserved for slow traffic, including bicycles, though you may be invited to bike on the sidewalk. Dozens of fishermen cast lines from the stone wall alongside lovers kissing and perhaps an old man playing the horn to no one in particular.

Fifth Avenue would be the most direct route out of the city, but bicycles are not allowed there, due to the imposed minimum speed limit along the stretch of foreign embassies. Cars speed along Fifth Avenue (Av 5ta) faster than any other street and do not make room for cyclists. Do not attempt to ride on it. Instead, follow this route along Third Avenue.

Third Avenue is an admittedly unpleasant route. It's a popular route for colectivo share taxis, so you will be breathing in exhaust and stopping frequently to allow for passengers exiting and entering cars. Trust that this is the most direct and safest route out of Havana. Eventually you'll be dropped back onto Fifth Avenue, which curves its way out of the city and turns into the Carrertera Panamericana. After about 15 kilometers, you'll finally feel like you're starting to leave the city, as wide roads lined with huge trees offer a bit of shade here and there.

Fusterlandia is an extensive ongoing mosaic art installation in Jaimanitas. It can be visited as a half-day excursion from Havana, or you could stop on your way to Bahía Honda, assuming you leave Havana around 8:30 a.m. Leaving any

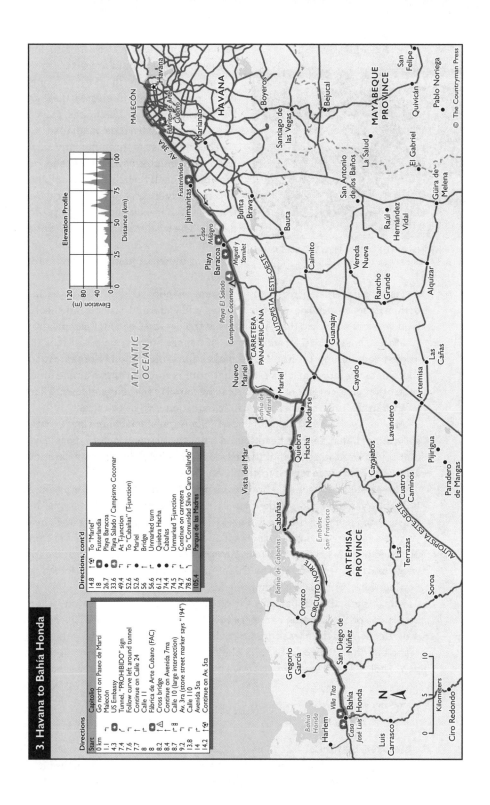

3. Havana to Bahía Honda

Directions

Start	Capitolio
0 km	Go north on Paseo de Martí
1.1	Malecón
4.3	US Embassy
7.4	Tunnel, "PROHIBIDO" sign
7.6	Follow curve left around tunnel
7.7	Continue on Calle 24
8	Calle 11
8	Fábrica de Arte Cubano (FAC)
8.2	Cross bridge
8.4	Continue on Avenida 7ma
8.7	Calle 10 (large intersection)
9.2	Av. 3ra (stone street marker says "194")
13.8	Calle 110
14	Avenida 5ta
14.2	Continue on Av. 5ta

Directions, cont'd

14.8	To "Mariel"
18	Fusterlandia
26.7	Playa Baracoa
33.6	Playa Salado / Campismo Cocomar
49.4	At T-junction
52.6	To "Cabañas" (T-junction)
52.6	Mariel
56	Bridge
56.6	Unmarked turn
61.2	Quiebra Hacha
74.4	Cabañas
74.5	Unmarked T-junction
74.7	Continue on carretera
78.6	To "Comunidad Silvio Caro Gallardo"
105.4	Parque de las Madres

© The Countryman Press

A FARMER POSING WITH THE AUTHOR'S BIKE SOMEWHERE BETWEEN BAHÍA HONDA AND VIÑALES

earlier would likely get you there before it opens. Official hours are 9:30 a.m. to 4 p.m., but staff say they're often open until 5 p.m. For those interested, there are half a dozen casas in Jaimanitas, most of which are visible from the main road.

This ride passes through many small towns with cafeterias along the road, but the small beach town of Baracoa makes an especially nice stop for a snack. See the "Playa Baracoa" box (opposite) for details. The road from Baracoa to Mariel continues flat, with a few bumps and pleasant views of fields and the sea in the distance.

For those interested in camping, the semi-abandoned Playa Salado is a nice option. Reggaeton music will welcome you, and you'll find a couple ramshackle food vendors servicing the few visitors at the nearby Coco Mar campismo.

Mariel, best known for its famous 1980 mass emigration boat lift, is the largest town along the route and makes for a nice midday break. About 1 kilometer before Mariel is a thatched-roof restaurant that's a nice lunch spot; otherwise, several restaurants can be found in the center of town. There is WiFi in the town's park and a public bathroom across the street.

Mariel is very industrial, and you will likely get stuck behind large trucks spewing exhaust as they head to and from the cement factory. Locals say that if you want to rent (an unlicensed) room, you should just ask around. The same holds true for the town of Cabañas.

The stretch between Quebra Hacha and Cabañas is quite bumpy, but it is doable on a road bike. Wide-open valleys welcome you, and tree-studded hills stretch as far as the eye can see. Families are likely to wave and cheer you on as you pass through their village. Note that there will be very few places to purchase water between Havana and Bahía Honda, so bring extra water and/or a water filter. The Cupet gas station (at 74k) typically stocks bottled water, but it is not guaranteed.

The stretch after Cabañas is the most gorgeous part of the route, where both sides of the winding carretera are lined with rolling hills. The valleys grow deeper and the horses grazing below look tiny. Palm trees dot the land-scape and the occasional banana plantation or patch of sunflowers offers a pop of color. The ride ends at the town park, which locals refer to as *el parque*.

ACCOMMODATIONS IN BAHÍA HONDA

Casa José Luis

4-8668466 or 5-2982036

Located next to the policlínico, this casa offers three nice rooms in the base-ment (CUC$25–$30). The hosts are very friendly and will let you test out the

About a quarter of the way to Bahía Honda is the fishing village of Baracoa, which has a small beach that makes for a nice day trip. The town has several nice casas, and the two listed here are particularly well suited to cater to cyclists. Some casas have addresses, but street names are not always used, so it will be easiest to find the casa using the descriptions below.

To get to Playa Baracoa, follow the directions from Havana to Bahía Honda, and at 26.5k, turn right toward Baracoa. About 100 meters later, take a left at Hotel Baracoa, which is usually full, hosting sports groups and organizations. A few blocks later, you'll arrive in the center of town. To reach casa Miguel y Yamilet, continue to 27.7k, turn right at the T-junction, and follow the curve until you see the house on your right.

Casa Milagro
5-2679038
milagropp@nauta.cu

This is a large red home on the main road from Havana, just before the right turn to Baracoa Beach. It's a modern home with two upstairs bedrooms (CUC$20–$30), but bikes can be kept on the ground floor. This casa is a bit farther from the beach but is conveniently located on the main road.

Miguel y Yamilet
4-7378113 or 5-2707936

This waterfront casa is along the main street in Baracoa, address #15408. The ground floor has a two-bedroom apartment (CUC$20–$30/room) and a ramp, making for easy bike storage. There is also a small, private swimming area behind the casa.

---

different beds to choose the firmness you prefer. This casa is the nearest to the main park but requires bringing your bike down a flight of stairs.

Villa Tita
Ave 23 #2005
5-5497774
villatita@nauta.cu

This is the first casa you'll pass as you enter Bahía Honda and is a five-minute walk to the park. It's a comfortable, modest casa with three rooms (CUC$20–$25 each, each with two or three beds). Tita is a gem, happy to offer laundry service and prepare fantastic, affordable meals. There are also four rocking chairs on the large front porch with a great view of the sunset.

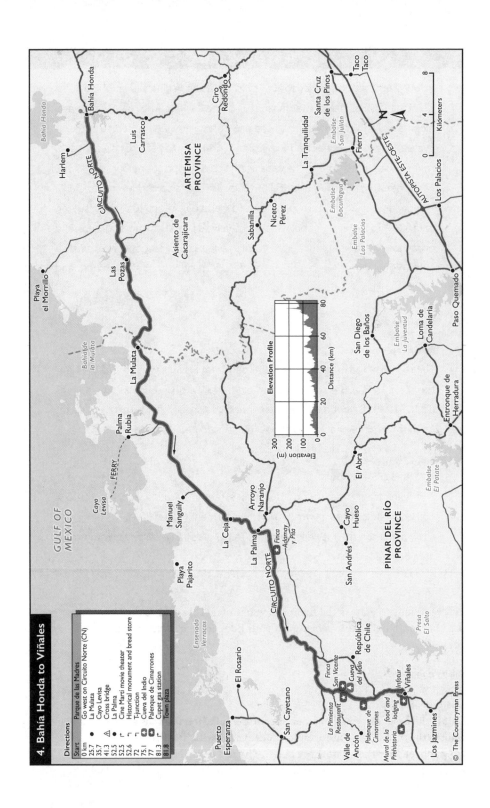

4. Bahía Honda to Viñales

Directions

Start	
0 km	Parque de las Madres
	Go west on Circuito Norte (CN)
25.7	La Mulata
35.7 •	Cayo Levisa
41.3 △	Cross bridge
52.5 •	La Palma
52.5 ┏	Cine Martí movie theater
52.6 ┏	Historical monument and bread store
72 ┏	T-junction
75.1 ┏✦✦	Cueva del Indio
77 ┏✦	Palenque de Cimarrones
81.3 ┏	Cupet gas station
81.8	Town plaza

© The Countryman Press

 # RIDE #4. BAHÍA HONDA TO VIÑALES

Distance: 50.8 miles/81.8 kilometers
Elevation: 2,752 feet/784 meters
Difficulty: Very Difficult
Time: 7–10 hours

This ride is easily one of the most beautiful in Cuba, but magnificent mountain views don't come easily. Be prepared for steep hills as you enter Viñales. The ride starts at the town park, where you head onto the *Circuito Norte* (North Circuit), which winds through wide-open valleys all the way to Viñales.

Men cutting grass with machetes or driving tractors will smile and wave, but the Circuito Norte (CN) is generally not frequently traveled, so you won't see many trucks or cars. The small town of La Mulata has a bakery and a casa particular. The 9-kilometer stretch between La Mulata and Cayo Levisa can get very bumpy at times, but most large potholes can be avoided. Smaller bumps are unavoidable but are manageable on any bicycle.

Small banana plantations and rice paddies dot the landscape. You may see long stretches of what looks like light brown gravel or dirt on the road, but it is actually rice left out to dry in the sun. About 2 kilometers before La Palma is a small shop selling fresh fruit, water, and other drinks on the side of the road. The shop has a small roof and some stools, a rare corner along this route to enjoy a snack in the shade. Though you'll pass through many small towns, there won't be many opportunities to buy water or substantial food. La Palma has a few pizzerias and small cafeterias, but the options are limited. There is WiFi in the park, and you'll find bathrooms across the street.

Approximately 3 kilometers past La Palma is Finca Adamay y Pita, a casa particular on an actual farm. (For those interested, the *finca* [farm] can be contacted at ady.ch@nauta.cu or 5-4314497.) The scenery soon turns to tobacco fields with triangular tobacco houses erected where farmers dry the leaves that will be rolled into cigars. Casas particulares pop up as far as 10 kilometers from the center of Viñales.

About 2 kilometers after the T-junction (72k) lie La Pimienta restaurant on the right and Finca San Vicente on the left. Both serve large plates of typical Cuban food. At 75.1k is Cueva del Indio, one of Viñales's most popular attractions, a cave that was an ancient indigenous dwelling where tourists take a short boat ride on an underground river. Ambitious cyclists who don't want to backtrack to visit the cave can leave their bikes with the parking attendant across the street and pay the CUC$5 admission fee. Another 2 kilometers down the road is Palenque de Cimarrones, an open-air museum, bar, and disco built into the side of a cliff. The ride ends at the town square locals refer to as el parque or la plaza.

4

PINAR DEL RÍO

QUICK LOOK

Pinar del Río is Cuba's westernmost province, famous for its limestone mogote mountains, lush valleys, tobacco fields in the north, and pristine scuba diving in the south. The central part of the province is punctuated with caves first used as hideouts by the Taíno; by Cubans fighting for independence from Spain; by guerilla revolutionaries set on overthrowing the Batista regime; and by Che Guevara, who set up his headquarters in a cave during the Cuban Missile Crisis. Some of these caves have since been converted into museums and nightclubs, while others serve as bases for scientific research.

Cuba's first tobacco factory opened in Pinar in the 1700s, and the region's primary draw continues to be the tobacco industry. Tobacco tours are conducted by foot, horseback, and classic car, but of course the best views are by bicycle. Cuba's world-famous cigars are sold everywhere in Cuba, but Viñales is the place to buy cigars directly from farmers.

No more than 1 square kilometer, the town of Viñales is a quaint town full of brightly colored homes, almost all of which are casas particulares. Most homes have porches equipped with rocking chairs, and some homes have rooftop patios where you can watch the sun set over the mogotes.

Highlights
- **Cayo Jutías** is a pristine, out-of-the-way beach that is challenging to get to (even by car!) but offers a unique, relaxed environment. The beach is a 3-kilometer blanket of white sand studded with pine trees and lined with gray mangroves.
- Dozens of farms offer **tobacco tours** where English-speaking farmers and tour guides walk you through the tobacco-growing and cigar-manufacturing process. At the end, you're invited to sample a cigar and given the opportunity to purchase some.
- **Cueva del Indio** (9 a.m.–5 p.m.) offers riverboat rides through the cave but is not nearly as impressive as the much larger **Gran Caverna de San Tomás** (one of the longest cave systems in the Western Hemisphere), which makes for an excellent day trip.
- **Palenque de Cimarrones** is a former runaway slave hideout and open-air

museum carved into the side of a mountain. The exhibit is open from 9 a.m. to 6 p.m. and the all-day bar converts to a disco at 10 p.m. on Saturday nights.

- The **Mural de la Prehistória** remains one of the most popular attractions in Viñales, though many find it cheesy. The 120-meter-long mural was completed by a follower of famed Mexican muralist Diego Rivera and took 18 people four years to complete.
- Several restaurants in Viñales offer some of the best views in Cuba, including **Balcón del Valle** and **El Paraiso,** an organic farm-to-table restaurant.

Need-to-Know

- As in many cities, just about everyone claims to be a tour guide. Should you choose to do a horseback tour, it's especially important to go with a good guide who will only lead you along safe paths. Speak with your casa to find a trusted guide.
- Excellent cycling paths exist leading you through the mountain valleys. Some of these routes are a series of unmarked turns through valleys with no reliable landmarks; thus, they were too complicated to include in this book. Speak with your casa if you'd like them to help find a local to accompany you, or call Daily, a local tour guide that can help arrange walking or cycling tours (5-8342922).

Terrain

All of the rides in this book passing through Pinar del Río are punctuated by steep mountain climbs offering rewarding views of misty mountain valleys and turquoise waters. The rides are very challenging and gratifying.

Special Events

While tobacco tours are available year-round, harvest season is January through April, which is when you're most likely to see campesinos harvesting full fields.

Tourist Information

Viñales is a tiny town, so just about everything can be found within a block of the town plaza on the main drag, Salvador Cisneros. The **Infotur** office (8 a.m.–5 p.m. Monday–Saturday) is located at Salvador Cisneros #63b. WiFi is available in the town plaza, and you can purchase Internet cards at the ETECSA office around the corner at Caferino Fernández #3 (8:30 a.m.–7 p.m. Monday–Saturday).

The **Banco de Crédito y Comercio** is on Salvador Cisneros #58 (8 a.m.–3 p.m.

CLASSIC CAR ON THE BEACH IN CAYO JUTÍAS

Monday–Friday,8a.m.–11a.m.Saturday)andhasanATM.The**CaDeCa**(8:30a.m.–4 p.m. Monday–Saturday, 8:30 a.m.–1 p.m. Sunday) is located on the corner of Salvador Cisneros and Adela Azcuy.

ACCOMMODATIONS IN VIÑALES

El Amanecer

Km 23 Carretera a Viñales (in front of the Centro Turístico)
4-8695858 or 5-4605172
anadelys.iglesias@nauta.cu or elamanecer@nauta.cu
Anita and her family offer three rooms (CUC$35 each) in a home with some of the best views in Viñales, enjoyed from the rooftop or the front porch's rocking chairs. One room has its own bathroom, while the other two share a bathroom. The family lives in the home directly behind the casa, so guests have full privacy while enjoying the convenience of having the hosts nearby. Anita is a fantastic cook who is very accustomed to preparing vegetarian food. She serves meals at a large open-air table behind the home. Note that this house is about 2.5 kilometers outside of central Viñales. Many travelers appreciate being a bit removed—and the views are remarkable—but a large hill separates you and the main part of town. If you're not in the mood to walk or ride, the house can easily call you a taxi to town, which costs CUC$5.

Cabaña La Cañada

Km 23 Carretera a Viñales (in front of the Centro Turístico)
5-2238888 or 5-4604011
denisis80@nauta.cu
Cabaña La Cañada is probably the closest you'll get to a rustic cabin (with all the amenities) in Cuba. This private cabin has two rooms (CUC$35 each), and Rayma and her friendly family live next door, eager to attend to guests. Note that this casa is just behind Casa El Amanacer, slightly down the hill. Large groups could spread guests across the two houses.

Villa Estrella y Yari

Calle Orlando Nodarse Interior #19
4-8796202 or 5-3642709
Estrella and Yari are a mother-daughter team providing top-notch hospitality to guests staying in their three rooms (CUC$25 each). The family lives in the same home, which is a five-minute walk from the town square. Both women are great cooks who are accustomed to preparing vegetarian cuisine, and they can even serve meals on the rooftop table so guests can enjoy the sunset at dinner.

Rafael Trejo #140

4-8793338

emilitin2009@nauta.cu or villapitinyjuana@gmail.com

Five very modern rooms (CUC$30–$35) in an expertly designed home set the bar extremely high. Request the back room, which has a huge window facing the mogotes. The home has a beautiful garden and patio, and very accommodating hosts are happy to help arrange local tours of the area.

RESTAURANTS IN VIÑALES

Balcón del Valle

Carretera a Pinar del Río

Daily noon–midnight

Mains CUC$8–$10

Come for the views and stay for the food. A wooden deck perches visitors directly above the mogote-studded valley. The restaurant specializes in fish, pork, and chicken dishes but also doubles as a great spot for a cocktail or fresh juice.

La Berenjena

Mariana Grajales, between Salvador Cisneros and Rafael Trujo

Daily 10 a.m.–10 p.m.

Mains CUC$4–$7

This vegetable-forward restaurant serves carefully prepared and artistically presented dishes using ingredients from its own garden. Its signature dish is the restaurant's namesake—aubergine, or eggplant—but they also serve chicken, lasagna, soups, and a wide range of tonics and fresh juices. For something different, try the *moringa* (a medicinal plant) noodles.

El Olivo

Salvador Cisneros #89

Daily noon–11 p.m.

Mains CUC$4–$7

Expect to wait in line at what appears to be Viñales's most popular restaurant. Mediterranean dishes such as seafood paella, mushroom risotto, and pasta round out the menu.

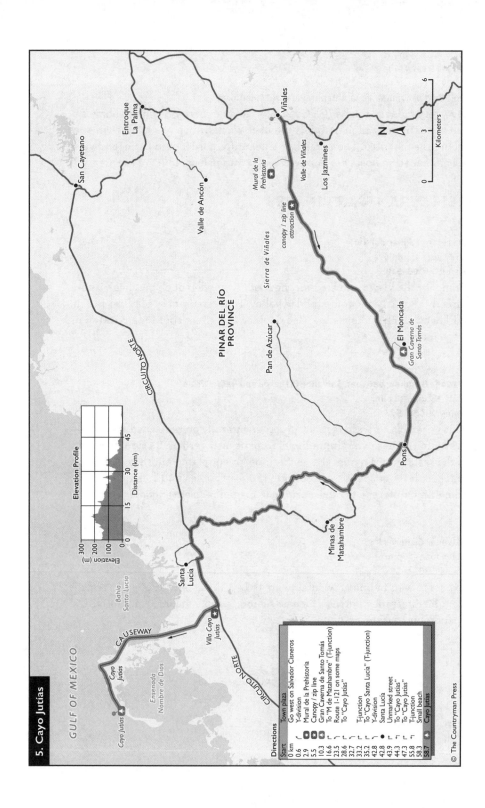

5. Cayo Jutías

GULF OF MEXICO

San Cayetano

Entroque La Palma

Viñales

Valle de Ancón

Valle de Viñales

Mural de la Prehistoria ★

Los Jazmines

Sierra de Viñales

canopy / zip line attraction ★

PINAR DEL RÍO PROVINCE

Pan de Azúcar

El Moncada

Gran Caverna de Santo Tomás

CIRCUITO NORTE

Pons

Minas de Matahambre

Santa Lucía

Bahía Santa Lucía

CAUSEWAY

Villa Cayo Jutías ★

CIRCUITO NORTE

Cayo Jutías

Ensenada Nombre de Dios

Cayo Jutías ✚

N

0   3   6
Kilometers

Elevation Profile

Elevation (m): 300 200 100 0

Distance (km): 0 15 30 45

Directions

Start		Town plaza
0 km		Go west on Salvador Cisneros
0.6		Y-division
2.9	★	Mural de la Prehistoria
5.5	★	Canopy / zip line
10.3	★	Gran Caverna de Santo Tomás
16.6	⌐	To "M de Matahambre" (T-junction)
23.5		Route I-121 on some maps
28.6	⌐	To "Cayo Jutías"
32.7	⌐	
33.2	⌐	T-junction
35.2	⌐	To "Cayo Santa Lucía" (T-junction)
42.8	•	Y-division
42.8	⌐	Santa Lucía
43.9	⌐	Unmarked street
44.3	⌐	To "Cayo Jutías"
47.3	⌐	To "Cayo Jutías"
55.8	⌐	T-junction
58.3		Small beach
58.7	✚	Cayo Jutías

© The Countryman Press

🚴 RIDE #5. CAYO JUTÍAS

Distance: 36.4 miles/58.7 kilometers
Elevation: 1,618 feet/493 meters
Difficulty: Very Difficult
Time: 6–8 hours

Cayo Jutías is an out-of-the-way beach that has enough amenities to keep you comfortable but few enough people that you feel like you've stumbled upon something special. Most tourists visiting the beach stay near the restaurant and the bathrooms, but if you climb over the gray mangroves scattering what appears to be the end of the beach, another kilometer of virgin beach (and perhaps a couple of starfish!) await you.

Though the total riding distance and elevation don't appear to be too overwhelming, what makes this ride so challenging is the condition of the road. Despite pleas from locals to repair the road, which has been increasingly battered as tourism to Viñales rises, the road hasn't been repaired in decades.

Potholes are deep and frequent, and while the worst can be avoided, some rough stretches are unavoidable. Local taxi and truck drivers say they frequently pick up cyclists who have exhausted themselves from the journey or who have busted a wheel. If you can manage, the views are lovely, but I recommend taking a colectivo for CUC$20 round-trip until the road is repaired. The condition of the road to Cayo Jutías is so bad that most local cars refuse to make the trip. Specific classic car colectivos make the trip every day, so if you would like to visit the beach on four wheels, ask your casa to call the taxi dispatcher.

The ride starts at the main town plaza and passes the Mural de la Prehistória, which many tourists find underwhelming but which is worth a five-minute stop (no need to pay the entrance fee if you are satisfied viewing it from a short distance). Mogotes and farms line the right side of the road, while tobacco fields decorate the left side. The first few kilometers out of Viñales reveal some of the most stunning scenery of the day. After passing the canopy/zip line attraction (CUC$8), the road becomes slightly bumpy, foliage thickens, and trees approach the sides of the street and then fall back, allowing better views of the mogotes.

Though this ride passes the Gran Caverna de Santo Tomás, do not attempt to visit the caves and the beach in one day. The cave tour can take several hours, and the challenging ride to Cayo Jutías requires all of your energy. After the T-junction (33.2k), the road begins to deteriorate considerably. Cars weave around the worst bumps, sometimes avoiding them by driving on the shoulder or wrong side of the road.

Keep your eyes open around the curves! Along some stretches, the road alternates between bumpy concrete and dusty gravel. Around 30k, the road becomes an uphill gravel and dirt road climb, which is especially unpleasant to ride through after it's been raining. Eventually you'll get to enjoy an expansive view of the valley and a downhill glide on smooth concrete, which you've surely earned. The road stays smooth for another 8 kilometers

STING RAY FLESH HANGING OUT TO DRY IN CAYO JUTÍAS

before the bumps start again in Santa Lucia, which has a few restaurants and a dozen casas.

The causeway that connects the mainland to the beach starts off bumpy, but you can find relief knowing this is your last stretch, made even sweeter by the turquoise ocean lining both sides of the path.

Just before the main entrance to Cayo Jutías is a small, tree-studded area that is popular with Cubans. Lean your bike against a tree and lay down a blanket next to locals. Colectivo taxi drivers usually park here and tell tourists to walk 500 meters down to the main beach, which has a restaurant, a bar, a bathroom, and changing facilities.

Note that camping on the beach is possible, but it gets very windy at night. Though the wind may be fierce at times, it keeps away some of the mosquitoes that would otherwise eat you alive. Sunset on the beach is magical, and since the area has no real development or light pollution, it's a great place to see stars. If camping isn't your thing, you can easily find accommodations at one of the casas in Santa Lucia and ride back to Viñales the following day. An especially spacious, green, and relaxing home is Villa Cayo Jutías (aylen.vento@nauta.cu, 5-3365574 or 5-4191595), located at the final right turn toward Cayo Jutías (47.3k) before riding across the causeway.

RIDE #6. CAYO JUTÍAS TO VIÑALES

Distance: 36.4 miles/58.7 kilometers
Elevation: 2,093 feet/638 meters
Difficulty: Very Difficult
Time: 6–8 hours

The return trip to Viñales has more hills, but some can be avoided by riding through Puerto Esperanza. The road is also in very bad condition, but there is far less traffic. This makes the ride more pleasant but also makes it much more difficult to find help or a ride should a pothole bust your rim. Note that if it's been raining the previous few days, it's riskier to go the Puerto Esperanza route, as flooding can shut down some of the roads along that route.

Alternate Puerto Esperanza Route: Follow the return directions to 16.9k, then follow the curve left toward Puerto Esperanza, onto the Circuito Norte. Follow the CN to San Cayetano, where the road splits. Either veer left to visit Puerto Esperanza or veer right to continue on the CN, as it bends south toward Viñales. Turn right at the T-junction in Entronque La Palma and follow the CN all the way to Viñales. Note that this route follows the last 9 kilometers of the Bahía Honda to Viñales route.

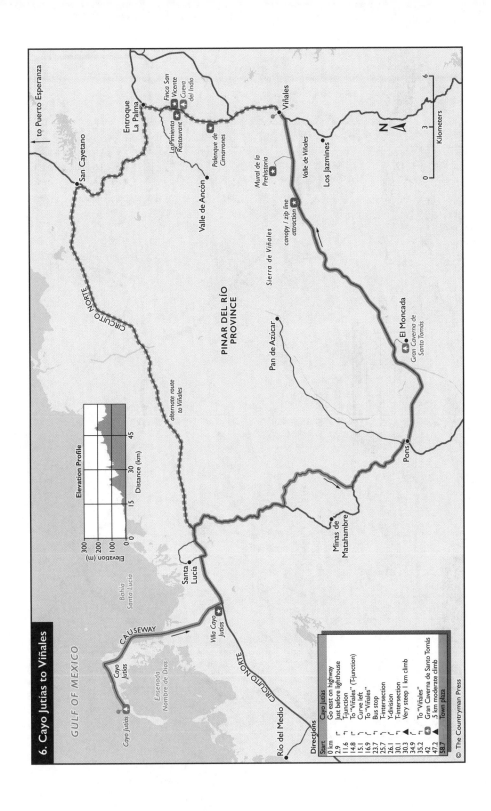

6. Cayo Jutías to Viñales

Elevation Profile

Distance (km): 15, 30, 45
Elevation (m): 0, 100, 200, 300

Directions

Start	Cayo Jutías
0 km	Go east on highway
2.9	Just before lighthouse
11.6	T-junction
14.8	To "Viñales" (T-junction)
15.1	Curve left
16.9	To "Viñales"
23.7	Bus stop
25.7	T-intersection
26.1	Y-division
30.1	T-intersection
30.3	Very steep 1 km climb
34.9	To "Viñales"
35.2	Gran Caverna de Santo Tomás
42	.5 km moderate climb
47.2	
58.7	Town plaza

© The Countryman Press

to Puerto Esperanza

San Cayetano

Entroque La Palma

Finca San Vicente

Cueva del Indio

La Pimienta Restaurant

Palenque de Cimarrones

Valle de Ancón

Mural de la Prehistoria

Viñales

Valle de Viñales

Los Jazmines

Sierra de Viñales

canopy / zip line attraction

PINAR DEL RÍO PROVINCE

Pan de Azúcar

El Moncada

Gran Caverna de Santo Tomás

Pons

Minas de Matahambre

CIRCUITO NORTE

alternate route to Viñales

Santa Lucía

Bahía Santa Lucía

Villa Cayo Jutías

Cayo Jutías

CAUSEWAY

Ensenada Nombre de Dios

CIRCUITO NORTE

Río del Medio

GULF OF MEXICO

Cayo Jutías

N

Kilometers: 0, 3, 6

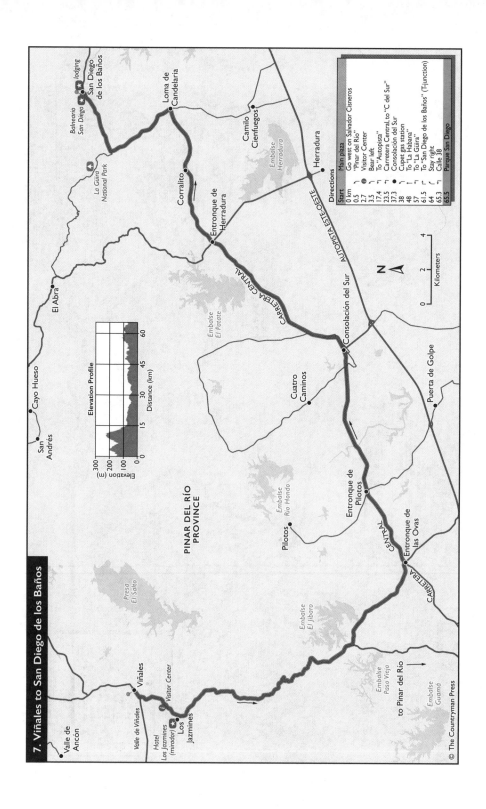

7. Viñales to San Diego de los Baños

Directions

Start	Main plaza	
0 km	Go west on Salvador Cisneros	
0.5	"Pinar del Río"	
2.7	Visitor Center	
3.5	Bear left.	
17.4	To "Autopista"	
23.5	Carretera Central, to "C del Sur"	
37.3	Consolación del Sur	
38	Cupet gas station	
48	To "La Habana"	
57	To "La Güira"	
61.5	To "San Diego de los Baños" (T-junction)	
64	Stay right	
65.3	Calle 38	
65.5	Parque San Diego	

Elevation Profile

Elevation (m): 0, 100, 200, 300
Distance (km): 0, 15, 30, 45, 60

PINAR DEL RÍO PROVINCE

N

Kilometers: 0, 2, 4

© The Countryman Press

RIDE #7. VIÑALES TO SAN DIEGO DE LOS BAÑOS

Distance: 40.7 miles/65.5 kilometers
Elevation: 1,575 feet/480 meters
Difficulty: Difficult
Time: 5–7 hours

The road out of Viñales is spectacularly beautiful and best enjoyed with a 7 a.m. departure because so many tour buses and colectivo taxis are on the road by 7:30 a.m. An early departure also means you'll get to enjoy the first 8 kilometers in the shade as the sun slowly rises over trees set close to the road. The road is in good condition and is generally maintained well enough to accommodate the tremendous number of tour buses and cars passing through every day.

The Viñales visitors center is a great place to stop for pictures of the mogotes and valleys below. Just past the visitors center is a road on the right that will take you up to the *mirador* (lookout) at Hotel Los Jazmines, an even better photo opportunity.

The next 2 kilometers are an extremely pleasant ride through rolling hills, mostly downhill. For those who want to visit Pinar del Río, keep straight instead of turning left at 17.4k. Some cyclists choose to go directly to Pinar del Río, a medium-sized city that puts you on the highway straight back to Havana. It is the most direct route, but the wide highway has a lot of traffic (for Cuba, at least), exhaust, and wind, and not a lot of scenery.

THE VIEW FROM HOTEL JAZMINES IN VIÑALES

The route detailed in the directions passes through quiet roads and mango groves where horse-drawn carts are more commonplace than cars.

I was surprised to find a casa particular at 22.4k. There's not much to see in the area, but it would be a nice option if the weather is very bad or if you'd like to experience staying in a tiny town that doesn't see much tourism. Few food options exist along this route, though small villages sell sandwiches and soda. Cosalación del Sur is the largest city with the most food options. The main park in the center of town also has WiFi, and there's a CaDeCa across the street.

San Diego de los Baños will welcome you with 4 kilometers of tree-lined streets offering a bit of shade in the hot afternoon sun. The ride ends at the town park.

San Diego de los Baños is a tiny town with only two restaurants and nothing going on at night. Its claim to fame is the Balneario San Diego, a recuperation facility with thermal pools, massages, and acupuncture services. Don't expect fluffy towels, slippers, or essential oils—this is as low-frills as they come—but it's definitely worth a visit. The "bathhouse" is located right across from the surprisingly lush and beautiful town park. Your host can arrange for massage service on-site using the same masseurs as the balneario. You'll pay an extra CUC$5 but won't be limited to the 8 a.m. to 5 p.m. balneario schedule. Be sure to get a good night's sleep for the intense hills the next day!

Camping Option

Instead of turning right at the junction at 61.5k, you can turn left toward La Güira National Park. The entrance fee is CUC$5, which may or may not include the cost for camping on-site, depending on who the guard is. Basic cabins rent for CUC$12 per night.

ACCOMMODATIONS IN SAN DIEGO DE LOS BAÑOS

At the time of writing, there were only two licensed casas in the city, and both border the main park.

Villa Julio y Cary
Calle 29 #4009
4-8548037
This small home offers two modest rooms (CUC$20–$25), a garden, and porches with rockers.

Casa Orduña
Calle 40 at corner of Calle 23
5-3443346 or 5-2684510
Two spacious bedrooms rent for CUC$20–$25 each, though one is larger, with its own small kitchen area. Enjoy the huge patio area with clotheslines and fans, which make it easy to wash and hang-dry clothing that will actually be dry by morning.

Hotel Mirador
Calle 23 at corner of Calle 40

4-8778338

This hotel is well landscaped, with comfortable rooms (CUC$40–$70) and an inviting outdoor pool and grill, but expect loud reggaeton music. There's a proper restaurant upstairs, decorated with tablecloths and cloth napkins, but at the time of research it only served pizza and spaghetti.

RIDE #8. SAN DIEGO DE LOS BAÑOS TO LAS TERRAZAS

Distance: 45.8 miles/73.7 kilometers
Elevation: 2,852 feet/787 meters
Difficulty: Very Difficult
Time: 7–9 hours

This is one of the most difficult—and most gorgeous—rides in this book. What makes the ride so difficult is not so much the steep elevation—and it is quite steep!—but rather the timing of the elevation. The steepest and longest hills come when you are precisely the most tired: the tail end of the ride. This ride can be broken up into two parts by spending the night in Soroa, a lush village in the mountains whose main draws are an orchid garden and gushing waterfall.

The ride begins in San Diego Park and quickly joins the Carretera Central (CC), which resembles any other street in the city. The first 8 kilometers are an easy ride on small, rolling hills dotted with potholes and bumps that are fairly easy to avoid. You'll enjoy the scent of freshly cut grass, thanks to the machete-wielding men lining the roads.

Unlike most cities, San Diego doesn't have breakfast stalls, so be sure to have a large breakfast at the casa or hotel. Fierro and Santa Cruz will be the first opportunities to find a cafeteria. Mango Jobo has a nice fruit market, and San Cristóbal will have the most options for a proper lunch. Instead of bearing right in San Cristóbal (38.1k), which is the most direct route, you can bear left to meander through the city a bit and then curve back onto the carretera.

Once you're on the Autopista, pay close attention to the several small bridges you'll cross, as many have gaps and holes of different sizes. About 2 kilometers after leaving the Autopista, you will begin seeing casas on both sides of the street. For those interested in stopping or staying in Soroa, see the boxed text "Soroa." For those continuing on to Las Terrazas, the hills have only just begun. A glorious downhill begins a few kilometers after casa and art gallery Sra. Aliuska (56.5k), but don't let it fool you. Follow the curve right and know the real hills are still to come!

The final stretch of the route has truly memorable scenery. The road is lined with thick green foliage, with trees overhanging and providing a bit of shade here and there. Several breaks in the foliage provide stunning views of tree-studded mountains and dense green valleys.

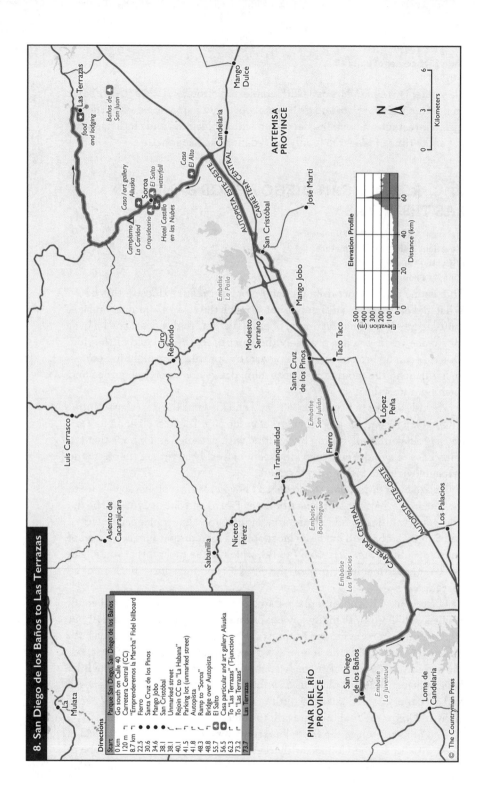

8. San Diego de los Baños to Las Terrazas

Directions

Start	0 km	Parque San Diego, San Diego de los Baños
Γ	120 m	Go south on Calle 40
Γ	8.7 km	Carretera Central (CC)
•	22.5	"Emprenderemos la Marcha" Fidel billboard
•	30.6	Fierro
•	34.6	Santa Cruz de los Pinos
•	38.1	Mango Jobo
•	38.1	San Cristóbal
Γ	40.1	Unmarked street
Γ	41.5	Rejoin CC to "La Habana"
L	41.8	Parking lot (unmarked street)
L	48.3	Autopista
Γ	48.8	Ramp to "Soroa"
Γ	55.7	Bridge over Autopista
🅧✚	56.5	El Salto
✚	62.3	Casa particular and art gallery Aluska
Γ	73.2	To "Las Terrazas" (T-junction)
🅧✚	73.7	To "Las Terrazas"
		Las Terrazas

PINAR DEL RÍO PROVINCE

ARTEMISA PROVINCE

Las Terrazas
food and lodging
Baños de San Juan
Mango Dulce

Casa / art gallery Aluska
Soroa
El Salto waterfall
Casa El Alto
Campismo La Caridad
Orquideario
Hotel Castillo en las Nubes

Candelaria

San Cristóbal
José Martí

AUTOPISTA ESTE-OESTE
CARRETERA CENTRAL

Mango Jobo
Embalse La Peña

Taco Taco

Ciro Redondo
Modesto Serrano

Santa Cruz de los Pinos
López Peña

Luis Carrasco

Embalse San Julián

Fierro

La Tranquilidad

Asiento de Cacarajícara

Sabanilla
Niceto Pérez

Embalse Bacunagua

Embalse Los Palacios

Los Palacios

CARRETERA CENTRAL
AUTOPISTA ESTE-OESTE

La Mulata

San Diego de los Baños

Embalse La Juventud

Loma de Candelaria

© The Countryman Press

Elevation Profile

Elevation (m): 500, 400, 300, 200, 100, 0
Distance (km): 0, 20, 40, 60

N

0   3   6
Kilometers

The ride ends in Las Terrazas. When you get to the T-junction (0.3k after the main entrance), turn left for casas or right for Hotel Moka. Casas are about half a kilometer down a gravel road, and Hotel Moka is about half a kilometer up a winding hill.

Las Terrazas is an eco-village known for hiking, bird-watching, and Baño San Juan, a refreshing river attracting Cubans and tourists who come to bathe in its cold water. The cool, misty mornings in Las Terrazas are unlike mornings anywhere else in Cuba, and lucky travelers will be able to spend two nights to be able to fully appreciate the area's charm.

ACCOMMODATIONS IN LAS TERRAZAS

Hotel Moka
www.hotelmoka-lasterrazas.com
4-8578600
Hotel Moka, the village's famed eco-hotel (CUC$150–$250) fills up well in advance and is worth a visit even if you don't stay there. The hotel can arrange tent camping, and you can ask the parking lot attendant to call the campground by walkie-talkie to see if there is availability.

Villa Maida y Mario
5-835944 or 5-4437044
This lovely "villa" rents two rooms within the family's home and another room in a private apartment in the backyard. The rooms run between CUC$20–$25, and your bike is welcome in the ground-floor living room.

Casa de Maria
5-6426648 or 4-8578813
One room is available (CUC$20–$25) within the family's home, which is surrounded by avocado and mango trees and a small park that Maria's husband, Miguel, is building for the neighborhood.

RESTAURANTS IN LAS TERRAZAS

El Romero
4-8578555
Daily 10 a.m.–9 p.m.
Meals CUC$3–$12
One of Cuba's only true eco restaurants, El Romero uses solar power, grows its own fruits and vegetables, and recycles, which may be standard in other countries but is far from the norm in Cuba. One of the country's only vegetarian restaurants, El Romero impresses even die-hard carnivores with its interesting and artfully prepared dishes, including soups, pastas, tempura, fried rice, home-baked herb breads, and vegetable tarts. Note that though there's no street address, the village is small and any local can direct you to the restaurant.

Even riders hearty enough to push all the way from San Diego de los Baños to Las Terrazas may want to spend the night to visit this lush village's waterfall and orchid garden. There are enough casas in town that it's very likely you'll be able to find a place to stay without a reservation. El Alto is a casa around the 52k mark—halfway between the highway and waterfall—where you can see the sun rise over the mountains. It's a nice option for anyone who wants to immediately jump on the highway in the morning. It comes before the hills but is a bit far from Soroa's main attractions. There's a handful of casas around the 55k mark that are very close to the waterfall, El Salto, and the orchid museum.

El Salto is open from noon to 8 p.m., costs CUC$3, and provides bicycle parking for CUC$1. Even if you don't visit the waterfall (which requires a short but steep hike), the restaurant and its clean bathrooms may come in handy! Fifty meters after the waterfall is a sign directing you to Castillo de Nubes, the *orquideario* (orchid garden), and the Villa Soroa cabins. The Hotel Castillo de las Nubes (Cloud House) offers gorgeous views of the surrounding area but is up an extremely steep and rocky hill. Cycling to it is not recommended.

About 2 kilometers past El Salto and the Orquideario is the casa of Sra. Aliuska. This charming casa particular doubles as an art gallery, with wood carvings, photographs, paintings, and ceramics adorning the home. Two independent rooms with two beds each are located behind the main home, nestled within a well-maintained garden overflowing with flowers. The beds are equipped with mosquito nets that are sometimes needed. You'll need to bring your bike up a few stairs, but it's worth it! Each room costs CUC$20–$25, but one is almost twice as large as the other. Make a reservation by emailing aliuska6911@nauta.cu or calling 5-3995091. For more modest accommodations, Campismo La Caridad is 1 kilometer past Casa Aliuska.

Cyclists interested in staying in Soroa and continuing on to Las Terrazas without as many hills can retrace the route back to the highway, turn left onto the Autopista, and follow signs directing you to Las Terrazas.

RIDE #9. LAS TERRAZAS TO HAVANA

Distance: 47.3 miles/76.1 kilometers
Elevation: 1,890 feet/576 meters
Difficulty: Moderate
Time: 5–7 hours

Some locals may encourage you to ride the 3-kilometer paved road to the Baño San Juan and then continue on the camino that is a direct path to the Autopista, allowing you to avoid the hills and additional kilometers on the main route. Note that this is a dirt and rock path that gets muddy after the rain, so it is not recommended. Besides, the main route is so pretty, why would you want to miss it?

Aside from a few hills at the beginning of the ride, the route is mostly flat, following the Autopista back to the capital city. The ride out of Las Terrazas is pleasant, with low-hanging clouds blanketing the dense foliage. Enjoy the smell of fresh air and minimally trafficked roads while you can—the ride into Havana could not be more different.

Riding along the Autopista is a great opportunity to see a variety of food vendors selling fruits, sandwiches, giant slabs of cheese, or whole roasted chickens. It's also a good opportunity to run into Cuban cyclists who train on this stretch of highway every morning. The road is in good condition, but you'll have to avoid some potholes and cracks.

Alternate route alert! If you'd like to take the northern route back to Havana, at 30.4k, bear right after the bridge toward Mariel to loop under another bridge ⇔. Follow the carretera 7 kilometers to Mariel and then follow the Havana to Bahía Honda route backward to Havana. The Autopista route is more direct, but the north shore route is more scenic.

The only food and bathroom stop along the route is Parador 6 Vías (57.5k).

CRUISING DOWN 23RD STREET IN VEDADO, HAVANA

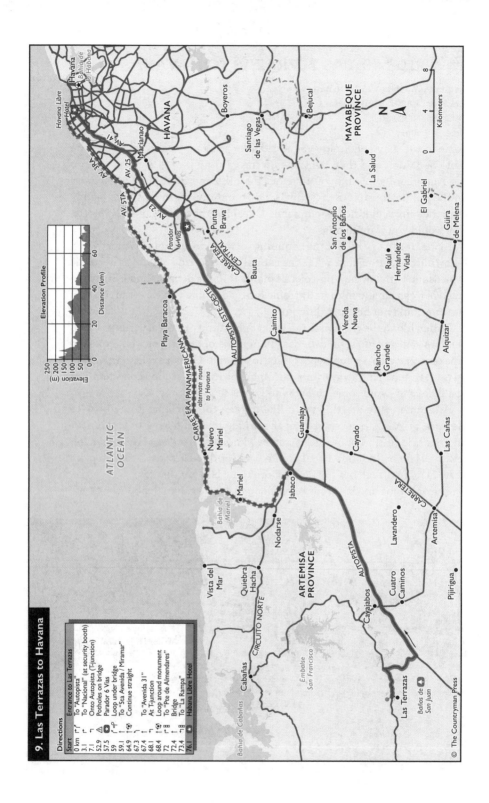

9. Las Terrazas to Havana

Directions

Start	
0 km	Entrance to Las Terrazas
	To "Autopista"
3.1	To "Nacional" (at security booth)
7.1	Onto Autopista (T-junction)
52.9	Potholes on bridge
57.5	Parador 6 Vías
59	Loop under bridge
59.1	To "5ta Avenida / Miramar"
64.9	Continue straight
67.3	
67.4	To "Avenida 31"
68.1	At T-junction
68.4	Loop around monument
72	To "Pte de Almendares"
72.4	Bridge
73.4	To "La Rampa"
76.1	Habana Libre Hotel

Elevation Profile

Elevation (m): 0, 50, 100, 150, 200, 250

Distance (km): 0, 20, 40, 60

ATLANTIC OCEAN

Havana Libre Hotel

Havana
Bahía de
La Habana

AV 41
AV 3RA
AV. 5TA
AV. 25
AV. 23
Parador 6 Vías

Marianao
Boyeros
HAVANA
Santiago de las Vegas
Bejucal

MAYABEQUE PROVINCE

La Salud
El Gabriel
Güira de Melena

Punta Brava
Bauta
San Antonio de los Baños
Raúl Hernández Vidal
Alquízar

CARRETERA CENTRAL
AUTOPISTA ESTE-OESTE

Caimito
Vereda Nueva
Rancho Grande
Las Cañas

Playa Baracoa
Nuevo Mariel

CARRETERA PANAMERICANA
alternate route to Havana

Guanajay
Cayado

Mariel
Bahía de Mariel
Jabaco
Nodarse

ARTEMISA PROVINCE

Lavandero
Artemisa

CARRETERA

Vista del Mar
Quiebra Hacha

CIRCUITO NORTE

Cuatro Caminos
Cayajabos

AUTOPISTA

Pijirigua

Cabañas
Bahía de Cabañas

Embalse San Francisco

Baños de San Juan
Las Terrazas

N
0 4 8
Kilometers

© The Countryman Press

They sell fried chicken, ham sandwiches, water, and sodas. Women, in particular, will have difficulty finding even an "outdoor bathroom" stop along this stretch, as there is minimal tree/bush coverage along the highway and the few green areas that would normally make for a nice squatting spot are located on a steep slope leading down to a barbed wire fence. Slipping is not an option.

Don't be fooled by the kilometer markers counting down to Havana. When you get to 1k, you are still on the outskirts. Depending on where you're staying, you may still have 15 or 20 kilometers to go.

Once you loop into Havana, you'll enjoy a long downhill ride along 23rd Avenue as it winds its way into the city. The road is busy and there's heavy traffic, but cars are respectful and slow traffic keeps to the right. The road takes you through Playa and Marianao, working-class neighborhoods where you will run into very few tourists (other than those visiting the Tropicana nightclub). The road confusingly changes name several times (Avenue 23, 25, 31, 41, then Calle 23), but continue on it as it winds its way through Havana and drops you in Vedado.

The ride ends at the historic Habana Libre Hotel, the former Havana Hilton, opened in 1958 and overtaken by Fidel Castro as his headquarters less than a year later. To continue to La Habana Vieja, keep straight on 23rd Street, which runs into the Malecón in a few blocks. Turn right and ride along the water to Old Havana.

5

SANCTI SPIRITUS

QUICK LOOK

Sancti Spiritus province contains some excellent—and very challenging—mountain cycling, but the rides in this book focus on the province's beaches, history, and culture. The most popular city in the province (and one of the most popular tourist destinations in the country!) is Trinidad, known for horse carriages trotting down cobblestone roads and pastel-colored homes with fortress-sized doors. It's also one of the best-preserved colonial cities in the Americas.

For generations, the local economy was sustained by a network of sugar mills, and Trinidad's old sugar-growing culture can still be explored by visiting former plantations and processing plants. The city has a thriving art scene, and painters can be seen crouched behind canvases on stoops across town. Many artists' homes double as art galleries, in addition to the many traditional galleries throughout the city.

Because Trinidad is so focused on tourism, the restaurants here serve very high-quality food. The downside is that the food is relatively expensive and there are very few peso restaurants, which is particularly problematic for locals who may have to save up for months to afford the standard CUC$10–$15 entrée.

Trinidadians are proud of their local drink, the *canchánchara*, a rum-based drink sweetened with honey. Other cities boast similar drinks and even try to claim it as their own, but Trinidadians are extremely proud to be the true creators. The drink was originally served warm and given to mambices fighters to energize them for battle, but ice eventually became (and remains) a key ingredient to help keep you cool.

Highlights
- Afro-Cuban music and culture is alive and well. Festive music is on nearly every corner but is especially lively at **La Casa de la Música** and **Casa de la Trova.** Head to **Rincón de la Salsa** if you'd like to practice dancing or take some classes.
- **Peninsula Ancón** is a long stretch of soft, white sand beach, perfect for sunbathing and swimming. Take your pick of touristy beaches with plenty of amenities or lesser-known nooks with little more than a rickety old palm umbrella.

- Climb an 18th-century tower at **Manaca Iznaga** plantation. Erected in 1750 to observe slaves working in the surrounding sugarcane fields, the tower sits seven stories high and still has its original bells intact.
- Check out the city's many art, craft, and souvenir markets. The largest **Arts & Crafts Market** is held Sunday through Friday from 9 a.m. to 6 p.m. next to Casa de la Trova on Cañada (Patricio Lumumba), near the corner of Jesús Mendéz and Valdéz Muñoz.

THE VEW FROM TRINIDAD'S TOURIST TRAIN

- Sip the town's famous drink, the *canchánchara*, and enjoy live salsa at **Taberna La Canchánchara**, which serves the rum and honey concoction out of terra-cotta mugs. This is the oldest building in town, and it still has its original floors and ceilings.
- If sore muscles require a day of rest but you'd still like to visit the sugar plantation and refinery, hop on the **Tourist Train,** which cuts right through the valley with stunning views of the mountains. Tickets go on sale at 9:10 a.m. (CUC$15) in the small house across from the train tracks.
- **Disco Ayala** (CUC$5) is considered overrated by some, but this nightclub inside a cave is one of the city's most popular attractions. The line forms at 9 p.m. and is crowded with jineteros. Once inside, expect loud reggaeton music, thick smoke, and wet floors due to moisture dripping from the cave walls—watch your step!

Need-to-Know
- Trinidad's streets may be beautiful, but they're covered in glass, so step and ride carefully.
- Just about every street in the city has two names, making address hunting endlessly confusing. Original street names are 500 years old and have saint names from Spanish and Catholic influence. After the Revolution, new names were given. Since people still use the old names, the government baptized the streets as having two names.
- Jinetero culture is strong in Trinidad, and street hustlers are known to be especially aggressive. Though the city is extremely safe, petty theft is most likely late at night, when travelers' judgment has been compromised by a few drinks. Stay alert after a night out.

Terrain
The Escambray Mountains run through Sancti Spiritus province and are extremely steep. While the Manaca Iznaga ride takes you along a few large

hills, it does not come anywhere close to mountain biking. Many of the streets within Trinidad are rocky, cobblestone streets that locals still manage to ride on, but the roads to the beach and sugar plantations are well-paved concrete.

Special Events
- Culture Week in Trinidad: early January
- Holy Week and Good Friday, in particular, is celebrated in Trinidad with a citywide procession: March/April
- Fiestas Sanjuaneras cowboy carnival in Trinidad: last weekend in June
- Ciudad Metal hardcore music festival in Santa Clara: December
- Las Parrandas Christmas Eve fireworks celebration in Remedios: December 24

Tourist Information
Cubatur (8 a.m.–8 p.m. Monday–Saturday) is at Antonio Maceo #447, and **Infotur** (9 a.m.–5 p.m. Monday–Saturday) is at Gustavo Izquierdo #112. WiFi is available in Parque Céspedes, Plaza Mayor, and on the steps leading to La Casa de la Música. Purchase Internet cards at the ETECSA office on the corner of General Lino Pérez and Francisco Patterson.

The **Banco de Crédito y Comercio** is at José Martí #264 (9 a.m.–3 p.m. Monday–Friday) and has an ATM. The **CaDeCa** is located on Maceo between Camilo Cienfuegos and Lino Pérez.

ACCOMMODATIONS IN TRINIDAD AND LA BOCA

Note that the final two accommodations are located about 4 kilometers out of town in La Boca, a small beach and fishing community. The village is perfect for those wanting to be closer to the beach or to relax away from the music, dancing, and large number of tourists that Trinidad is known for. Find more casa options at www.trinidadrent.com.

Cabaña Marla y Fernando
Calle Gustavo Izquierdo (Gloria) #103-A e/Simón Bolivar y Piro Guinart
4-1993910
Hidden behind fortress-sized wooden doors is a gorgeous home with high ceilings, an outdoor patio with an antique well, and two immaculately clean upstairs bedrooms (CUC$25–$35). The family lives downstairs and is happy to cook up fantastic meals and arrange activities. Bike storage is available on the ground floor. The home is on the same block as the Viazul bus terminal.

Hostal Pino
Antonio Guiteras #223, between Frank País and Miguel Calzada
4-1992909, 5-3376803, or 5-2993439
b.pino2014@gmail.com
Pino and Belkys rent several homes within a few blocks of each other, all

near Parque Céspedes. Two rooms (CUC$25–$30) are available in their large family home, which includes a lovely outdoor patio, and two additional rooms are available in a private apartment nearby. Need more space? Their neighbor, Olga, rents several rooms in her spacious home next door. Pino is a wealth of information and can help arrange activities and excursions around the city.

THE VIEW FROM THE BELL TOWER IN TRINIDAD'S MUSEUM OF THE STRUGGLE AGAINST BANDITS

Casa Sotolongo
Real de Jigue #33, between Desengaño and Rosario
4-1994169
casasotolongo@gmail.com

Three gigantic bedrooms await you in this classic Colonial home with massive doors and walkways originally built large enough for horse carriages to walk through. The inner courtyard is decorated with plants, the upper patio provides lovely views of the city, and the entire home has its own WiFi connection (though you'll still need Internet scratch-off cards). Ask if Carlos is around; the owners' son, a local journalist, leads excellent city tours.

Iberostar Grand Hotel
Corner of José Martí and Lino Pérez, in front of Parque Céspedes
4-1996070
www.iberostar.com

Cyclists wanting to relax in more luxurious accommodations (CUC$350–$400/night) would do well at the Spanish-run Iberostar Hotel. Nineteenth-century colonial charm accompanies modern conveniences such as designer toiletries and in-room minibars. Tourists flock to the hotel just to take pictures in the fern-filled lobby and dine in the hotel's restaurant, where classical and jazz musicians perform nightly.

Hostel El Ocaso
Avenida del Mar #28 (La Boca)
4-1993063 or 5-4082975
alinaocaso@nauta.cu

This clean, spacious home has three bedrooms (CUC$35–$40) and a terrace with an excellent view of the sea. It's just outside the center of La Boca, so it's especially quiet.

B&B El Capitan

Playa La Boca #82 on the Ancón-Trinidad highway (La Boca)
4-1993055 or 5-2909238
captaincasanovatrinidad@yahoo.es

Hands down, this is the most luxurious casa in La Boca. Have your pick of four bedrooms (CUC$50–$70, including breakfast), relax on the patio, or take a nap in a hammock overlooking the ocean.

RESTAURANTS IN TRINIDAD

Trinidad has far too many good restaurants to list here, but many of them are located along Maceo, including Restaurant San José (pasta, pizza, soup, seafood) and La Redacción Cuba (lamb or chickpea burgers, mushroom tort, pasta with lobster), which could easily be mistaken for a Brooklyn outpost.

Sol Ananda

Rúben Martínez Villena #45, corner of Simón Bolivar
Daily 11 a.m.–11 p.m.
Mains CUC$10–$20

Grandfather clocks, 18th-century chinaware, and even an antique bed might cause you to mistake this restaurant for a museum. Located right off Plaza Mayor, Sol Ananda is owned by a vegetarian yogi, hence the vegetable-forward and Indian-themed dishes (curries, samosas). Ropa vieja and several Cuban and fusion dishes are on the menu, for diners who can't be persuaded by plant-based fare.

Guitarra Mia

Jesús Menendéz #19, between Camilo Cienfuegos and Lino Pérez
Daily 12:30–11 p.m.
Mains CUC$9–$15

Unsurprisingly, music is the theme of this restaurant, and diners are serenaded by smooth live guitar music during their meals. Ropa vieja, vegetable paella, and seafood dishes stand out on the eclectic menu. Dishes are artistically presented, and meals end with a complimentary cigar.

Taberna La Botija

Corner of Amargura and Boca
Open 24 hours
Small plates CUC$4–$8

MANY RESTAURNATS IN TRINIDAD RESEMBLE MUSEUMS AND ANTIQUE SHOPS

Equal parts must-try restaurant and lively nightclub, Taberna is the place to be! Lines are consistently out the door, so arrive very early if you're hungry. The house band belts out jazz and soul music as the kitchen churns out huge, artfully arranged plates of Cuban and fusion food.

Café el Mago
Ciro Redondo #264 between Juan Manuel Marquez and Echerri
Daily 10 a.m.–1 a.m.

Rum-based cocktails, coffee, and snacks are served as a DJ spins alternative, house, and funk music. Because the owners offer affordable drinks for young Cubans, you will mingle with everyday locals instead of the jineteros plaguing more touristy spots.

RIDE #10. PLAYA ANCÓN

Distance: 18.1 miles/29.1 kilometers
Elevation: 456 feet/139 meters
Difficulty: Easy
Time: 2 hours

Playa Ancón is considered by many to be the nicest beach in Southern Cuba. The sand is soft and white, the water is warm and turquoise, and you can have your pick of small and large beaches, depending on how many other people you'd like to share the sand with. This ride stops at several beaches that are close enough to each other that you could make a quick stop at each. At most beaches, plastic chairs, or *camas*, cost CUC$2 and bike parking is CUC$1.

DAY TRIP TO PLAYA ANCÓN IN TRINIDAD

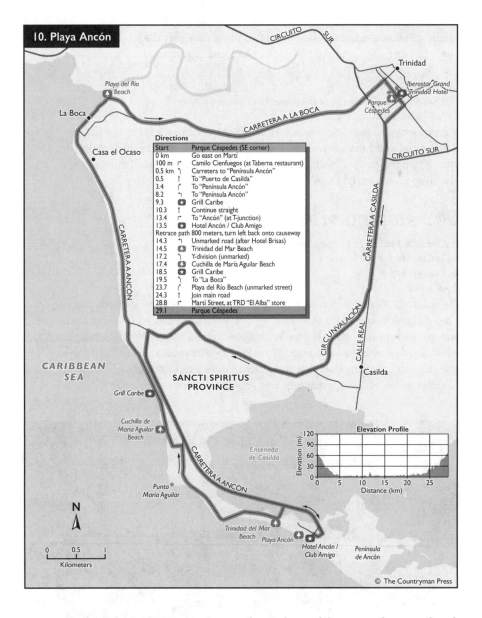

10. Playa Ancón

CIRCUITO SUR

Trinidad

Iberostar Grand
Trinidad Hotel

Playa del Río
Beach

Parque
Céspedes

La Boca

CARRETERA A LA BOCA

Casa el Ocaso

CIRCUITO SUR

Directions

Start		Parque Cèspedes (SE corner)
0 km	↱	Go east on Martí
100 m	↱	Camilo Cienfuegos (at Taberna restaurant)
0.5 km	↰	Carretera to "Península Ancón"
0.5	↑	To "Puerto de Casilda"
3.4	↱	To "Península Ancón"
8.2	↰	To "Península Ancón"
9.3	★	Grill Caribe
10.3	↑	Continue straight
13.4	↱	To "Ancón" (at T-junction)
13.5	★	Hotel Ancón / Club Amigo
Retrace path 800 meters, turn left back onto causeway		
14.3	↰	Unmarked road (after Hotel Brisas)
14.5	⬆	Trinidad del Mar Beach
17.2	↰	Y-division (unmarked)
17.4	⬆	Cuchilla de María Aguilar Beach
18.5	★	Grill Caribe
19.5	↰	To "La Boca"
23.7	↰	Playa del Río Beach (unmarked street)
24.3	↑	Join main road
28.8	↱	Martí Street, at TRD "El Alba" store
29.1		Parque Céspedes

CARRETERA A ANCÓN

CARRETERA A CASILDA

CIR CUNVALACIÓN

CALLE REAL

CARIBBEAN
SEA

SANCTI SPIRITUS
PROVINCE

Casilda

Grill Caribe ★

Cuchilla de
María Aguilar
Beach

Ensenada
de Casilda

Elevation Profile

120
90
60
30
0

Elevation (m)

0   5   10   15   20   25
Distance (km)

CARRETERA A ANCÓN

Punta
María Aguilar

N

0   0.5   1
Kilometers

Trinidad del Mar
Beach   Playa Ancón

Hotel Ancón /
Club Amigo

Península
de Ancón

© The Countryman Press

This ride starts in Parque Céspedes, in front of the iconic Iberostar hotel. Instead of curving right at 3k, you can stay left to ride through Casilde, a small fishing village that used to be an important port.

Grill Caribe is a waterfront restaurant and beach bar that has a small dive center with snorkel rental. The beach here is a bit rocky, but it's still a top choice since it's a calm, lesser-visited beach. You are unlikely to be approached by jineteros or salespeople here.

Hotel Club Amigo offers the widest variety of food on the beach. A single buffet meal is CUC$10, while a day pass (CUC$25) includes all-you-can-eat and drink in the buffets and snack shops until 6 p.m. Bike parking is available along the street, but bikes are not allowed on the beach itself. A diving center near the hotel offers daily scuba diving and snorkeling trips, though they're not as good as at Playa Girón (Bay of Pigs).

To return to the main route from Club Amigo, retrace your steps to the causeway and main road you came in on. Do not take the road that continues to the other hotels, as you will be turned around by security guards.

Trinidad del Mar is a popular beach to bike to, evidenced by the dozen or so bikes you'll see resting against the trees. Add your bike to the pile and pay the attendant $1. Otherwise, follow the curve right to continue on the route. You will pass several small beaches, all of which have palm umbrellas and make for a lovely swim or snack stop. These smaller beaches don't have beach chairs and may have limited snack options. As such, they also have far fewer tourists. Cuchilla de María Aguilar Beach is a quiet beach for relaxing and snorkeling but doesn't have beach chairs. Note that beaches get progressively rockier as you head east.

La Boca is a small fishing village with a pebbly beach that is a quieter alternative to Trinidad. Casas begin appearing around the 22.5k point. The first few houses you pass are some of the nicest and most modern ones, with the best views of the sea. The ride ends at Parque Céspedes.

RIDE #11. MANACA IZNAGA

Distance: 24.8 miles/39.9 kilometers
Elevation: 1,235 feet/376 meters
Difficulty: Moderate
Time: 3–4 hours

This ride begins in Parque Céspedes, in front of the Iberostar hotel, and takes you through a part of Trinidad few tourists pass. Birdcages hang on the front porches of modest homes while pigs squeal and roosters crow in the yard. Just after leaving town, the ride passes the mirador, a beautiful lookout point (and zip-lining attraction) that requires a short ride up a steep hill. Kids run barefoot along the highway as men cut grass with machetes.

The Manaca Iznaga tower will be visible before you approach the turn. Lock up your bike, pay $1 admission, and climb the 136 steps to the top to view the Valle de los Ingenios (Valley of Sugar Mills). Be sure to check out the old sugar press behind the restaurant, which serves food from noon to 4 p.m. You'll also find bathrooms back there. Before returning back to the Circuito Sur (CS), stop by the guarapo stand next to the train tracks and enjoy a cup of fresh sugarcane juice.

Just as with the Manaca Iznaga tower, you will see the Central FNTE sugar refinery before you arrive. The tall smoke stacks are more recognizable than the small cafeteria and railroad tracks that mark the turnoff to the refinery. The old sugar refinery turned museum (8:30 a.m.–4 p.m. daily) is worth the CUC$1 admission price (CUC$1 more if you'd like to take pictures).

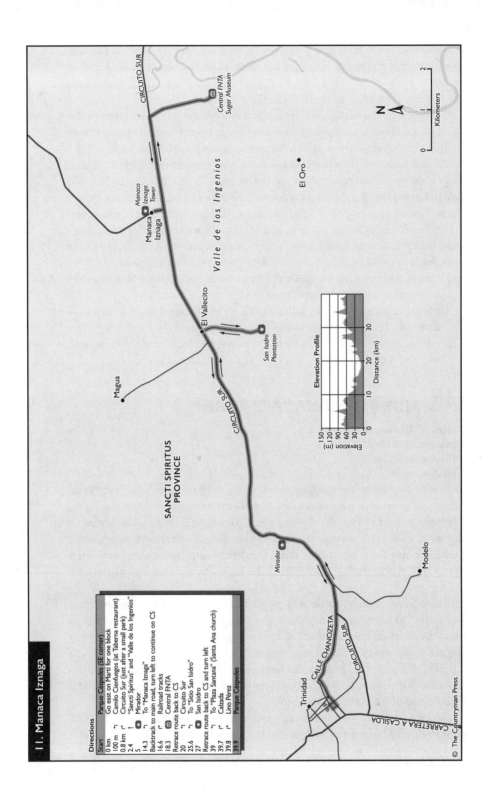

11. Manaca Iznaga

Directions

Start		Parque Céspedes (SE corner)
0 km		Go east on Martí for one block
100 m	⌐	Camilo Cienfuegos (at Taberna restaurant)
0.8 km	r	Circuito Sur (just after a small park)
2.4	⌐	"Sancti Spiritus" and "Valle de los Ingenios"
5		Mirador
14.3	⭑r	To "Manaca Iznaga"
		Backtrack to main road, turn left to continue on CS
16.6	⌐	Railroad tracks
18.3	🏛	Central FNTA
		Retrace route back to CS
20	r	Circuito Sur
25.6	r	To "Sitio San Isidro"
27	⭑	San Isidro
		Retrace route back to CS and turn left
39	r	To "Plaza Santana" (Santa Ana church)
39.7	r	Calzada
39.8	r	Lino Pérez
39.9		Parque Céspedes

CIRCUITO SUR

Central FNTA
Sugar Museum 🏛

N

Kilometers
0   1   2

Manaca
Iznaga Tower

Manaca
Iznaga ⭑

El Oro •

Valle de los Ingenios

El Vallecito

San Isidro
Plantation ⭑

Magua •

CIRCUITO SUR

SANCTI SPIRITUS
PROVINCE

Elevation Profile

Elevation (m)

150
120
90
60
30
0

0   10   20   30

Distance (km)

Mirador ⭑

CALLE CHANOZETA

CIRCUITO SUR

Trinidad •

Modelo •

CARRETERA A CASILDA

© The Countryman Press

Also worth CUC$1 is the cup of sugarcane juice, fresh pressed next to the admission table. Is there such a thing as too much sugarcane juice?

On the way to San Isidrio, you'll pass a large propaganda billboard that says YO SOY EL MAESTRO ("I am the teacher"). This billboard refers to Manuel Ascunse, one of the teachers that Fidel sent out to eradicate illiteracy among rural populations during the Revolution. When contra-Revoluciónarios asked who the teacher was, 16-year-old Ascunse came outside and responded, "Yo soy el maestro." Both he and the student who came out to defend him were shot and hung on a tree to scare people in the area.

San Isidro was a typical sugar plantation, operated with slave labor. Remnants of the plantation survive, including an impressive slaveholder's house, three-story watchtower, cistern, distillery, and slave quarters, among other buildings. Nearly all of the buildings are in ruins—some in danger of imminent collapse—and are an important part of the region's history.

 RIDE #12. TRINIDAD TO CIENFUEGOS

Distance: 51.3 miles/82.6 kilometers
Elevation: 1,848 feet/563 meters
Difficulty: Difficult
Time: 6–8 hours

This ride begins at the familiar Parque Céspedes, but instead of starting on the corner in front of the Iberostar hotel, you'll start at the northwest corner of the park, in front of the elevated performance area. You'll turn onto an unmarked "highway" that looks like any other small street but turns into the Circuito Sur (CS).

The road winds a bit, but continue following it and look for the frequent and visible signs directing you to Cienfuegos. A few moderate climbs await you as you leave Trinidad, but the steepest hills come toward the end. You don't have to wait long for the best scenery of the day to begin, including views of the Escambray Mountains on the right and sweeping coastal views on the left.

Río Hondo can be a nice beach for swimming, where the cool fresh water from the river meets the warmer salt water of the ocean. As you approach the bridge (19.3k), a small path to the right takes you down to the water, where you can rest your bike against the rocks. After Río Hondo, you may begin seeing crabs in April and May, but most don't come out until evening. Many small beaches present themselves on this ride, but their viability as swimming spots depends on the season and recent rainfall, which can muddy the water.

Very few turns are required on this route, as you'll stay on the CS most of the way. After passing the Yaguacam shrimp farm (25.7k), the ocean opens up in front of you and you catch a view of Playa Yaguacam, which is also a nice swimming option with palm umbrellas and a snack shop to cater to the nearby hotel and guest houses. The CS then curves inland for the remainder of the ride, offering views of the mountains along your right side. A few

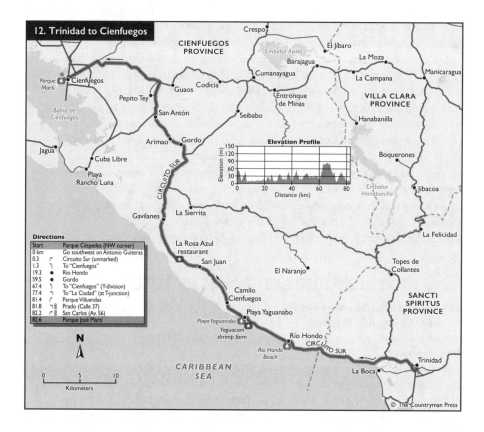

12. Trinidad to Cienfuegos

bumpy sections exist, mostly due to sloppy road repair jobs, but the highway is in very good condition for the majority of the route.

You will pass several small cafeterias, including La Rosa Azul (39.6k), a lovely little ranchón that makes for a great midway rest stop. In the town of Gordo, there is a small snack stall on your left that sells sandwiches in case you need an energy boost for the rest of the ride. As usual, drinks typically consist of homemade sodas and juices with questionable water, so coffee is your safest bet. Right after the snack stall is a fruit market that, for some reason, has painted Santa Claus with fruit to advertise its offerings.

Around 64.4k, ignore the sign that says CIENFUEGOS on the left. That is a longer route that leads to the flamingo reserve and beach or, more indirectly, to Cienfuegos. Continue straight on the main highway and enjoy views of large mango orchards lining the road and horses grazing in front of small, humble homes.

The CS turns into Calzada de Dolores, which has terrible traffic and exhaust but is the most direct and easy-to-follow route. You won't be on the street for long and will soon arrive at the town's main park, Parque Martí.

6

CIENFUEGOS

QUICK LOOK

Referred to as Cuba's "Pearl of the South," Cienfuegos is best known for its distinctively French architecture (due to it being the only area colonized by the French, not the Spanish) and for its hometown talent, Benny Moré. The mambo singer and bandleader who described Cienfuegos as the city he liked best is memorialized across the city in statues, billboards, and on nightclub awnings.

Sun worshippers can make their way to Rancho Luna beach, while nature lovers can embark on flora and fauna tours to a flamingo reserve or hike an enchanted trio of waterfalls at El Nicho in the Sierra del Escambray mountain range. The city's quiet charm is a welcome alternative to nearby tourist meccas, and its location on the Bay of Cienfuegos makes striking sunsets possible across the city.

RANCHO LUNA BEACH IN CIENFUEGOS

Highlights

- Head to the French- and Italian-influenced **Teatro Tomás Terry** on the north side of Parque José Martí to marvel at the 950-seat auditorium adorned with gold-leaf mosaics, marble statues, and ceiling murals.
- Cienfuegos's main street, **Prado** (Av 37), turns into the **malecón,** cutting right through the bay and connecting the center of the city with the southern zone. The stretch livens up in the evening and is the perfect place to observe city life.
- **Santa Isabel Boulevard** (Calle 29) is considered Cienfuegos's second boulevard, lined with shops, art galleries, and souvenirs. At the end is a bar locals have dubbed the **Piña Colada,** where cheap drinks are served along with lovely views of the bay.
- **Cementerio La Reina** is the only colonial cemetery in Cuba where people were buried in above-ground walls, referred to as nichos, due to high groundwater levels.
- **Punta Gorda** is a charming area at the southern tip of Cienfuegos, where a waterfront gazebo is the perfect place to watch the sunset.
- **Palacio de Valle** is an incredibly ornate palace with Spanish and Moorish influences. An upscale(ish) restaurant is located on the first floor, and a rooftop bar and patio afford stunning views of the bay.
- **Rancho Luna** beach makes for a wonderful day trip. You can pedal both ways or hop the ferry back to town.
- Join a tour at **Laguna Guanaroca** (CUC$10), where local guides will point out flora and fauna, including the tocororo, Cuba's national bird, before rowing you in a small canoe to observe the local flamingo population. Arrive early or book ahead via Ecotur, Infotur, or Cubatur during peak season, as the park caps attendance at 40 people per day.

Need-to-Know

- Many streets go by two names (such as Prado/Calle 37).
- Cienfuegos is one of the cleanest cities in Cuba—enjoy it and be extra sure to keep trash to yourself.

Terrain

The Escambray Mountains run through Cienfuegos, presenting very challenging cycling, but the rides outlined in this book are close to the coast, making them far less hilly.

Special Events

Benny Moré International Music Festival: November

Tourist Information

Cubatur (9 a.m.–7 p.m.) is located at Calle 37 #5399, between 54th and 46th Avenues. **Infotur** (9 a.m.–6 p.m.) is at Calle 56 #3117, between 31st and 33rd Avenues. WiFi is available in Parque Martí and Hotel Unión in the city center and in Hotel Jagua in Punta Gorda. Internet cards can be purchased at

Hotels Unión and Jagua and at the ETECSA office at Calle 31 #5402, between 54th and 56th Avenues.

The **Banco de Crédito y Comercio** (9 a.m.–5 p.m. Monday–Friday) is on the corner of Av 56 and Calle 31 and has an ATM. The **CaDeCa** (9 a.m.–5 p.m. Monday–Friday) is located at Av 56 #3316, between Calles 33 and 35.

ACCOMMODATIONS IN CIENFUEGOS

Casa de Cecilia

Av 54 #5505, between 55 and 57
4-3516063 or 5-8352185
dailymd@nauta.cu
Cecilia's lovely three-bedroom home (CUC$20–$25 each) has high ceilings and classic wooden furniture. She welcomes you with a smile and sits you down at a table full of maps and travel brochures to give you a city orientation. She also speaks fluent English.

Casa Roberto Carlos

Av 54 #3922, between 39 and 41
5-53668761, 5-3284566 or 4-3517137
carlos.chavez@nauta.cu or robert71@nauta.cu
Roberto and his husband Carlos rent three rooms in their own home and three more in a private apartment across the street (CUC$30–$35 each). The family home is a traditional, French-inspired Cienfuegos home with high ceilings and decorative pillars, while the three-story apartment is modern and sunny, with several small balconies and a rooftop terrace and patio. The men are loads of fun and offer a wealth of information about the city's nightlife.

Hostal Colonial

Av 52 #4114, between Calles 41 and 43
4-3555590
manolitolujan@nauta.cu
Large groups will love this five-bedroom home (CUC$35–$40 per room) and its delightful patio. Be sure to dine here, as the food is excellent.

La Casita de Oshun

Calle 35 #16, Punta Gorda
4-3519449 or 5-2381610
Aleja2303@yahoo.es or Alejandra.lopez@ nauta.cu
This charming casa is a Cuban National Heritage home and offers two rooms (CUC$40–$45 each) and a waterfront patio with a wide view of the bay. The

A HOME BICYCLE REPAIR STATION IN CIENFUEGOS

home is located in Punta Gorda, a bit removed from the town center but also more relaxed.

RESTAURANTS IN CIENFUEGOS

Paladar Aché

Av 38, between Calles 41 and 43
4-3526173
Monday–Saturday noon–10:30 p.m.
Mains CUC$10–$15

This restaurant, tucked away on a quiet residential street, is one of only two remaining private restaurants from the 1990s. Roast pork headlines the menu, but the restaurant is testing out new vegetarian dishes relying on mushrooms and garbanzos. The large patio is inviting and doubles as indoor bike parking.

Palacio de Valle

Corner of Calle 37 and Av 2, Punta Gorda
Daily 10 a.m.–10 p.m.
Mains CUC$7–$13

Seafood dominates the menu, which is good, but the real draw is the building itself. Already-extraordinary Spanish and Moorish architecture is enhanced by fine stucco walls, mosaics, high ceilings, and chandeliers. Be sure to climb the spiraling staircase to grab a drink on the upstairs patio, where live musicians make the stunning view of the city even more enjoyable.

Restaurante Villa Lagarto

Calle 35 #4b, Punta Gorda
Daily noon–11 p.m.
Mains CUC$10–$20

Come for the food, stay for service. Enjoy succulent shish kebobs and roast pork while overlooking the stunning bay. Did you stuff yourself so much you're not ready to get back on the bicycle? Have a quick rest on one of the restaurant's hammocks and rocking chairs, or consider booking one of the rooms in the hostel the restaurant operates.

RIDE #13. CIENFUEGOS CITY RIDE

Distance: 6.5 miles/10.5 kilometers
Elevation: 287 feet/87 meters
Difficulty: Easy
Time: 1–2 hours

Today's city exploration begins at Parque Martí, where you can visit the Teatro Tomás Terry, check out various art galleries, and grab a drink on one of several cafés' plant-filled patios. On the way to La Reina cemetery, you'll pass the "locomotive graveyard," where old trains rust away, serving little purpose other than as a backdrop for travel photographs. This ride takes you past the Piña Colada waterfront bar before curving along the coast toward

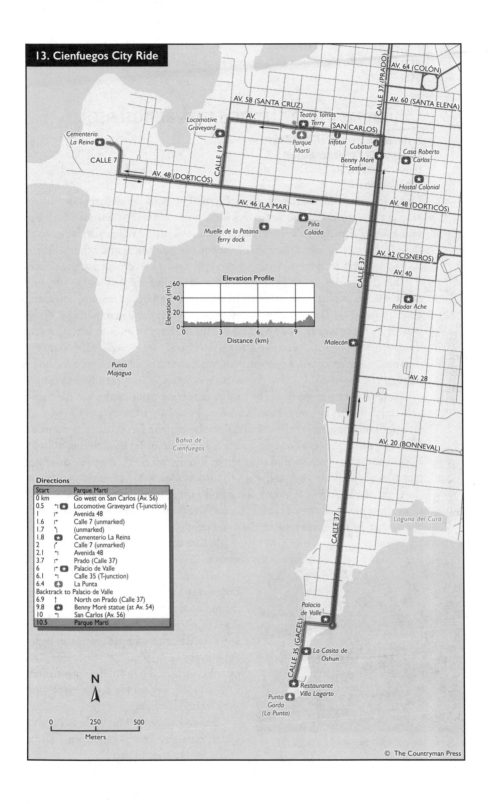

13. Cienfuegos City Ride

AV. 64 (COLÓN)
CALLE 37 (PRADO)
AV. 60 (SANTA ELENA)
AV. 58 (SANTA CRUZ)
AV.
Locomotive Graveyard
Teatro Tomás Terry (SAN CARLOS)
Cementerio La Reina
Parque Martí
Infotur
Cubatur
Casa Roberto Carlos
CALLE 7
CALLE 19
Benny Moré Statue
AV. 48 (DORTICÓS)
Hostal Colonial
AV. 46 (LA MAR)
AV. 48 (DORTICÓS)
Muelle de la Patana ferry dock
Piña Colada
AV. 42 (CISNEROS)
AV. 40
CALLE 37
Paladar Ache

Elevation Profile

Elevation (m)
60
40
20
0
0   3   6   9
Distance (km)

Malecón

Punta Majagua

AV. 28

AV. 20 (BONNEVAL)

Bahía de Cienfuegos

CALLE 37

Laguna del Cura

Directions

Start		Parque Martí
0 km		Go west on San Carlos (Av. 56)
0.5	⌐ ★	Locomotive Graveyard (T-junction)
1	⌐	Avenida 48
1.6	⌐	Calle 7 (unmarked)
1.7	⌐	(unmarked)
1.8	★	Cementerio La Reina
2	⌐	Calle 7 (unmarked)
2.1	⌐	Avenida 48
3.7	⌐	Prado (Calle 37)
6	⌐ ★	Palacio de Valle
6.1	⌐	Calle 35 (T-junction)
6.4	★	La Punta
Backtrack to Palacio de Valle		
6.9	↑	North on Prado (Calle 37)
9.8	★	Benny Moré statue (at Av. 54)
10	⌐	San Carlos (Av. 56)
10.5		Parque Martí

Palacio de Valle

CALLE 35 (GACEL)

La Casita de Oshun

N

Restaurante Villa Lagarto
Punta Gorda (La Punta)

0   250   500
Meters

© The Countryman Press

the southern end of the city. At the southern tip, you'll find Punta Gorda and Palacio de Valle before heading back north to the city's famous Benny Moré statue.

RIDE #14. RANCHO LUNA BEACH RIDE

Distance: 15.2 miles/24.5 kilometers
Elevation: 743 feet/226 meters
Difficulty: Moderate
Time: 2–3 hours

In order to fully maximize this route, you'll want to leave early so you can stop at the Refugio de Fauna Guanaroca for one of their 90-minute flora and fauna tours. If you haven't reserved tickets, it would be wise to arrive no later than 8:30 a.m. to guarantee your chance to see flamingos and other wildlife. If the park isn't of interest, simply ride right past it and onward to the beach.

This ride begins at the Benny Moré statue (corner of Av 54 and Prado) and quickly takes you to rural roads lined with coconut palms. Horses, cows, and goats graze in the fields and rest under the shade of large mango trees. When you arrive at the beach, leave your bike in the parking lot on your left. Bringing a lock is always best, but you can also tip the attendant to watch it. I brought my bike onto the beach during a recent visit, but it is very uncommon for bikes to be allowed onto beaches in Cuba. Proper parking in the lot is typically mandatory.

The quickest way back to the city is to retrace your route, but for those seeking different scenery, more adventure, and superb views of the bay, an alternate return option takes you back to the city via ferry, which is detailed here. Note that the ferry dock is located below the Hotel Pascaballo, but you cannot see it from above and the path to it is not marked. The path does not look like a legitimate path and you will no doubt question whether you are on the right track. Follow the directions and ask for help if needed. It's a short route, but there are several small, unmarked paths and trails, so it may look confusing. Allow extra time in case you take the wrong path.

TRANSPORTING OUR BIKES ON THE PASCABALLO FERRY TO CIENFUEGOS

Be sure to confirm the boat you get on goes to Cienfuegos, and not to El Castillo, the city and fort across the water. Some boats may stop at the fort and then continue to Cienfuegos, but not all of them. As of this writing, boats leave Cienfuegos at 8 a.m., and then they leave Hotel Pascaballo at 1 and 3 p.m. It's worth stopping by the boat landing in Cienfuegos to confirm, as ferry schedules are subject (and very likely) to change.

The ferry docks at Muelle de la Patana, which puts you five blocks from Parque Martí, where the ride ends.

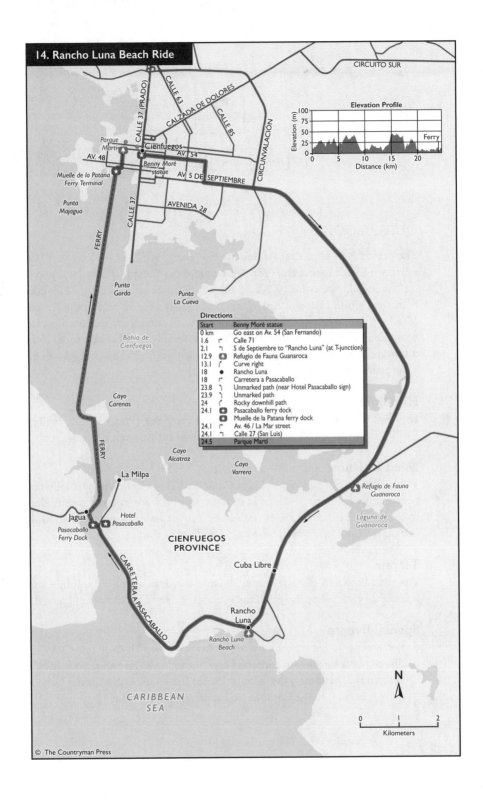

14. Rancho Luna Beach Ride

Elevation Profile

Directions		
Start		**Benny Moré statue**
0 km		Go east on Av. 54 (San Fernando)
1.6	↱	Calle 71
2.1	↰	5 de Septiembre to "Rancho Luna" (at T-junction)
12.9	🅰	Refugio de Fauna Guanaroca
13.1	↱	Curve right
18	●	Rancho Luna
18	↱	Carretera a Pasacaballo
23.8	↳	Unmarked path (near Hotel Pasacaballo sign)
23.9	↳	Unmarked path
24	↱	Rocky downhill path
24.1	⛴	Pasacaballo ferry dock
24.1	⛴	Muelle de la Patana ferry dock
24.1	↱	Av. 46 / La Mar street
24.1	↰	Calle 27 (San Luis)
24.5		Parque Martí

7

MATANZAS

QUICK LOOK

The province of Matanzas (which means "slaughter") is best known for its northern beach resort city, Varadero, one of the most beautiful and popular beaches in the country. Along the southern coast, the Bay of Pigs has historical significance to Americans and Cubans for its role in the Cuban Missile Crisis but is now known as one of the country's top destinations for scuba diving and wildlife viewing. The provincial capital of Matanzas is an underappreciated and up-and-coming city with splendid coastal views and a burgeoning art scene.

Highlights

Highlights for each city within Matanzas province (Playa Girón, Jagüey Grande, Varadero, and Matanzas) are detailed within each city's section.

Need-to-Know

While camping is allowed in Playa Girón and Playa Larga, it is usually not possible in Varadero. I've met bike tourists who were granted permission by local police officers to camp in Varadero, but that's not guaranteed. In all camping situations, strong mosquito repellent is a must.

Terrain

The road between Matanzas and Havana includes some large hills—and incredible views—but the province is mostly flat and roads are well paved.

Special Events

- Festival de Bailador Rumbero in Matanzas's Sauto Theater: mid-October
- The region's significant Santería population celebrates religious festivals year-round, including the celebration for Babalu Ayé, the Yoruba Orisha corresponding to the Catholic St. Lazarus, on December 18

🚲 RIDE #15. CIENFUEGOS TO PLAYA GIRÓN

Distance: 49.7 miles/80 kilometers
Elevation: 758 feet/231 meters
Difficulty: Difficult
Time: 5–6 hours

The road from Cienfuegos to Playa Girón is a pretty ride without too many hills; the difficulty level can be mainly attributed to the distance and the heat. The *Circuito Sur* is a flat, tree-lined (though shadeless) road that crosses over small rivers and passes by cornfields, banana plantations, and mango orchards. The CS curves a bit and you'll see smaller roads veering off, but stay on the main highway until Yaguaramas.

A few small cafeterias can be found in Yaguaramas, though bottled water is unlikely. There are a few quick turns onto unmarked streets in the town, so if you get confused, just ask someone, "Girón?" (pronounced "Hee-rone") and they'll point you in the right direction. The tiny town of Horquita has a small cafeteria offering simple sandwiches and bocadillos.

The ride ends at the photo-worthy Playa Girón billboard, which will be facing the other direction. Most casas are located on or near this main stretch—you will already have passed dozens by the time you get to the billboard. You can turn left at the billboard to ride to the beach, museum, or Hotel Playa Girón.

Playa Girón is quite small and you can find the **CaDeCa**, **Viazul** bus office, souvenirs, and snack shops all right next to each other across from the newly renovated **Playa Girón Museum.** Water and snacks are also available in the shop attached to Hotel Playa Girón, which has bathrooms open to the public.

Try out different spots along the beach and be sure to walk along the breakwater at sunset. There's a lesser-known beach about 1 kilometer east, where you'll find locals cracking open coconuts with machetes and frying up fresh fish for a few CUCs. The beach is rocky but the water is warm and clear, and it's the perfect sunset picnic location. Be sure to bring bug spray!

Cuisine in the region is known to include a much broader range of animals (crab, lobster, octopus, crocodile, etc.). Be very wary of ordering crocodile, as some of the meat served in casas and restaurants may be illegally poached. The crocodile meat served at the area's crocodile farm is sourced from the farm's own breeding program.

Bypassing Girón: To bypass Girón and go straight to Jagüey, skip the left turn toward the power towers in Yaguaramas and continue straight on the Circuito Sur until it runs into the Autopista. Turn left toward La Habana then right toward Jagüey Grande.

ACCOMMODATIONS IN PLAYA GIRÓN

Note that most casas in Playa Girón don't use addresses; rather, homeowners rely on travelers to ask a local to direct them to a particular house. Because

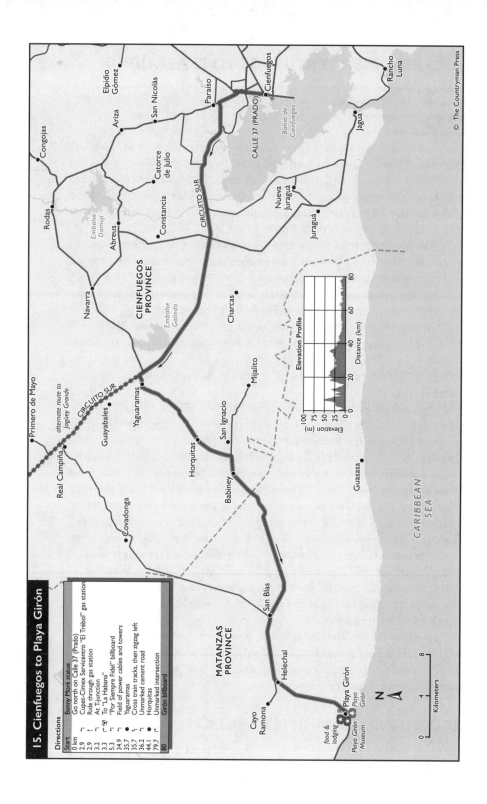

15. Cienfuegos to Playa Girón

Directions

	Start	Benny Moré statue
	0 km	Go north on Calle 37 (Prado)
⌐ ↑	2.9	Cupet-Cimex Servicentro "El Trébol" gas station
⌐ ↑	2.9	Ride through gas station
⌐ ↑	3.2	At T-junction
⌐ ↑ ⚲	3.3	To "La Habana"
⌐ ↑	5.3	"Por Siempre Fidel" billboard
⌐ ↑	34.9	Field of power cables and towers
⌐ ●	35.7	Yaguaramas
↺ ⤴	35.7	Cross train tracks, then zigzag left
⌐ ↑	36.2	Unmarked cement road
⌐ ↑	44.1	Horquitas
⌐ ↑	79.7	Unmarked intersection
	80	Girón billboard

© The Countryman Press

the town is small and everyone knows everyone, you shouldn't have much difficulty finding your destination. Just say the name of the casa you're looking for or show the name in this book.

Villa Castellaños

5-4220092, 5-4348092, or 5-2292437

This husband-wife team of doctors provides excellent hospitality and fabulous food (including great veggie options) in their two casas. Two rooms are available in the couple's home, which includes a large outdoor patio, grill, and garden; and two more are available in a large private apartment (several blocks away), complete with front porch and rockers.

Ivette and Ronel

5-3117389

micha@infomed.sld.cu

Ivette and Ronel have access to at least a dozen rooms across various casas they run in conjunction with neighboring families. Ronel is a diving instructor, so many of his rooms tend to be filled with divers. Their main house is one of the last ones on the main road leaving from Girón (or the first if coming from Havana/Jagüey Grande).

Camping Option

Camping in the Bay of Pigs is possible, both on the beach at Playa Girón and farther along in Playa Larga. In either instance, know that bug spray is absolutely mandatory. The beach is relatively calm, and you can purchase food and water at nearby hotels, restaurants, and casas, but you won't get any sleep unless your tent is completely sealed and you have good bug spray.

 RIDE #16. PLAYA GIRÓN TO JAGÜEY GRANDE

Distance: 39.4 miles/63.4 kilometers
Elevation: 482 feet/147 meters
Difficulty: Moderate
Time: 4–5 hours

This is the most straightforward route in the book, and one of the easiest. There's not a single turn for 60 kilometers—just follow the road as it curves! This is also one of the best areas in Cuba for unique propaganda billboards that go beyond the usual VIVA LA REVOLUCIÓN. They are specific to the US invasion and tend to reference the "imperialist mercenaries" who attempted to thwart the Revolution.

After a few kilometers, the ocean comes into view but is then often hidden behind a mixture of dead and living trees. The ocean appears here and there, offering spectacular views of turquoise and blue water while the Ciénaga de Zapata swamp occupies the entire right side of the path. The road is flat and in fairly good condition, except for some cracks and bumps due to patchy repair jobs. Aside from a few tour buses and colectivo cars,

Some of Cuba's best (and cheapest!) scuba diving and snorkeling can be found in Playa Girón. Excellent diving also exists in Maria La Gorda (Pinar del Río), Cayo Coco (Ciego de Avila), and Jardin de la Reina (Camagüey and Ciego de Avila), but all are difficult and expensive to get to. Dives in the Bay of Pigs run about CUC$25-$30 each and include transportation and gear. Two of the most popular dive sites are Punta Perdiz and Cueva de los Peces. Ask your casa to make you a reservation with the dive center, which can send an open-air bus to pick you up the next morning. Alternatively, you could cycle 8 kilometers to Caleta Buena beach, a nonresort, unpretentious, all-inclusive beach (CUC$15/person). The beach offers excellent snorkeling and scuba diving in salt and fresh water, making for a truly unique underwater experience.

SCUBA DIVING IN PLAYA GIRÓN (BAY OF PIGS)

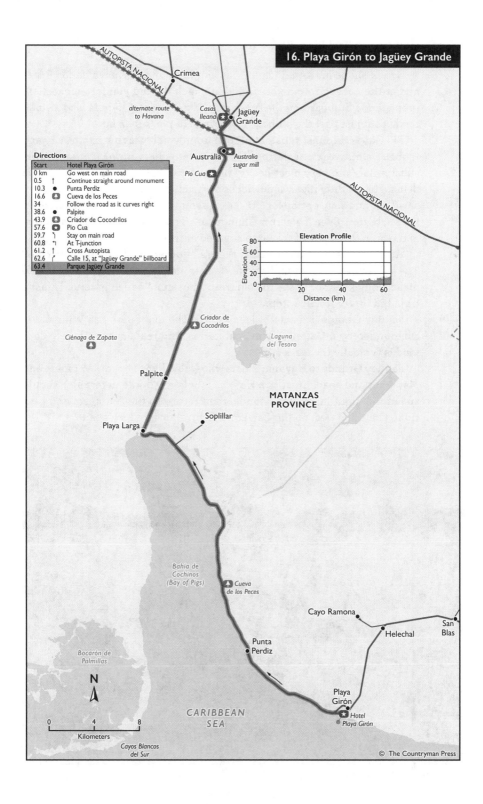

16. Playa Girón to Jagüey Grande

Crimea

AUTOPISTA NACIONAL

alternate route
to Havana

Casas
Ileana

Jagüey
Grande

Australia · Australia
sugar mill

Pío Cua

AUTOPISTA NACIONAL

Directions

Start		Hotel Playa Girón
0 km		Go west on main road
0.5	↑	Continue straight around monument
10.3	●	Punta Perdiz
16.6	⬆	Cueva de los Peces
34		Follow the road as it curves right
38.6	●	Palpite
43.9	⬆	Criador de Cocodrilos
57.6	★	Pío Cua
59.7	⌐	Stay on main road
60.8	⌐	At T-junction
61.2	↑	Cross Autopista
62.6	⌐	Calle 15, at "Jagüey Grande" billboard
63.4		Parque Jagüey Grande

Elevation Profile

Elevation (m) — 0 20 40 60 80
Distance (km) — 0 20 40 60

Criador de
Cocodrilos

Ciénaga de Zapata

Laguna
del Tesoro

Palpite

MATANZAS
PROVINCE

Soplillar

Playa Larga

Bahía de
Cochinos
(Bay of Pigs)

Cueva
de los Peces

Cayo Ramona

San
Blas

Helechal

Punta
Perdiz

Bocarón de
Palmillas

N

Playa
Girón

Hotel
Playa Girón

CARIBBEAN
SEA

0	4	8

Kilometers

Cayos Blancos
del Sur

© The Countryman Press

your road companions are local farmers in rubber boots riding bicycles or steering horse-drawn carts.

Snack shops and small cafeterias can be found at Cueva de los Peces and at the curve around 34k. In Palpite, look behind you for an excellent propaganda billboard on the other side of the street. There is also a small restaurant just past the billboard, offering simple Cuban fare.

Pio Cua is the most substantial restaurant you'll pass during the day and is open 8 a.m. to 4 p.m., catering mostly to the tour bus crowd. It offers a fairly substantial (and very meat-heavy) buffet for CUC$10, including juice or a drink. For a lighter meal, sandwiches are available, as is a small vegetarian salad bar and soup option for CUC$5 (the soup and salad bar are included in the $10 buffet). Even if you're not hungry, it's a good spot to use the bathroom and rest in the shade of the large covered entryway.

At the T-intersection at 60.8k, there's another great billboard of Fidel. The old Australia sugar mill smoke stack is visible on the right. Feel free to make a quick detour to see the old train "museum," which is actually just a train but is still worth a stop.

Jagüey Grande is a small, sleepy town. The main park has WiFi and is surrounded by a **CaDeCa**, bank, cafeterias, and restaurants (though casa food is typically the tastiest).

Jagüey Grande to Havana: Riders who would like to bypass Varadero and Matanzas and head directly to Havana (about a 150-kilometer ride), should spend the night in Jagüey Grande, then return to the Autopista and turn right. Continue west on the Carretera Central toward La Habana.

A PLANTAIN VENDOR ON THE HIGHWAY OUTSIDE JAGÜEY GRANDE

ACCOMMODATIONS IN JAGÜEY GRANDE

Casas Ileana
Calle 15 #5831 between 58 and 60
4-5914178 or 5-2442117
Ileana.fente@nauta.cu
Ileana offers two clean rooms, one with two double beds, the other with one double bed. Her home has a nice upstairs patio and terrace, and she serves excellent food. If she can't host you, she can find you a room in another nearby casa.

RIDE #17. JAGÜEY GRANDE TO VARADERO

Distance: 52.6 miles/84.7 kilometers
Elevation: 974 feet/297 meters
Difficulty: Difficult
Time: 6–8 hours

This ride begins in the town park, in front of Palacio del Pueblo, and quickly leads into agriculture country. Some small passenger trucks and cars will be on the road, but the route is fairly quiet. The first half of the long stretch to Jovellanos (3-202 on some digital maps) is lined with miles and miles of grapefruit, orange, and lemon groves. Smiling farmers will look up from the fields to wave and cheer you on.

Finding a bathroom along the route can be a challenge, and I wound up asking to use the bathroom of a home operating a fruit stand around the 32k mark. Should you do this, be sure to tip. Small cafeterias selling sandwiches, pizza, and snacks are available in Isabel and Jovellanos. At the 35.6k mark, turn right in Jovellanos. You'll see a bridge about a block ahead of you; this is the Carretera Central that you need to get on, but it can only be accessed via a roundabout series of turns.

The best lunch option is Coliseo, where the corner cafeteria serving pizza and spaghetti has plenty of seating and room for your bike. Cardenas would be the next good lunch option but would require you to ride an additional few kilometers into town. Cardenas, about 16 kilometers before Varadero, has lots of casas, making it a great stop for anyone wanting to break up the route. The ride ends at the Gran Caribe Hotel Sun Beach, which is a public WiFi hotspot and a short walk/ride to the casas listed here.

Varadero is one of Cuba's top beach destinations and is, by far, the most popular beach in western Cuba. Though it's known for its all-inclusive resorts, some of which are extremely luxurious, moderately priced casas are also available. Prices for casas, restaurants, souvenirs, and just about everything else tend to be higher here. On the flip side, the sand is also softer and cleaner, and the water is clearer than most Cuban beaches. Don't expect a lot of cultural sites here. Nobody goes to Varadero to visit museums or take historical walking tours—it's all about the sun and sand!

Every local has his or her opinion about the best beach in Varadero, but

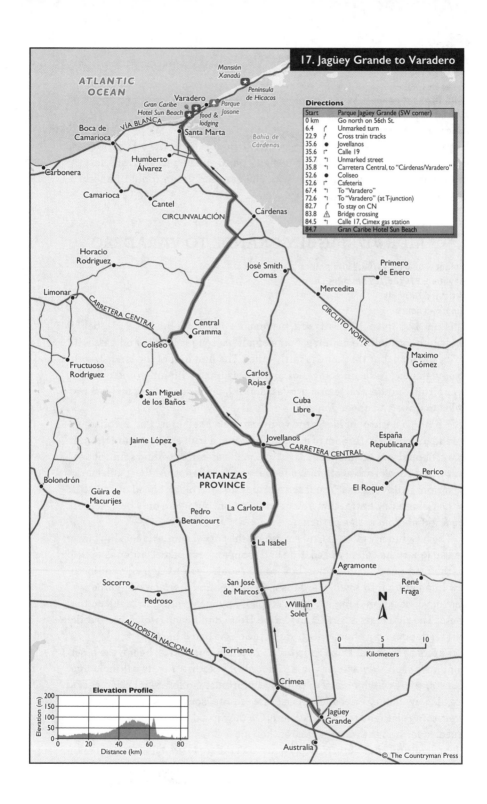

17. Jagüey Grande to Varadero

ATLANTIC OCEAN

Mansión Xanadú

Peninsula de Hicacos

Varadero
Gran Caribe Hotel Sun Beach
VÍA BLANCA
Parque Josone
food & lodging
Santa Marta

Boca de Camarioca

Bahía de Cárdenas

Carbonera

Humberto Álvarez

Camarioca

Cantel
CIRCUNVALACIÓN

Cárdenas

Directions

Start	Parque Jagüey Grande (SW corner)
0 km	Go north on 56th St.
6.4	Unmarked turn
22.9	Cross train tracks
35.6	Jovellanos
35.6	Calle 19
35.7	Unmarked street
35.8	Carretera Central, to "Cárdenas/Varadero"
52.6	Coliseo
52.6	Cafeteria
67.4	To "Varadero"
72.6	To "Varadero" (at T-junction)
82.7	To stay on CN
83.8	Bridge crossing
84.5	Calle 17, Cimex gas station
84.7	Gran Caribe Hotel Sun Beach

Horacio Rodriguez

José Smith Comas

Primero de Enero

Limonar
CARRETERA CENTRAL

Mercedita

CIRCUITO NORTE

Central Gramma

Coliseo

Maximo Gómez

Fructuoso Rodriguez

Carlos Rojas

San Miguel de los Baños

Cuba Libre

Jaime López

Jovellanos

España Republicana

CARRETERA CENTRAL

Bolondrón

MATANZAS PROVINCE

Perico

Güira de Macurijes

El Roque

Pedro Betancourt

La Carlota

La Isabel

Agramonte

Socorro

San José de Marcos

René Fraga

Pedroso

William Soler

N

AUTOPISTA NACIONAL

Torriente

0   5   10
Kilometers

Crimea

Jagüey Grande

Australia

© The Countryman Press

Elevation Profile

Elevation (m)

200
150
100
50
0

0   20   40   60   80
Distance (km)

everyone agrees that the beach around the Meliá hotel and **Mansion Xanadu** (a magnificently restored old mansion that used to belong to the Dupont family) is one of the best crescents of sand. There may not be a parking attendant, so bring a lock and leave your bike in the lot. The ride along the Autopista Sur that takes you to Xanadu is absolutely stunning and best enjoyed in the morning, before tour buses hog the roads.

Just about every stretch of beach along Varadero's picturesque coastline is packed with tourists. On the weekends, the section along the 40s and 50s becomes even more crowded when locals come to enjoy the weekend. A quieter stretch can be found in the high teens and low 20s.

Parque Josone provides a nice escape from the bustling traffic and tour buses. You can relax in the shade, enjoy a drink

A LOCAL MAN TRANSPORTING "MILK FOR THE BABIES" OUTSIDE CARDENAS, MATANZAS

at the bar overlooking the lake, or rent a bike paddleboat (CUC$5/hour).

The **Tourist Information Center** is on the corner of Avenida 1ra and Calle 23, and the **CaDeCa** money exchange is on Calle 44 and Avenida 1ra in the Comercial Hicacos shopping complex. The **Banco de Crédito y Comercio** is on the corner of Avenida 1ra and Calle 36, and the **Banco Financiero Internacional** is on the corner of Avenida 1ra and Calle 32.

ACCOMMODATIONS IN VARADERO

Casa Lola

First Avenue (Avenida 1ra) #1602, between 16/17
4-5613383

Guests will spot this home by the well-maintained front garden, overflowing with plants and flowers and decorated with rainbow-colored patio chairs and a large swing that's just calling your name! Three rooms are available for CUC$40 each.

Casa Fara

Calle 18 #101, between First and Second Avenue (Avenida 1ra y 2da)
faramaria68@nauta.cu

Just 50 meters from the beach, this home within a garden offers two rooms for CUC$30–$40 each. The larger room is actually a private apartment with its own kitchen and direct patio access. It rents for the same price as the smaller room, so try to snag it if it's available!

Casa Santa María

Calle 17 #103, between First and Second Avenue (Avenida 1ra y 2da)
3-915969, 5-610103, or 5-612479
davidestradalon22@yahoo.com

This nicely furnished ground-floor apartment rents two rooms, each with two beds, for CUC$40–$45 each. Though you'll enjoy the privacy of your own apartment, the owners are just around the corner, should you need help.

Villa Pla

Calle 31 #108C
4-5612375 or 5-2846553
orestepla3@yahoo.com

This home offers two rooms with double beds and a nice back patio with a lounge chair. It's a few blocks from the beach and near one of the city's best restaurants, Salsa Suarez.

RESTAURANTS IN VARADERO

Salsa Suarez

Calle 31 #103, between Av 1 and Av 3
Daily 1 p.m.–10:30 p.m.
Mains CUC$8–$13

Can't decide what to eat? Head to this crisply decorated modern restaurant serving up everything from sushi and tapas to risotto and quesadillas. Meals are colorful, artistically presented, and delicious.

Paladar Nonna Tina

Calle 38, between Av 1 and Av de la Playa
Tuesday–Sunday noon–11 p.m.
Mains CUC$6–$11

If you ask a local what the best restaurant in town is, most would recommend Paladar Nonna Tina. While most Cuban "Italian" food is synonymous with mushy spaghetti, Nonna Tina is known for al dente tagliatelle al ragú, flavorful gnocci, and wood-fired pizza. Try to snag a table in the front patio, and be sure to order a proper cappuccino and tiramisu.

Dante

Inside Parque Josone
Daily noon–10:30 p.m.
Mains CUC$7–$12

Varadero's ratio of Italian to Cuban restaurants is much higher than in other cities, but what's more impressive than Dante's à la carte pasta menu (from lasagna to fusilli with shrimp) is the wide assortment of domestic and imported drinks. Dante is located near the edge of Parque Josone's artificial lake, and the restaurant's large windows and romantic terrace afford a panoramic view of the water.

Corner of Av 1 and Calle 62
Daily noon–midnight
Mains CUC$7–$13

For a fun snack or a meal out of the ordinary (in Cuba, at least), swing by what locals rate one of the best state-run restaurants in town. Though many people are happy to have a change from the usual rice and beans, don't expect Swiss standards. Small, hot cauldrons bubble with melted cheese, chicken, beef, shrimp, and lobster fondue.

RIDE #18. VARADERO TO MATANZAS

Distance: 23 miles/37 kilometers
Elevation: 546 feet/166 meters
Difficulty: Easy
Time: 2–3 hours

The ride from Varadero to Matanzas is short and mostly flat along a well-paved highway. Your first turn at the Cimex will put you right onto the Autopista Sur, which crosses a bridge and eventually turns into the Via Blanca. Follow the Via Blanca highway as it curves toward La Habana and turns into the Circuito Norte (CN). Traffic moves very quickly along the Via Blanca, but cars are respectful, so you're able to enjoy the sweeping views of the water crashing against the coast to your right. A large emergency shoulder also doubles as a bike path along some stretches.

A potential interesting and very popular (i.e., crowded) side trip would be to the Saturn caves about halfway to Matanzas. Around 24k, you may also want to stop and snap a picture of a colorful *bloqueo* (embargo) propaganda billboard facing the other direction.

When you are near the Matanzas city center, you'll see an old, crumbling building ahead to your left with a mural painted on it. This is Calle 79. Continue straight to arrive at Parque Libertad, where the ride ends.

Bypassing Matanzas: To skip Matanzas and continue on to Jibacoa, instead of continuing straight onto Calle 79 (at 36.5k), turn right just after the railroad tracks to continue on the Autopista. Cross the metal bridge and curve right around the bay. Pick up the remaining directions during the Matanzas to Havana ride.

Matanzas: The main attractions in Matanzas are **Taller-Galería Lolo**, a busy riverfront artists' collective full of surreal sculptures crafted out of

PARQUE LIBERTAD IN MATANZAS

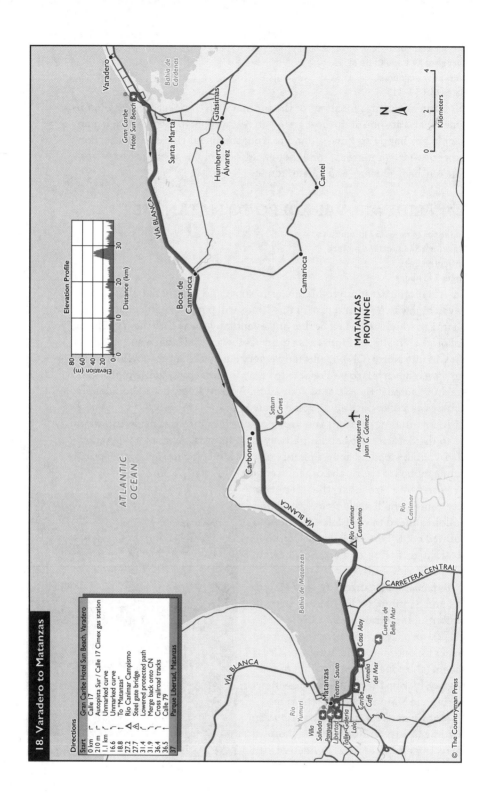

18. Varadero to Matanzas

Directions

Start	Gran Caribe Hotel Sun Beach, Varadero
0 km	Calle 17
210 m	Autopista Sur / Calle 17 Cimex gas station
1.1 km	Unmarked curve
16.6	Unmarked curve
18.8	To "Matanzas"
27.2	Río Canímar Campismo
27.7	Steel gate bridge
31.4	Lowered protected path
31.9	Merge back onto CN
36.4	Cross railroad tracks
36.5	Calle 79
37	Parque Libertad, Matanzas

Elevation Profile

ATLANTIC OCEAN

Varadero

Bahía de Cárdenas

Gran Caribe
Hotel Sun Beach

Santa Marta

Guásimas

Humberto
Álvarez

Cantel

VÍA BLANCA

Boca de
Camarioca

Camarioca

MATANZAS
PROVINCE

Saturn
Caves

Carbonera

Aeropuerto
Juan G. Gómez

VÍA BLANCA

Río Canímar
Campismo

*Río
Canímar*

Bahía de Matanzas

CARRETERA CENTRAL

Cuevas de
Bella Mar

Casa Aloy

Amelia
del Mar

VÍA BLANCA

*Río
Yumurí*

Matanzas

Teatro Sauto

Caribe
Café

Villa
Soñada

Parque
Libertad

Taller-Galería

Lolo

© The Countryman Press

salvaged materials, and the **Cuevas de Bella Mar** (CUC$5), a stalactite- and stalagmite-filled cave system. The caves are an easy 2-kilometer ride from the main road. From Caribe Café, take Calle 254 (Levante) two blocks and turn left onto Calle 159/Carretera a las Cuevas de Bellmar. It's a straight shot from there. On most days, a bus runs between the caves and **Iglesia Monserrat** approximately every 45 minutes. Ask the parking attendant if you are interested. Also, be sure to stop by **Teatro Sauto** (Calle 272 near Calle 129), a beautiful neoclassical building decorated with marble statues and paintings. Matanzas's famous Hershey Train to Havana was closed indefinitely for repairs at the time of research but will hopefully reopen.

Tourist Information: WiFi is available in Parque Libertad, and Internet cards can be purchased at the **ETECSA** on the corner of Calles 83 and 282.

The **Banco de Crédito y Comercio** (9 a.m.–5 p.m.) has an ATM and is on Calle 85 #28604, between Calle 286 and 288. The **CaDeCa** is around the corner on Calle 286 between Calles 83 and 85.

ACCOMMODATIONS IN MATANZAS

Casa Alay
Calle Larga de Escoto #21608 between Doblada and Bajada Streets (one block from Centro Commercial la Sirenita on the beach)
5-2952260
alain.donaedita@gmail.com
Alay and his family rent out three private bungalows in a lush, secluded, mini-paradise that will make you forget you're in the city. Hammocks hang around small ponds, where you can lounge and read a book from the home's small library. The three rooms in the garden are the best option, but if they're taken, ask about the private apartment next door, which also allows access to the main garden and patios. Note that if you are riding from Varadero, you'll pass this house (it's one block off the main road) about 2 kilometers before you reach the town center.

Villa Soñando
Calle 290 #6701, corner of Santa Isabel
4-5242761
mandy_rent_habitaciones@yahoo.com
A "Villa of Dreams" that may quite possibly be the most modern and luxurious casa in Matanzas (and all of Cuba). Three spacious, glass-brick bedrooms with sleek bathrooms and minibars rent for CUC$30–$35 per night. Huge, delicious dinners are served on the upstairs terrace.

RESTAURANTS IN MATANZAS

Caribe Café
Corner of Levante (Calle 254) and the Carretera
Daily 7 a.m.–10 p.m.
Meals CUC$3–5
This nautically themed waterfront restaurant has a good selection of coffee, alcoholic and nonalcoholic drinks, breakfast, spaghetti, pizza, and salads.

Amelia Del Mar
Calle 129 #22014 between 220 and 222
4-5261653
Thursday–Tuesday noon–midnight
Meals CUC$4–$10

This unsuspecting restaurant opens into a huge garden patio where tables and sofas are hidden within plant-filled nooks. Soups, salads, and plantains stuffed with shrimp or tuna are given romantic albeit slightly cheesy names like "lovers meeting," "fragile trembles," and "summer promises."

 RIDE #19. MATANZAS TO HAVANA

Distance: 58.8 miles/94.6 kilometers
Elevation: 2,000 feet/610 meters
Difficulty: Difficult
Time: 6–8 hours

The ride from Matanzas to Havana is beautiful and includes coastal views both at the beginning and end of the ride. The route begins with a long and slow climb with tour buses, taxis, and trucks transporting Cubans whizzing by to Havana. The most difficult hills are within the first 25 kilometers, and there are several lodging options for riders interested in breaking up the route. After 7 kilometers, the road flattens out briefly and the expansive Yumurí Valley opens to your left. Around 14.5 kilometers, there is a large cafeteria and snack shop with bathrooms on the left.

The Mirador de Bacunayagua makes for a nice rest stop or bathroom break. Those who wish to visit the lookout point will have to loop around to climb the hill near the control point. Those who don't want to climb or lock up can still find bathrooms and snacks at the Playa Azul cafeteria just past the mirador. Plenty of food options are available along the route, including a particularly nice cafeteria around 32.2k.

Those wanting to break up the route should consider stopping in or near Jibacoa. Several casas are conveniently visible from the highway. A hotel option would be Villa Loma. Just before the 57k highway marker and yellow bridge, take the unmarked concrete path next to a large tree with a bus stop, likely full of people waiting for a ride. This path leads to the Villa Loma hotel, which is made up of small cabana apartments on a well-landscaped lawn full of magenta bougainvillea bushes. It has a pool and nice views of the water (phone: 4-7295316 or 4-7295332).

Just past the yellow bridge are two casas on the left side of the street. Rooms are basic, and one of the hosts is a diving instructor and can take you diving or snorkeling. One kilometer later (at the 55k road marker) is Pedro's House (4-7294389), renting two nice rooms a five-minute walk to the water, though it's too rocky to swim. A bar and restaurant across the street make for a nice lunch spot for those who want to continue on to Havana.

Between Jibacoa and Guanabo, there are several industrial stretches, and the ride to Havana doesn't offer much in the way of scenery aside from

19. Matanzas to Havana

Elevation Profile

Ciclobus stop

Elevation (m)

250
200
150
100
50
0

0   20   40   60   80

Distance (km)

Ciclobus

Directions

Start	Parque Libertad, in front of Hotel Velasco
0 km	North on Calle 288
50 m	Calle 77 (Manzano)
0.5	At park, Calle 270
0.6	Cross bridge over Río Yumurí
0.8	Train tracks
1.3	To "La Habana" and "Guanabo"
20.1	Mirador de Bacunayagua
32.2	Stay on highway
72.4	Guanabo
88.5	To "Nacional"
90.1	Follow signs to "túnel"
93.2	Military hospital
93.3	Ciclobus stop
93.8	Ciclobus stop (Old Havana)
93.8	Second exit (left turn)
93.8	Ride in direction bus was going (SW)
94	Agramonte to "Monumento José Martí"
94.6	Parque Central

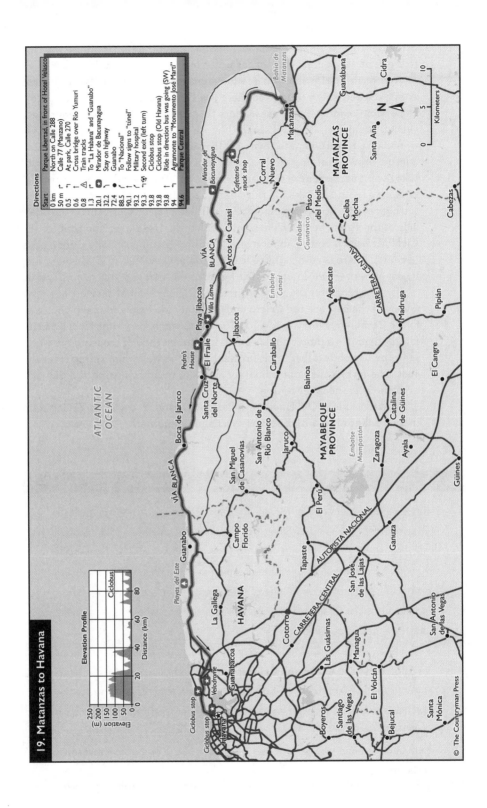

ATLANTIC OCEAN

Bahía de Matanzas

Matanzas

MATANZAS PROVINCE

Mirador de Bacunayagua

Cafetería & snack shop

Corral Nuevo

Paso del Medio

Ceiba Mocha

Santa Ana

Guanábana

Cidra

Cabezas

VÍA BLANCA

Arcos de Canasí

Embalse Caunavaco

Embalse Canasí

Aguacate

CARRETERA CENTRAL

Madruga

Pipián

Playa Jibacoa

Villa Loma

Jibacoa

Caraballo

Bainoa

Catalina de Güines

El Cangre

El Fraile

Pedro's House

Santa Cruz del Norte

Jaruco

San Antonio de Río Blanco

MAYABEQUE PROVINCE

Zaragoza

Ayala

Boca de Jaruco

San Miguel de Casanovias

Embalse Mampostón

Güines

Guanabo

Campo Florido

El Perú

Tapaste

Ganuza

AUTOPISTA NACIONAL

Playas del Este

La Gallega

Cotorro

Las Guásimas

San José de las Lajas

San Antonio de las Vegas

HAVANA

CARRETERA CENTRAL

Managua

El Volcán

Santa Mónica

Boyeros

Santiago de las Vegas

Bejucal

Guanabacoa

Velódromo

Ciclobus stop

Habana

Ciclobus stop

N

0   5   10
Kilometers

© The Countryman Press

occasional ocean views. Guanabo is another potential stop for those wanting to break up the route. Loads of casas can easily be found in the city.

Approaching Havana, you'll follow signs toward the *túnel* (tunnel). Bikes aren't allowed in the tunnel, so there is a Ciclobus, a bus that carries bicyclists, motorcyclists, and passengers through the 3-kilometer underwater tunnel. Around 91.2k, you'll see the blue velodrome on the left. This is where cyclists train and compete. Just past the velodrome is the military hospital, a large, brown building set back from the highway. This is where you will take the unmarked curve right and circle around the roundabout, essentially making a left turn. Take the third exit to continue in the same direction as the highway for about two blocks. You will see a raised platform on the other side of the street, across from a small cafeteria. Head over and wait for the Ciclobus, which comes about every 20 minutes and costs one Cuban peso (5 cents). There is zero signage leading to the Ciclobus, so if you can't find it, just ask—*everyone* knows it. The bus runs daily from 6:30 a.m. until 7 p.m.

If you arrive later than 7 p.m., find the Ciclobus out of service, or prefer a view of the bay, see the **Cristo and Cojímar** ride map and make your way to the Casablanca ferry (page 90). The Casablanca ferry runs from 5 a.m. to midnight and is a more reliable and beautiful method of crossing the water than the Ciclobus, albeit a bit farther out of the way when riding from the east. The ferry runs approximately every 15 minutes during the day and every hour in the late evening.

The ride ends in Old Havana, in Parque Central. You will see El Capitolio in the background, which serves as a helpful landmark.

PICK A BEACH: PLAYAS DEL ESTE RIDE

About 30 kilometers east of Havana is a beach strip known as *Playas del Este* (Eastern Beaches). These white sand beaches are only a 20-minute drive from Havana, so they attract both tourists and locals and are especially crowded on weekends. Expect lots of loud music and beach vendors selling jewelry and trinkets all day. Grilled fish and cold beer are readily available. The most popular beach is Playa Santa María del Mar, where lounge chairs and shade umbrellas can be rented.

To get to Santa María, Megano, Mar Azul, Guanabo, or any of the Playas del Este, follow the **Cristo and Cojímar** ride and continue east on the highway until you see signs for the beach of your choice. Highway turnoffs to the beach will have you turn right, then loop back under the freeway (essentially a left turn ↰ to get to the beach. To return to Havana, follow the same route back or jump on the Ciclobus (directions at the end of the **Matanzas to Havana** ride).

8

HOLGUÍN

QUICK LOOK

Christopher Columbus first landed in Cuba in what is now Holguín and described it as "the most beautiful country human eyes had ever seen." Cubans debate exactly where Columbus docked, but by most accounts it was somewhere near what is now the sleepy fishing village of Gibara. Holguín is now best known for the northern beach resort town of Guardalavaca, but an increasing number of tourists (and locals) are flocking to Gibara, which holds the annual Cine Pobre film festival.

Highlights
- **Cine Pobre** is an offbeat, somewhat makeshift weeklong festival held in Gibara each April, showcasing Cuban and international films that have been produced on a small budget. Note that some festival films are screened in Holguín.
- Within the capital city of Holguín, cycle the steep hill or walk up 465 steps to **La Loma de la Cruz,** the city's highest point, where a restaurant, bar, small art gallery, and panoramic views await you. A cross was raised here in 1790 in hopes of relieving a drought. Devotees now climb to the summit on May 3 during the Romerías de Mayo.
- Holguín hosts the **Fiesta de Cultura Iberoamericana** each October, when big name musicians from across Latin America take over the city for a week.
- Holguín's **Fábrica de Órganos** is the only organ factory in Cuba. It has irregular and unreliable hours, but there's usually a neighbor nearby happy to let you in, in exchange for a tip.
- **Guardalavaca's** white sand and turquoise waters make it one of the country's best beaches.
- For live music, head to **Casa de la Música** on Parque Calixto García or **Casa de la Trova** at Maceo #174. On most weekends you'll find live music in Plaza de la Marqueta.

Need-to-Know
- Some routes in and through Holguín may seem roundabout; this is because several main streets prohibit cycling.

A HORSE CART IN GIBARA, HOLGUÍN

- In some cases, directions include walking your bike a block or two, or they suggest riding on parallel streets to avoid further complications with pedestrian-only walkways and car-only avenues.

Terrain

The terrain surrounding the city of Holguín is hilly, but flat agricultural lands make up the south and the marshy northern coast.

Special Events

- Cine Pobre, film festival in Gibara: April
- Romerías de Mayo procession and celebration in Holguín: May 3
- Festival de Cultura Iberoamericana in Holguín: late October

Tourist Information

Cubatur and **Infotur** are located inside the Pico Cristal building on the corner of Martí and Manduley. Infotur (Monday–Friday 8 a.m.–4 p.m.) sells the helpful *Carreteras* map book. WiFi is available in Parque Calixto García, and you can purchase Internet cards at the main ETECSA office at Martí #122 or at their smaller office on the corner of Martí and Maceo.

The **Banco de Crédito y Comercio** is on Arias Street in front of Parque

Céspedes, and the **Banco Financiero Internacional** is at Manduley #165, between Frexes and Aguilera. Both are open 9 a.m. to 3 p.m. Monday through Friday and have ATMs. The **CaDeCa** is located at Manduley #205, between Luz Caballero and Martí.

ONE OF HOLGUÍN'S FAMOUS SIDE-CAR BICYCLE TAXIS

ACCOMMODATIONS IN HOLGUÍN

Casa Sigfredo

Luz Caballero #48A
2-4423057 or 5-5985543
Sigfredoj76@nauta.cu

Though this well-furnished apartment (CUC$20–$25) is located up one flight of stairs, Sigfredo's father is happy to store your bike in his ground-floor apartment below. Sigfredo is extremely friendly and highly knowledgeable about the city.

Villa Oscar

Luz Caballero #74A
2-4471457 or 5-5839351
nirde88@nauta.cu or nirdeperezrodriguez@gmail.com

Oscar (known as "Pino") has two large, well-furnished apartments (CUC$25–$35) on the second and third floor of his home, where a huge balcony and in-house WiFi make hauling a bike up the stairs worthwhile. Oscar will likely insist on bringing the bike up for you.

Villa Liba

Maceo #46, corner of 18th (Línea)
villaliba@nauta.cu or mariela.gongora@infomed.sld.cu
2-4423823 or 5-2896931

Jorge and Mariela offer two ground-floor rooms (CUC$25–$30 each) in a quiet, suburbanesque corner of Holguín, slightly removed from the city center. Bonus: Mariela is a massage and Reiki specialist.

RESTAURANTS IN HOLGUÍN

El Aldabón

Mártires #81 (between Frexes and Aguilera)
Daily 11 a.m.–11 p.m.
Mains CUC$2–$4

Knock on the large wooden door and wait for someone to unlock it and let you into a proper dining room that leads to a back patio decorated with flags from around the world. Portions are generous, and the peso menu is affordable enough that you'll see many locals dining alongside tourists.

Mártires #143 (between Luz Caballero and Ariochea)
Daily noon–midnight
Mains CUC$8–$12

This elegant restaurant is one of the city's best, offering artistically prepared plates of octopus, pasta, and steaks. Reservations are recommended on the weekend.

🚲 RIDE #20. HOLGUÍN TO GIBARA

Distance: 21.3 miles/34.3 kilometers
Elevation: 1,370 feet/418 meters
Difficulty: Moderate
Time: 3–4 hours

This ride starts in front of Panamericana market in Calixto García park. Head north on Manduley ("Bulevar" or "Libertad" on some digital maps), walking your bike the first two blocks through the pedestrian-only "boulevard," then continue biking on Manduley. You'll turn onto Avenida Cajigal right after Parque Infantil and the Ministerio de Agricultura. This road turns into Carretera Gibara (6-221 on some digital maps). Once you are 2 kilometers out of town, traffic thins considerably, and you'll be the only one on the road much of the way. In the absence of cars, there will be farmers hauling loads on horse-drawn wagons. The road is bumpy at times and potholes have been patched repeatedly, but with the virtually nonexistent traffic, large bumps are easily avoidable.

Aside from a small food stand and a local entrepreneur who may set up in front of her home, the only food stop is the Parador San Marcos in Floro Pérez, offering juice, drinks, and sandwiches. A large GIBARA sign welcomes you to the city, where vendors will surely call to you from their small stalls and pushcarts to offer you fresh *camarones*, shrimp cocktails.

Gibara fills to the brim each April, when Cubans from across the country (and a handful of international film buffs) travel there to attend the Cine Pobre film festival. In fact, so many people attend that the government allows regular, unlicensed homes to host tourists to meet the demand. Any other time of year, expect empty streets and a relaxed vibe. If you're

A COUPLE EAGER TO CHAT IN GIBARA, CUBA

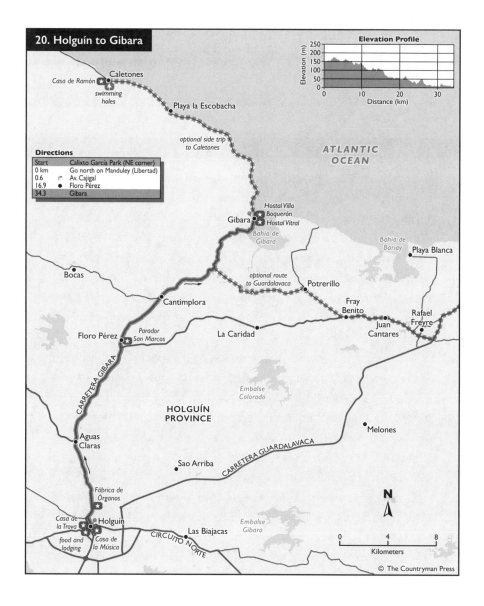

Elevation Profile

Elevation (m)

Distance (km)

Casa de Ramón
Caletones
swimming
holes
Playa la Escobacha

optional side trip
to Caletones

ATLANTIC
OCEAN

Directions

Start	Calixto García Park (NE corner)
0 km	Go north on Manduley (Libertad)
0.6	Av. Cajigal
16.9	Floro Pérez
34.3	Gibara

Hostal Villa
Boquerón
Gibara   Hostal Vitral
Bahía de
Gibara

Bahía de
Bariay
Playa Blanca

Bocas

optional route
to Guardalavaca
Potrerillo

Cantimplora

Fray
Benito

Rafael
Freyre

Floro Pérez
Parador
San Marcos
La Caridad

Juan
Cantares

Embalse
Colorado

HOLGUÍN
PROVINCE

Melones

CARRETERA GIBARA

Aguas
Claras

Sao Arriba
CARRETERA GUARDALAVACA

Fábrica de
Órganos

Casa de
la Trova
Holguín

Embalse
Gibara

food and
lodging
Casa de
la Música
Las Biajacas
CIRCUITO NORTE

N

0   4   8
Kilometers

© The Countryman Press

interested in historical tours of the city, excursions to the surrounding cave system, or guided dives in Caletones, contact José Corella at 5-3979096 or Josélin54@nauta.cu.

Continuing to Guardalavaca: To return to Holguín, follow the same route back. Though it's possible to go directly from Gibara to Guardalavaca, the road is very bumpy and dusty and is an absolute mess if it's been raining. Cyclists with mountain tires will have better luck and can reach Guardalavaca by turning left toward Fray Benito and continuing toward Rafael Freyre. Another option would be to catch a ferry. Cubatur runs day trips along the north coast, stopping in Gibara and Playa Blanca, among other places. The schedule varies, but if you ask ahead (ideally in Holguín, before heading to Gibara), you may be able to catch a one-way ride to Playa Blanca, then ride on to Guardalavaca.

PLAYA CALETONES

Caletones is a poor village that recently opened several casas particulares to accommodate tourists. There's not much to do, but it's a quiet and relaxing escape to a corner of the island that few tourists see. It's about a 20-kilometer ride from Gibara along a very dusty, rocky coastal road. The ride is a straight shot and could be tacked on to the end of the Holguín-Gibara ride, or it could serve as a day trip. Mountain tires are ideal but not necessary. Locals take this route on all types of bicycles. If you'd like to explore Caletones without the dust, bumps, and potential flat tires, a taxi would cost about CUC$25 round-trip.

Follow signs to Caletones, where a single winding coastal road leads you to the center of town, marked by a Red Cross sign. Just behind the sign is a TRD store with drinks and snacks. A bakery is farther down the road on the left, but you may not find any proper restaurants open. Opposite the Red Cross sign and TRD store is an unmarked street. Half a block down this street is Casa de Ramón (5-4095670 or 5-2193337), a blue house with red trim and a rooftop patio with a hammock.

Gibara residents enjoy visiting Caletones to swim in its various swimming holes—Tanque Fría and Tanque Azul, in particular. Tanque Fría is near the entrance of town, whereas Tanque Azul is accessed by hiking along a rocky 3-kilometer path. While it's possible to visit on your own, a guide (about CUC$5) is recommended, because the path is not well marked and tourists have gotten lost in the past. During slow periods and weekdays, it may be difficult to find an official guide, but you can ask around and will surely find a local happy to accompany you. Be sure to tip. The surface water is warm, but if you jump off a ledge (and you should!), you will plunge into colder water below. A yellowish film coats the edge of the pool, but locals insist that it's harmless algae.

ACCOMMODATIONS IN GIBARA

Hostal Vitral
2-4844469
Calle Independencia #36 between J. Peralta and C. García

One beautiful room (CUC$30) is available in this well-maintained home that could almost be mistaken for a museum. Expect high ceilings, fresh flowers, and even a wishing well!

Hostal Villa Boqueron
Ave Rabí #53 between J. Peralta and Luz Caballero
2-4844087 or 5-3139421
isidroramon@naut.cu

Two rooms (CUC$30 each) are available in this plant-filled waterfront home. The front room gets especially good breezes.

RIDE #21. HOLGUÍN TO GUARDALAVACA

Distance: 36 miles/58 kilometers
Elevation: 1,263 feet/385 meters
Difficulty: Moderate
Time: 4–6 hours

The ride from Holguín to Guardalavaca is a pleasant, hilly ride during which you are sure to see other cyclists, including small, supported bike tours to and from the beach resorts. Should you wish to visit Guardalavaca by four wheels, private taxis are available for hire, and shared colectivo taxis and buses make trips throughout the day.

This ride starts in front of the Tienda La Campana and Pico Cristal buildings in Calixto García park, then zigzags its way to the highway. It's a long, gradual climb out of town, and the road is in generally good condition. This is the main and most popular route in the region, so there are a lot of vehicles on the road. Some may honk very loudly to let you know they are passing. It's a well-intentioned notification but can be startling nonetheless.

You'll pass several fruit stands along the way, and about 1 kilometer before arriving in Guardalavaca you'll spot a Tienda de Acsesorios gas station next to an El Rápido snack bar. Between the two you should be able to find drinks and snacks. There's also a bathroom behind the gas station. After enjoying a day (or days) of swimming in crystal blue water and laying on soft white sand, return to Holguín by the same route, being sure to stock up on water at the Tienda.

Guardalavaca is one of Cuba's top beach destinations and is known for its all-inclusive resorts, though moderately priced casas are also available. A cluster of rooms are available for rent in the apartment buildings on the right side of the road, immediately before making the final left turn to the beach. Others are located farther east along the coast.

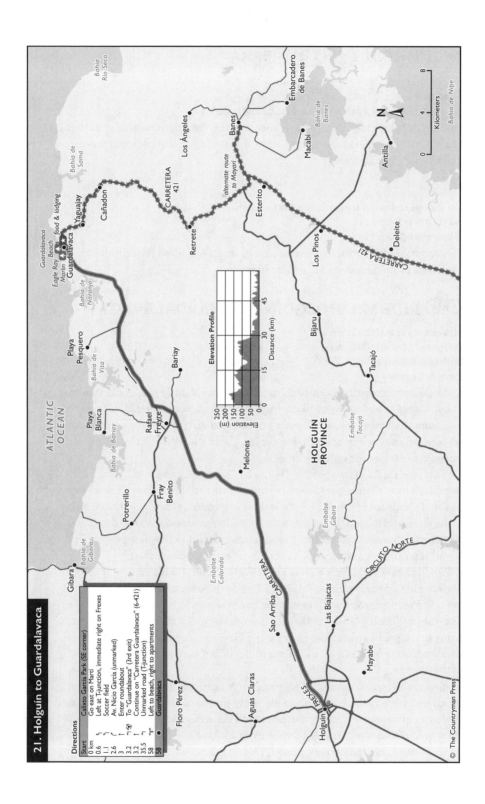

21. Holguin to Guardalavaca

Directions

Start		Calixto García Park (SE corner)
0 km		Go east on Martí
0.6	⌐	Left at T-junction, immediate right on Frexes
1.1		Soccer field
2.6	⌐	Av. Nicio García (unmarked)
3	⟳	Enter roundabout
3.2		To "Guardalavaca" (3rd exit)
3.2		Continue on "Carretera Guardalavaca" (6-421)
35.5	⌐	Unmarked road (T-junction)
58	⊤	Left to beach, right to apartments
58	●	Guardalavaca

ATLANTIC OCEAN

Gibara

Bahía de Gibara

Playa Blanca

Bahía de Bariay

Playa Pesquero

Bahía de Vita

Guardalavaca Beach
food & lodging
Eagle Ray Marti
Guardalavaca
Yaguajay
Cañadon

Bahía de Naranjo

Bahía de Samá

Bahía Río Seco

Retrete

CARRETERA 421

Los Ángeles

Embarcadero de Banes

Banes

Macabí

Bahía de Banes

Antilla

Bahía de Nipe

alternate route to Moyari

Esterito

Los Pinos

Deleite

CARRETERA 421

Bijaru

Tacajó

Embalse Tacajó

HOLGUÍN PROVINCE

Bariay

Rafael Freyre

Potrerrillo

Fray Benito

Melones

Embalse Gibara

Embalse Colorado

Floro Pérez

Aguas Claras

Sao Arriba

CARRETERA

Las Biajacas

Mayabe

CIRCUITO NORTE

Holguín

FREXES

Elevation Profile

Elevation (m)
250
200
150
100
50
0

Distance (km)
0 15 30 45

N

Kilometers
0 4 8

© The Countryman Press

The first hotel you'll see entering Guardalavaca is **Club Amigo** (CUC $80–150). Inside, you'll find a **CaDeCa** (8:30 a.m.–noon and 1–5:30 p.m.). WiFi cards can be purchased in the lobby. Just past Club Amigo is **Hotel Brisas** (CUC $100–170), which has a quieter beach than Club Amigo. Brisas has a decidedly older crowd than Club Amigo, which is cheaper and has more of a party scene. You are more likely to mingle with locals (including jineteros) at the bars, restaurant, and disco around Club Amigo.

Nonhotel guests are welcome at most areas on the beach, though you won't be allowed into hotel restaurants, pools, or bars without a guest wristband. Beach chairs are available everywhere.

Cafetería Pirata is a beachfront restaurant serving large plates of fresh seafood and sautéed vegetables (CUC$5–$15) until 4 p.m. **Rico Pizza** serves CUC$2 pizzas until 8 p.m., but I've seen them run out sooner. For finer dining, head to **El Ancla** at the west end of the beach, where glass walls offer stunning views of the sea, and lobster is served on tables with linen tablecloths. Closer to the main resort area, it can be hard to find food in the evening, so if you're not staying at an all-inclusive hotel (if you are, don't miss mealtimes!), be sure to arrange dinner at your casa.

Eagle Ray Marlin is a dive center on the beach offering one dive for CUC$45 and two for CUC$60. Snorkeling (CUC$20 on the boat) is better along the coast, where it only costs CUC$10. I camped under a large tree in front of Eagle Ray Marlin in 2016 and got stuck in the bathroom overnight when the lock jammed in the door. The staff still laughs about the event and assures that the bathroom door has been fixed. Mention it to the dive center staff, who will surely enjoy another good laugh and happily let you set up a tent.

Guardalavaca to Mayarí Shortcut: Cyclists on tight schedules who enjoy grueling climbs can save time by following the routes in the *Carreteras* map book from Guardalavaca to Banes (via 421, through Yaguajay and Retrete). After an overnight in Banes, you'll jump back on 421 and take it south along a much flatter road to 123 (Carretera Mayarí), which takes you straight to Mayarí. Hearty cyclists may be able to tackle the 86-kilometer route in one day, but steep hills and high temperatures make the ride more pleasant when broken up.

A CYCLIST TRANSPORTING A BIKE IN GUARDALAVACA, HOLGUÍN

ACCOMMODATIONS IN GUARDALAVACA

Marlene Claro: "La Orquidia"
Edificio #7 (Building #7), Apartment #18
5-3139490
This apartment building is located on the main road from Holguín, near the turnoff to the beach. You'll see plenty of "Room for Rent" signs in the building, but this apartment (CUC$25–$30) stands out. The room is clean, comfortable, sunny, and only five minutes from the beach. Sra. Marlene lives in the home and is happy to prepare meals.

Villa Lago Mar
Los Cayuelos #46
5-2193867 or 5-8105917
nildamian@nauta.cu
This waterfront home is a bit removed from the resort area but is a quick bike ride or a lovely stroll to the main beach stretch. Meals are served on the breezy patio, and the home's two welcoming rooms (CUC $30–$45) fill up quickly during peak season.

 # RIDE #22. HOLGUÍN TO MAYARÍ

Distance: 55 miles/88.5 kilometers
Elevation: 2,218 feet/676 meters
Difficulty: Difficult
Time: 6–9 hours

Libertadores Avenue is the only direct way to the main highway to Mayarí. Technically, bikes are not allowed during peak hours, but many bicyclists risk the 30-peso fine (about CUC$1.25) and ride beside trucks, buses, cars, taxis, horse carriages, and an extraordinary variety of makeshift vehicles. Some parallel streets exist but only run for a few blocks before dead-ending. Given that most cyclists wind up riding on Libertadores to prevent getting lost, directions will be given along this main avenue, but you can follow the web of small side streets on a digital or printed map if you like. Libertadores eventually turns into Circuito Norte, which stretches across the entire northern coast of the island.

The ride begins in front of the Pico Cristal building in Calixto García park. Once you are out of Holguín, there isn't much traffic, but you will surely pass trucks and buses spewing thick black exhaust. Aside from exhaust, the ride is mostly green, even during dry season, and the landscape is dotted with small farms and pastel-colored cottages. Large bougainvillea bushes overflow with bright pink and magenta flowers. The road to Mayarí is a series of climbs of various difficulty, but the road is in good condition. You'll pass small banana plantations, herds of wandering goats that never seem to get sick of eating, and carts pulled by horses so skinny that their ribs are showing.

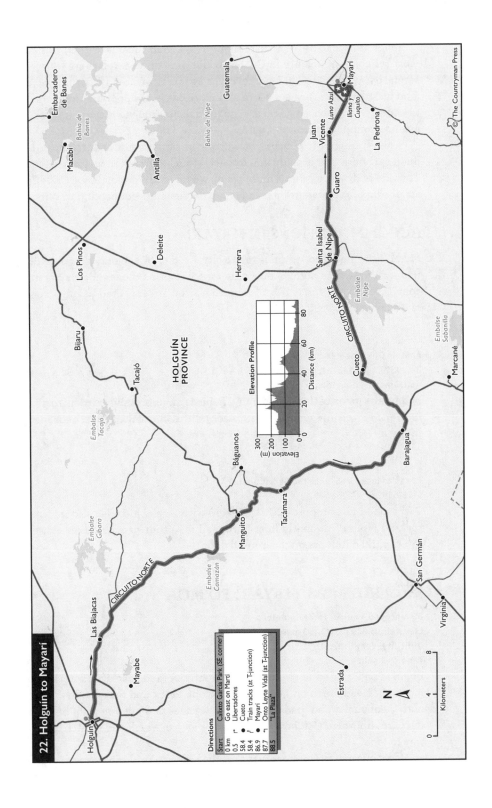

22. Holguín to Mayarí

HOLGUÍN PROVINCE

Directions

Start	Calixto García Park (SE corner)		
0 km	⌐		Go east on Martí
0.5			Libertadores
58.4	●		Cueto
58.4	⌐		Train tracks (at T-junction)
86.9	●		Mayarí
87.7	⌐		Onto Leyre Vidal (at T-junction)
88.5			"La Plaza"

Elevation Profile

CIRCUITO NORTE

© The Countryman Press

Snack stalls can be found in Manguito (29k) and Tacamara (39k), but the most reliable options are in Cueto. At the time of research there were no official casas in Cueto, but I met several bike tourists who stayed in unofficial (and less than ideal) casas. More and more casas are popping up in small towns all over Cuba, so if you are too tired to continue to Mayarí, it's worth asking around for a casa in Cueto.

When you arrive in Mayarí, you will see the sign to continue straight as the main carretera that brought you from Holguín bends left to go toward Moa. The ride ends at the town's main plaza, which is surrounded by a **CaDeCa**, small shops, and restaurants, and is full of teenagers connecting to WiFi.

ACCOMMODATIONS IN MAYARÍ

Motel Bitiri, near the entrance to the city, used to be the only accommodation available. The hotel is now only for Cubans, as the standards are not considered to be high enough for tourists, who are expected to stay in one of a dozen casas particulares.

Luna Azul
Antonio Guiteras #24
2-4503737, 5-5562561, or 5-8258685
ltoll@mayari.hlg.sld.cu
Behind the gates of this unassuming home is an impressive garden, restaurant, and two clean rooms (CUC$30 each) with some of the softest bedsheets in Cuba.

Iliana y Cuquito
Avenida Maceo #65, near the ServiCupet
5-2615192 or 5-3266809
Two second-floor rooms (CUC$30 each) with large balconies and inviting rocking chairs frequently host European bike tour groups. Bikes can be safely parked indoors on the ground floor.

 # RIDE #23. MAYARÍ TO MOA

Distance: 60.1 miles/96.7 kilometers
Elevation: 3,800 feet/1,158 meters
Difficulty: Very Difficult
Time: 7–9 hours
Begin at La Plaza, which is buzzing with activity (and snack vendors) in the morning. Head north on Leyte Vidal for one block and take the first right onto Valenzuela. The road will bend a few times and put you right back on the Circuito Norte (Highway 123 on some maps), which will stretch all the way to Moa.

Gorgeous mountain scenery makes the hills you're climbing seem not so bad. The region is quite green, but the trees lining the road offer no shade

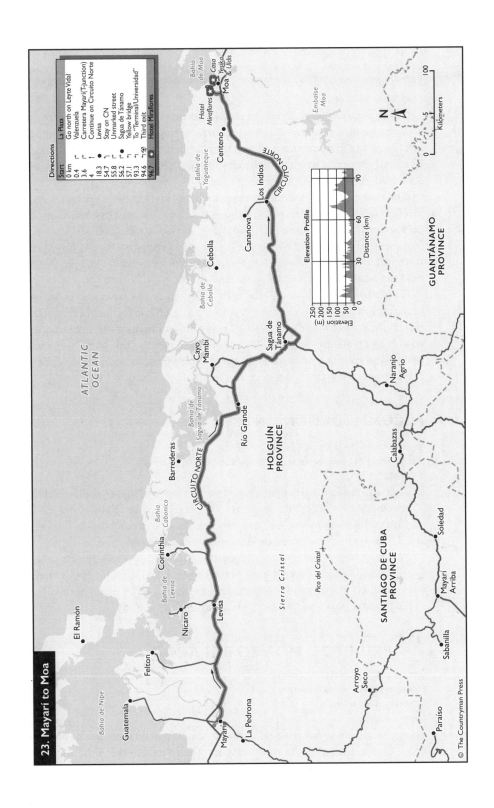

23. Mayarí to Moa

Directions

Start	La Plaza
0 km	Go north on Leyte Vidal
0.4	Valenzuela
3.6	Carretera Mayarí (T-junction)
4	Continue on Circuito Norte
18.3	Levisa
54.7	Stay on CN
55.8	Unmarked street
56.2	Sagua de Tánamo
57.1	Yellow bridge
93.3	To "Terminal/Universidad"
94.6	Third exit
96.7	Hotel Miraflores

ATLANTIC OCEAN

Bahía de Moa

Casa Yesika
Moa & Uldis

Hotel Miraflores

Centeno

CIRCUITO NORTE

Los Indios

Cananova

Bahía de Yaguaneque

Cebolla

Bahía de Cebolla

Elevation Profile

Cayo Mambí

Sagua de Tánamo

Naranjo Agrio

Bahía de Sagua de Tánamo

Río Grande

HOLGUÍN PROVINCE

Calabazas

CIRCUITO NORTE

Barrederas

Bahía Cabonico

Soledad

Corinthia

Bahía de Levisa

Sierra Cristal

Pico del Cristal

SANTIAGO DE CUBA PROVINCE

Mayarí Arriba

Nicaro

Levisa

Felton

Sabanilla

El Ramón

Bahía de Nipe

Guatemala

Arroyo Seco

Mayarí

La Pedrona

Paraíso

Embalse Moa

N

Kilometers

GUANTÁNAMO PROVINCE

© The Countryman Press

to weary riders. Around the 45k mark, the road condition deteriorates for several kilometers. Snacks are available outside the bus terminal in Levisa, and cafeterias are the most likely lunch option in Sagua de Tanamo (referred to simply as "Sagua").

There is no proper signage for the curves and unmarked turns in Sagua, so if you believe you made a wrong turn, refer to your digital map or simply ask "Moa?" to virtually anyone and they'll point you in the right direction. The road continues to wind all the way to Moa, a nickel-mining town known for its bright red (clothing-staining) soil.

The ride ends at Hotel Miraflores, which has WiFi and hosts Cubans and foreigners alike. Rooms are CUC$30–$40/night, but tourists complain of cold water, broken AC, and bad food. You'll be better off in one of the town's four casas particulares. It's unlikely all casas will be booked at the same time, but it's possible when a large cycling or church group visits, in which case the hotel may be your only option.

To get to Casa Yesika y Uldis, take a left out of the hotel and continue straight through the roundabout. If you skip stopping at the hotel altogether, turn right at the roundabout (94.6k), ride about 1 kilometer, then turn right onto Mariana Garajes at the T-junction. Just before you reach the small bridge and roundabout, turn right on the unmarked street, Mario Muñoz. The house is a few doors down on the left.

ACCOMMODATIONS IN MOA

Casa Yesika (Jessica) and Uldis
Mario Muñoz #11 between Mariana Grajales and Final Aserrio
5-8024071
Yesika, who is a fantastic cook, hosts travelers in three rooms, each of which has two beds. The back patio overlooks a small river, although this is a nickel-mining town, so the view isn't entirely scenic. If Yesika's place is booked, she'll happily find you accommodations in another nearby home.

You may have a hard time finding this casa. In my case, the first five people consulted had never heard of the street in question, and two others gave conflicting directions. When in doubt, mention the name of the casa or simply ask, "Casa particular?" for more clear directions.

RIDE #24. MOA TO BARACOA

Distance: 47 miles/45.6. kilometers
Elevation: 2,883 feet/879 meters
Difficulty: Very Difficult
Time: 7–10 hours
This ride begins at the Hotel Miraflores, where you'll take a left out of the hotel, take a right at the first roundabout, then turn left on to the Circuito Norte, which takes you all the way to Baracoa. You'll bear right at the small nickel mine on your left before passing the large nickel mine on your right,

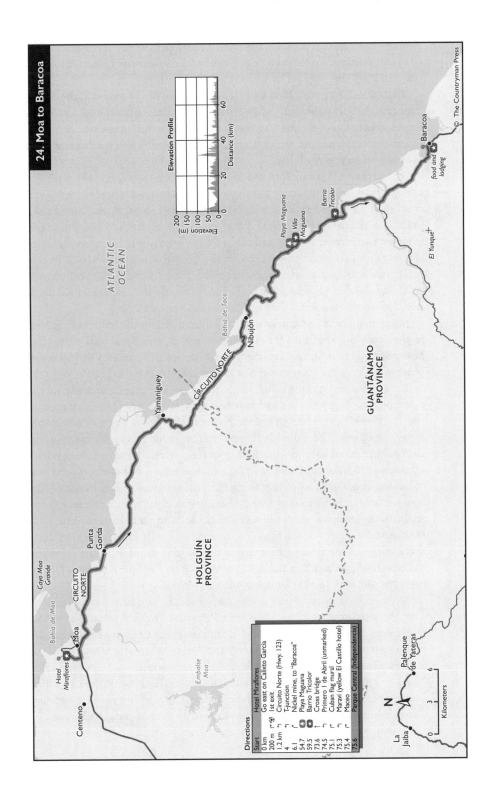

named after Che Guevara. Do not attempt to take pictures of the sign, mine, or surrounding area, as Cuba does not like its dirtiest city documented and you will likely be stopped by police or pedestrians.

The stretch between Moa and Baracoa is one of the worst in the entire country. Potholes abound and the steep hills make gravel and dirt roads impossible to climb at times. There has been talk of fixing the road for many years and residents remain optimistic, so it's possible the roads have been repaved when you read this.

At the time of research, the road out of Moa was dusty and the potholes and gravel began after about 15 kilometers, but the road is in relatively good condition compared to what's ahead. When the red earth and dusty road ends, the alternating gravel and dirt roads begin. Around the 37k mark, when you are reaching your pothole limit, the road somehow manages to get worse, making it easier to walk than ride a bike up steep gravel hills. At this point, you may begin seeing vendors selling cucurucho. Stop for the sweet treat and enjoy a quick rest, because the road gets even worse with a deep, pothole-ridden descent before another steep, rocky climb.

Many maquinas and trucks will have joined you on the road leaving Moa in the morning, shuttling Cubans between Moa and Baracoa. By the time afternoon rolls around and you approach Baracoa, the streets will be much quieter, making the rough road conditions slightly more tolerable.

For anyone tiring of the rough roads and steep hills, consider breaking the ride into two days and find accommodations near Playa Maguana, around the 55k mark. Several casas are visible from the street, and two additional casas, along with the Villa Maguana hotel, are hidden 150 meters away on the beach, tucked behind a thick layer of trees. Even if you're able to power all the way to Baracoa, Playa Maguana makes for a nice beach stop instead of having to make a return trip along the gravel to visit it another day. (The beach can also be visited by private taxi or colectivo from Baracoa.) Those wishing to be closer to the beach should take the left turn toward Villa Maguana. When the ocean appears, the road will split three ways, and there are no signs. Keep straight to arrive at the two beach casas or turn left to go to the villa. Try Casa Yan-Inolvis (5-2780678) on the beach or Casa Carlos (6-3670098), a bit farther back but with a great view.

To reach Baracoa, continue on the same road. Look out for Barrio Tricolor, a brightly painted neighborhood that Venezuela helped rebuild after the 2016 hurricane. Homes are decorated with patriotic slogans such as *Unidos por la patria* ("United in patriotism") and *Hasta la victoria siempre* ("Until victory, always"), Che Guevara's famous victory quote.

As you approach Baracoa, more trucks are out kicking up dust and dirt, making for an unpleasant gray stretch before the road improves in the city. The ride ends at Parque Central, also known as Parque Independencia.

9

GUANTÁNAMO

QUICK LOOK

Known to many Westerners (Americans, in particular) only for its controversial US military base and detention center, Guantánamo is actually one of the most beautiful and biologically diverse regions in Cuba. The southern part of the province is dry and arid, whereas the north is lush, green, and wet. Though brutally battered by Hurricane Matthew in October 2016, the far eastern city of Baracoa is being rebuilt and remains the province's main draw. The small city is bursting with music, culture, and some of the country's best food, which goes beyond traditional Cuban cuisine and takes on a broader Caribbean flare by incorporating coconut milk in many dishes.

Baracoa is the oldest Spanish settlement in Cuba and was its first capital, but up until the Cuban Revolution, it was only accessible by sea. In the 1960s, Fidel Castro built La Farola, a 120-kilometer-long road through the mountains from Guantánamo to Baracoa, showcased as a large success for the Revolution. The road removed Baracoa from isolation and soon brought tourists eager to explore the region's forests, mountains, beaches, and cuisine.

The town of Baracoa is quaint, quiet, and decorated with brightly colored homes, many of which are casas particulares. Take your pick of quiet hillside bungalows perched high above the city or seaside casas on the quiet bay overlooking *El Yunque* (the anvil), the region's famous 575-meter-high, table-shaped mountain. Most visitors traveling Cuba by bus or car go directly from Baracoa to Santiago de Cuba, overlooking the scrawny city of Guantánamo. Though its few museums and cultural and historic sites seem to be forever closed for repairs, the city is home to one of the country's three famed *Tumba Francesa* (French Haitian song and dance) troupes, and it's the best place to hear the province's own indigenous music genre, changüí.

Highlights

- Delightful **Baracoa** is the perfect base for exploring the region's history, beaches, and national parks.
- **Baracoa's cuisine** is unique on the island, incorporating coconut and coconut milk into sweet and savory dishes, the most famous of which

is **cucurucho,** grated coconut mixed with sugar, orange, pineapple, and guava juices, wrapped in a palm leaf.

- The best chocolate in Cuba comes from Baracoa, the center of the country's chocolate industry. It can be purchased in town at the **Casa del Cacao,** but the best treats are homemade chocolates made with honey. Attend a chocolate-making demonstration and purchase the freshly made chocolate at various casas de cacao, homes along the hilly road to **Boca de Yumurí** (look for the sign outside that says CASA DE CACAO or CASA DE ZOILA, CASA DE MARIA, etc.).
- Visit the bust of **Chief Hatuey** in front of **La Catedral de Nuestra Señora de la Asunción.** Chief Hatuey was a Taíno leader who led a war of resistance against the Spanish, who then captured him. Before being burned alive, he was told that if he renounced his gods and became Christian, he would go to heaven. Hatuey asked if there were Spaniards in heaven, and when he was told there were, proclaimed that he had no interest in going anywhere that would have such cruel people.
- **Museo Arqueológico Cueva el Paraíso** (CUC$3, CUC$5 with pictures) is a museum inside a cave that explores Taíno culture (700–1500 AD) before they were wiped out by the Spanish.
- Additional **archaeological remnants** of indigenous Taíno culture, including caves filled with glyphs, can be explored by bicycle, foot, or car. To arrange a private tour with Dr. Robert Orduñez, the director of the Baracoa Archaeological Society, stop by his home at Flor Crombet #245 or call 2-1643862.
- **Playa Maguana** makes for a lovely day trip (by bike or by car) or serves as a pleasant midway stop between Moa and Baracoa. Rent a snorkel and mask to find large seashells and conches—just be sure to leave them where you found them.
- **La Farola highway** is a marvelously gorgeous—and very challenging—ride through the mountains of Baracoa.

Need-to-Know

- Should you wish to stay in Cajobabo, Yacabo, or other campismos in Guantánamo province, make a reservation at the Campismo Popular office or the Havanatur office in Baracoa.
- Cyclists who wish to save time can take a bus from Baracoa to Guantánamo or Santiago. The bus follows the same route, along La Farola, which is the most beautiful route in the region but also one of the most challenging.
- The Viazul bus to Guantánamo leaves at 9 a.m. and costs CUC$10, plus CUC$2–$5 per bicycle. The bus leaves for Santiago at 2 p.m. for CUC$15. Those who want to save time but not go all the way to Guantánamo can get dropped off in Imías for CUC$6. During off-peak season, the bus is almost empty, but be sure to book ahead during high season. Talk with the driver to see if he will stop at the mirador lookout point on La Farola for two minutes so you can take a picture.

Terrain

Guantánamo province is covered with mountains and smaller yet still challenging foothills that reach to the sea. The steepest hills you'll encounter will be the rides into and out of Baracoa, which are some of the most difficult in Cuba.

Special Events

- Antonio Maceo Carnival in Baracoa: April
- Festival Nacional de Changüí in Guantánamo: June

Tourist Information

Cubatur (Antonio Maceo #181) and nearby **Ecotur** (on Parque Independencia) are good places to book excursions and find updated information on hard-to-reach sights, such as Punta Maisí. **Infotur** (Antonio Maceo #129a, near Maraví) sells the helpful *Carreteras* map book. **Havanatur** is at Martí #225, inside the old campismo office (there is still a large CAMPISMO sign outside). Here you can book tours, make campismo and hotel reservations, and book airfare and Viazul bus tickets. The actual **Campismo** office is now at Martí #80, near 24 de Febrero Street, inside a cafeteria called La Esquina.

WiFi is available in Parque Independencia, and you can purchase Internet cards at the nearby **ETECSA** office at Antonio Maceo #182 (next to Cubatur). If ETECSA is closed, head to Rumba en el Parque cafeteria in front of the main plaza to purchase WiFi cards.

The **Banco de Crédito y Comercio** (8 a.m.–2:30 p.m. Monday–Friday) is at Antonio Maceo #99, and the **Banco Popular de Ahorro** (8–11:30 a.m. and 2–4:30 p.m. Monday–Friday) is located at José Martí #166. Both have ATMs. The **CaDeCa** (8:30 a.m.–4 p.m. Monday–Friday and 8:30–11:30 a.m. Saturday–Sunday) is located at José Martí #241.

ACCOMMODATIONS IN BARACOA

Casa Yoco y Mima

Rubert López #91 López, between Limbano Sanchez and Ramón López Peña
5-8028779
yocolondres@nauta.cu

Yoco and his wife, Mima, rent three bedrooms above their family home just a few blocks from the town center. Bike parking is available on the ground floor, next to Yoco's own folding bike. The three rooms have access to a shared kitchen, though the family can also prepare meals, which are served on an inviting, sunny terrace with lovely views of the city.

BARACOA, GUANTÁNAMO

Moncada 92-B between Paraíso Abajo and Calle
2 2-1645618 or 5-3019085
VillaParadisoBaracoa@gmail.com
www.villaparadisobaracoa.com
Though the house is a bit farther from the city center and requires climbing a small hill, it just might be the nicest casa in all of eastern Cuba. Manuel and his partner, Roberto, are generous and kind hosts, offering three gorgeous, modern rooms (CUC$25–$35). This multilevel home is surrounded by a lush, flower-filled garden that gives the home a secluded feel and has several terraces overlooking the entire city. It's easily the best view from any casa in Baracoa.

Vista Bahía
Calle Calíxto García #57, corner of Coliseo
2-1643967, 5-4069002, or 5-4968788
vistabahiabaracoa@gmail.com
If relaxing on a rocking chair overlooking Baracoa's bay and famous Yunque mountain is your ideal way to spend the evening, this is the place for you. Daniel rents two comfortable rooms (CUC$20–$30 each), with two beds each, but the real draw is the stunning view from the front porch.

Casa El Ciclista
Avenida Malecón #82, between Gliserio and Moncada
2-1641685 or 5-5302082
llacermachadorolbis@yahoo.es
Former professional cyclist Llacer Machado now runs a casa particular that's extremely easy to spot on the malecón waterfront. The home is near the Christopher Columbus statue and has a large cyclist painted on the front.

RESTAURANTS IN BARACOA

Baracoando
Flor Crombet 9 Interior (one block from the malecón)
2-1644008 or 5-2589319
Daily 10 a.m.–7 p.m.
Mains CUC$5–$8
Tucked back on an unassuming street that still shows evidence of Hurricane Matthew's extensive destruction in 2016 is Baracoando, a mostly vegetarian restaurant aiming to bring diners back to basics through flavorful, home-cooked food. Eggplant, chickpeas, lima beans, lentils, and greens are sautéed and slowly simmered with coconut milk, curry powder, and other spices you're unlikely to find elsewhere in Cuba. Have a seat on the front patio, furnished with tables and chairs made from repurposed wood, and sip a fresh-brewed herbal infusion while you wait for your meal.

DINNER AT BARACOANDO, A MOSTLY VEGETARIAN
RESTAURANT IN BARACOA

BARACOAN CUISINE IS KNOWN FOR USING LOTS OF
COCONUT MILK

Las Terrazas

Flor Crombet #143 between Ciro Frías and Pelayo Cuervo2-1643123 or 5-2718556
abadcub@gmail.com
Daily noon–3 p.m. and 6:30–11 p.m.
Mains CUC$7–$15

Chef Nilson serves up some of the best and most authentic food in the city—
pescado con leche de coco (fish fillet in coconut milk) is their specialty.
Vegetarians can enjoy their own menu, which features mixed vegetables
simmered in coconut milk, wine, or chocolate sauce. Reservations are recommended for dinner, but if you want to ensure you get a highly sought-after
table overlooking the ocean, come for lunch.

Cafetería el Parque

Antonio Maceo #142, on the main plaza
Open 24 hours
CUC$1–$3

This no-frills cafeteria offers little more than sandwiches and beer, but it's
the favored meeting point in the city, so it's a fantastic place to people-watch
and make friends. It's one of the only places open all night, and you can even
catch the WiFi signal from the park.

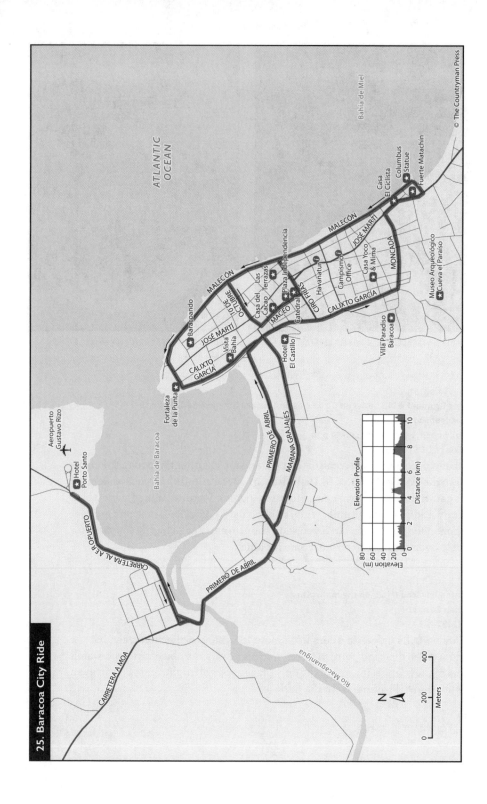

25. Baracoa City Ride

Elevation Profile

Elevation (m)

Distance (km)

ATLANTIC OCEAN

Bahia de Miel

Columbus Statue
Casa El Ciclista
Fuerte Matachín
Museo Arqueológico
Cueva el Paraíso

MALECÓN
JOSÉ MARTÍ
MONCADA
Casa Yoco & Mima
Campismo Office
Havanatur
Villa Paradiso Baracoa
CALIXTO GARCIA
CIRO FRÍAS
Plaza Independencia
Catedral
Casa del Cacao
Las Terrazas
MACEO
Hotel El Castillo
10 DE OCTUBRE
MALECÓN
Baracoando
JOSÉ MARTÍ
Vista Bahia
CALIXTO GARCIA
Fortaleza de la Punta

PRIMERO DE ABRIL
MARIANA GRAJALES
PRIMERO DE ABRIL

Bahía de Baracoa

Aeropuerto Gustavo Rizo
Hotel Porto Santo
CARRETERA AL AEROPUERTO
CARRETERA A MOA

Río Macaguaniagua

N

0   200   400
Meters

© The Countryman Press

RIDE #25. BARACOA CITY RIDE

Distance: 6.5 miles/10.5 kilometers
Elevation: 380 feet/116 meters
Difficulty: Easy
Time: 1–2 hours

This is a leisurely ride that begins in Plaza Independencia. Head south on Maceo to the bust of **Chief Hatuey** in front of **La Catedral de Nuestra Señora de la Asunción.** Take a left on Ciro Frías, then another left at the **malecón.** The road is rough with lots of bumps, potholes, and glass, but the view is incredible. Strong, salty waves crash onto the street as you ride along Baracoa's beautiful waterfront and curve around the **Fortaleza de la Punta,** a small fort that now doubles as a restaurant. Turn left onto Calixto García, where a quiet row of houses with porches offers the best place to catch a view of El Yunque.

Turn right onto Mariana Grajales at 1.7k, then left onto Primero de Abril (1 de Abril) to circle around the **Bahía de Baracoa** (Baracoa Bay). The ride curves right and follows the road along the bay to the Hotel Porto Santo, a beautiful hotel 4 kilometers from town that provides a lovely view of Baracoa in the distance. Note that the view of the bay is especially beautiful and photogenic in the early evening.

Return to town via Primero de Abril and turn right at the mural of revolutionary heroes (7.5k) onto Calixto García. You'll see the yellow **El Castillo** hotel towering over the city. You can pedal up for a view of Baracoa and of El Yunque or continue on Calixto García another half kilometer and walk up to the **mirador** for another spectacular view.

Moncada Street will take you to Av José Martí and down to **Fuerte Matachín,** a municipal museum that was under repair at the time of research, and on to a shady waterfront park that's home to the town's **Christopher Columbus statue.** Continue north on the malecón and take a left on 10 de Octubre (10.4k) to return to the center of Baracoa. There is no street sign, but there's a large white and red apartment building on one corner and a mural depicting waves on the other. Note that this ride can begin and end anywhere along the route.

CUCURUCHO AND COCONUT SNACKS FOR SALE AT PLAYA MAGUANA, BARACOA

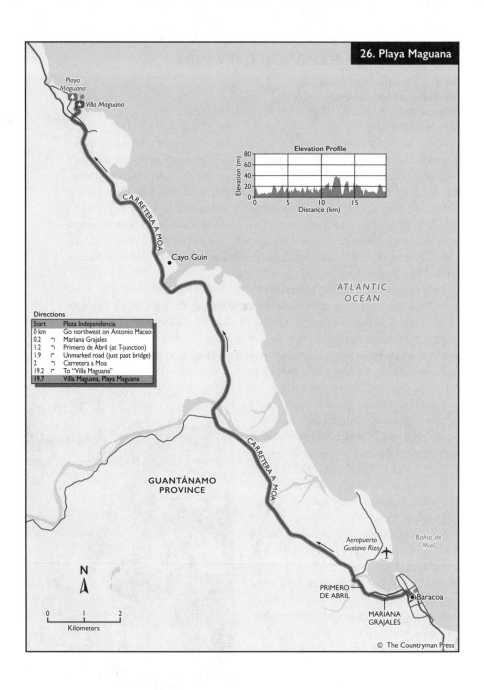

26. Playa Maguana

Elevation Profile

Directions

Start		Plaza Independencia
0 km		Go northwest on Antonio Maceo
0.2	↰	Mariana Grajales
1.2	↰	Primero de Abril (at T-junction)
1.9	↱	Unmarked road (just past bridge)
2	↰	Carretera a Moa
19.2	↱	To "Villa Maguana"
19.7		Villa Maguana, Playa Maguana

GUANTÁNAMO
PROVINCE

ATLANTIC
OCEAN

Bahia de
Miel

Aeropuerto
Gustavo Rizo

PRIMERO
DE ABRIL

MARIANA
GRAJALES

Baracoa

Playa
Maguana

Villa Maguana

CARRETERA A MOA

Cayo Güín

N

0   1   2
Kilometers

© The Countryman Press

RIDE #26. PLAYA MAGUANA

Distance: 24.5 miles/39.4 kilometers
Elevation: 877 feet/267 meters
Difficulty: Moderate
Time: 2 days

Though this ride could be completed in a day (three hours each way), it's much more pleasant to break it up into two days. Those with limited time or interest in day trips should consider staying at Playa Maguana on the way from Moa before continuing on to Baracoa. Alternatively, the beach can be reached by colectivo taxi. The ride is not particularly difficult and most bumps can be easily avoided, but as you approach the beach, large dust clouds will whip up as vehicles pass you on the dirt road. In any scenario, consider staying in one of the casas detailed in the ride from Moa to Baracoa, which stops at Playa Maguana (page 168). You can also stop at Hotel El Castillo or Hotel La Habanera in Baracoa to make a reservation for Villa Maguana, a former private villa that is now owned and run by the state. It just might be the only accommodation in eastern Cuba where you'll have WiFi on the beach.

This ride ends at Villa Maguana, which has a small strip of beach sheltered in a tiny cove. Even if you don't stay at the hotel, you can use the bathroom, dine in the restaurant, relax on the sunny strip of sand, or rent a lounge chair (CUC$2) in the shade. This small stretch of beach is quiet, and the only other people you'll see are likely to be a few tourists staying at the hotel. The larger main strip of beach is a 10-minute walk north along the coast. You could also ride directly there and lock your bike under a tree.

The main beach area will have more tourists and also a good number of Cubans enjoying the water and listening to salsa and reggaeton. You'll also be approached by lots of vendors selling fried fish, handmade chocolates, cocoa butter cream sold in small wooden jars (a popular souvenir in the region), and cucurucho. To return to Baracoa, follow the directions in reverse.

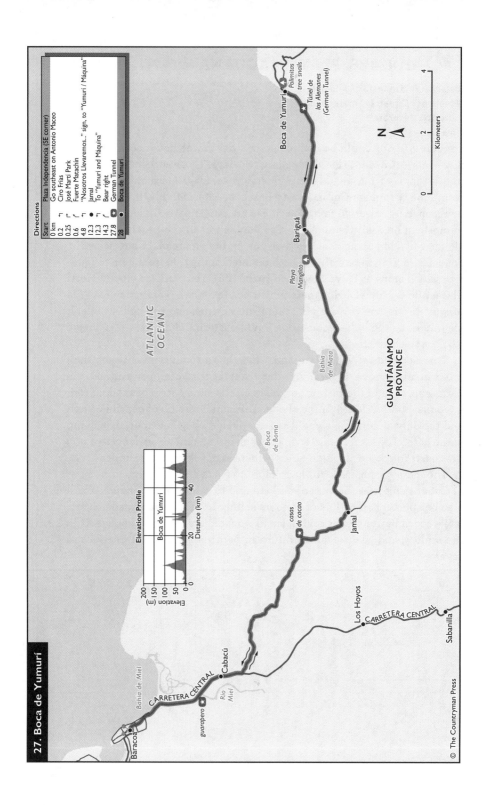

27. Boca de Yumuri

Directions

	Start	Plaza Independencia (SE corner)
	0 km	Go southeast on Antonio Maceo
⌐	0.2	Ciro Frías
⌐	0.25	José Martí Park
⌐	0.6	Fuerte Matachín
●	4.8	"Nosotros Llevaremos..." sign, to "Yumuri / Máquina"
⌐	12.3	Jamal
⌐	12.3	To "Yumuri and Máquina"
●	14.3	Bear right
✱	27.8	German Tunnel
●	28	Boca de Yumuri

ATLANTIC OCEAN

GUANTÁNAMO PROVINCE

Polimitas tree snails

Túnel de los Alemanes (German Tunnel)

Boca de Yumuri

Bariguá

Playa Manglito

Bahía de Mata

Boca de Borna

casas de cacao

Jamal

Los Hoyos

CARRETERA CENTRAL

Sabanilla

Bahía de Miel

CARRETERA CENTRAL

Cabacú

Río Miel

guarapero

Baracoa

Elevation Profile

Boca de Yumuri

Elevation (m): 200 150 100 50

Distance (km): 0 20 40

N

0 2 4
Kilometers

© The Countryman Press

RIDE #27. BOCA DE YUMURÍ

Distance: 34.8 miles/56 kilometers
Elevation: 2,000 feet/610 meters
Difficulty: Difficult
Time: 3–5 hours

Boca de Yumurí means "Mouth of Yumurí," referring to the Yumurí River that flows through the area. The dark sand beach and quiet community make this a great day trip. To make the ride more educational and more challenging (8 to 10 additional kilometers that will add about 600 meters of elevation), arrange with Dr. Ordoñez for one of his archaeology students to take you on an archaeology bike tour along this route (see Baracoa highlights for more information).

The ride begins at Parque Independencia and follows José Martí (Carretera Central or Farola) for several kilometers. At 2.9k is a guarapero that's open until around 6 p.m., so you could also stop on the way back to Baracoa for some fresh sugarcane juice.

The kilometer marks on the road signs indicate the number of kilometers traveled off the main road, Martí, in Baracoa. Several casas del cacao (see "The Best Chocolate in Cuba" box) can be found between kilometer marks 9 and 10.

Bring a swimsuit and towel to turn the ride into a beach trip. Several small beaches exist along the route, the most popular being Manglito. Just beyond Manglito, back on the main road, is El Rey, a good option for grabbing lunch to eat on the beach. If you can hold out for a couple more kilometers, you will have your pick of four more restaurants offering waterfront views. Some even have tables set up in the shade on the sand.

Just before arriving in Yumurí, you'll ride through the **Túnel de los Alemanes** (German Tunnel), an amazing natural arch of trees and foliage. After the tunnel and just before the bridge, you can turn right and head down the small hill to take a boat ride with local "guides" who will show you flora and fauna in the area (negotiate a price before beginning the tour). A "natural pool" is a popular stop, but if it's been raining it's more like a muddy swamp. Local women also sell cocoa butter in small wooden jars to help sustain themselves. The village is exceedingly poor, and it's very likely that people will ask if you have clothing to donate (bras are especially appreciated). The ride ends here in the village, but you can continue on across the bridge.

Take extreme care crossing the bridge over the river, as there are massive gaps that reveal construction cables and the

A MAN GATHERS COFFEE BEANS IN BOCA DE YUMURI, GUANTÁNAMO

Anyone in Cuba will tell you that the best chocolate in the country comes from Baracoa, and the best of the best is the homemade variety, made with fresh cacao and local honey. Several casas de cacao (chocolate houses) can be found between the 9- and 10-kilometer marks on the Boca de Yumurí ride. One of them has a small, hidden-by-foliage, easy-to-miss sign that says CASA DE ZOILA. Another is directly across the street. The women who own these homes make chocolate on the premises and are happy to give you an educational presentation of the cacao production process. Free samples of cocoa beans at various fermentation, roasting, and final product stages are available for tasting, including toasted cacao beans, bars of chocolate made with honey, chocolate bonbons stuffed with banana filling, and a dried cacao and banana powdered mix used to make a beverage similar to hot cocoa. This chocolate is completely different from what is sold in the stores in Baracoa and is of much higher quality. Bars range from three for CUC$1 to CUC$1 each. There will be more of a selection in the morning, but it's safer to pick up the chocolate in the evening so it doesn't melt in your bags.

THE CHOCOLATE SPREAD AT ONE OF BARACOA'S CASAS DE CACAO

water below. Just past the bridge is a sign directing travelers to the left for Maquina (Maisí). If you take a right and navigate around large boulders, you will climb—and surely need to walk your bike up—an extremely steep hill. This is the old road to Maisí, which was repaired after Hurricane Matthew. About 50 meters farther up is a viewpoint over the river on the right. On the left is a small house that sells souvenirs and drinks (the father is pictured on the previous page collecting coffee beans outside his house). They are also known to let tourists use their bathroom—be sure to bring your own toilet paper, hand sanitizer, and a tip for the family. The family also welcomes tourists to view dozens of the endangered *polimitas* tree snails in the large tree in their yard. While some people illegally sell the shells and make jewelry out of them, this family participates in conservation efforts by providing a habitat for the snails and not allowing them to be removed or sold. If you view the snails, leave a tip for the family to encourage them to continue protecting the animals.

When you're ready, follow the same route back to Baracoa, and don't forget to stop for that guarapo!

🚲 RIDE #28. BARACOA TO IMÍAS/PLAYA YACABO

Distance: 47.5 miles/76.4 kilometers
Elevation: 3,321 feet/1,012 meters
Difficulty: Very Difficult
Time: 7–10 hours

The ride from Baracoa to Imías, along the extremely challenging (and rewarding!) La Farola, is easily one of the most beautiful rides in the country. La Farola is a long, winding series of steep curves through dense mountains, offering breathtaking views of the surrounding hills and valleys. Good signage will alert you to sections with particularly sharp curves. The road is in good condition and drivers are respectful of bikes, but some curves are narrow, so keep your eyes on the road.

A small shoulder exists along most of the route, but it is often interrupted by a drainage dip or the occasional metal grate or gaping hole. These shoulders and drainage areas get muddy and slippery if there has been a lot of rain. Given Baracoa's microclimate, it's very possible you'll encounter rain at some point, albeit light and brief. Downpours can be quite strong during rainy season.

Along the way, you may see wooden pushcarts with flat bottoms and tall handles on one side. Locals use these *chivichanas* to ride down the mountain using a simple foot braking mechanism, then push them back up the hill or put them on a truck heading up. Chivichanas are unique to Baracoa and have proved especially necessary in medical emergencies, when a person has required immediate transportation to a hospital.

The Alto de Cotillo (33.8k) summit has a mirador at the highest point in the region, 650 meters above sea level. There

ONE OF GUANTÁNAMO'S FAMOUS CHIVICHANAS

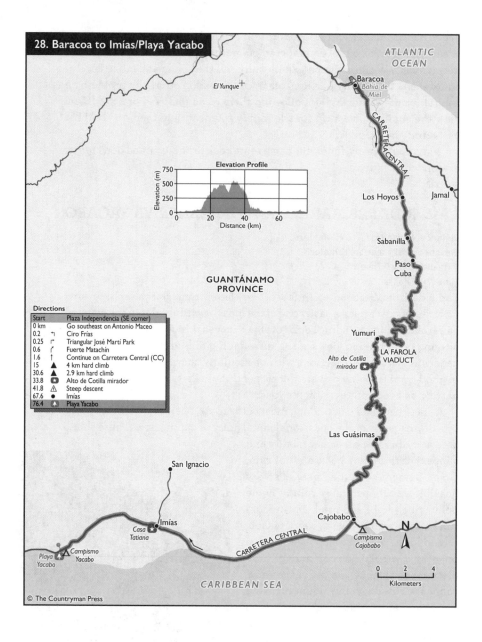

ATLANTIC
OCEAN

El Yunque

Baracoa
Bahía de Miel

CARRETERA CENTRAL

Los Hoyos   Jamal

Sabanilla

Paso
Cuba

Elevation Profile

GUANTÁNAMO
PROVINCE

Yumuri

Alto de Cotilla mirador   LA FAROLA
VIADUCT

Directions

Start		Plaza Independencia (SE corner)
0 km		Go southeast on Antonio Maceo
0.2	↰	Ciro Frías
0.25	↱	Triangular José Martí Park
0.6	↱	Fuerte Matachín
1.6	↑	Continue on Carretera Central (CC)
15	▲	4 km hard climb
30.6	▲	2.9 km hard climb
33.8	✪	Alto de Cotilla mirador
41.8	⚠	Steep descent
67.6	●	Imías
76.4	⬥	Playa Yacabo

Las Guásimas

San Ignacio

Cajobabo

Casa   Imías
Tatiana   Campismo
                                     Cajobabo
Playa   Campismo
Yacabo   Yacabo

CARRETERA CENTRAL

N

0   2   4

Kilometers

CARIBBEAN SEA

© The Countryman Press

are still a few tough climbs ahead, but the ride is mostly downhill from here. There's a small collection of food stalls offering simple sandwiches (bread with cheese), bananas, cucurucho, and juice that may use questionable water. The views of the southern coast begin a few kilometers past the mirador.

Once you leave the mountains, the road is in good condition. If you can't make it all the way to Imías, you can stop at Campismo Cajobabo and rent a basic room. There are additional campismos in Imías and Yacabo. At the time of research, the cabins at Playa Imías (2 kilometers before Imías city center) were still badly damaged by hurricanes, and the rocky beach was littered with garbage and beer bottles. The staff hope that the cabins will be repaired in the future.

A BIKE SHOP IN IMIAS, GUANTANAMO

This ride ends at the Campismo Yacabo, about 5.6 kilometers past Imías and the center point between Baracoa and Guantánamo. It's a very modest campsite, and while the buildings are new and in relatively good condition and the air-conditioning works, there is not always hot water. Cajobabo is newer, better maintained, and in much better condition all around, but the best option is to stay at the casa of Tatiana and Josue. You will be more comfortable, you will not have to listen to reggaeton blasting at 2 a.m., and Josue can help you fix your bike and tell you about his experience cycling across Cuba in 2015.

ACCOMMODATIONS IN IMÍAS/PLAYA YACABO

To make a reservation at either Cajobabo or Yacabo, stop by **Havanatur** (Martí #225) or the Campismo Popular office (Martí #80) in Baracoa, or contact the latter at 2-1642776 or commercial.baracoa@campismopopular.cu.

Casa Tatiana
Calle B #233, Imías
2-1880993, 5-3210861, or 5-3677258
tatiana33@nauta.cu or clubciclofarola@nauta.cu
Tatiana and her husband, Josue, rent one very comfortable room in their home and are in the process of building a second casa particular. The home is one block from the public WiFi hotspot, and the bicycles on the home's sign make it easy to spot. Josue believes he is the first Cuban to cycle across Cuba from Punta Maisí (the easternmost point in Cuba) to María la Gorda in Pinar del Río.

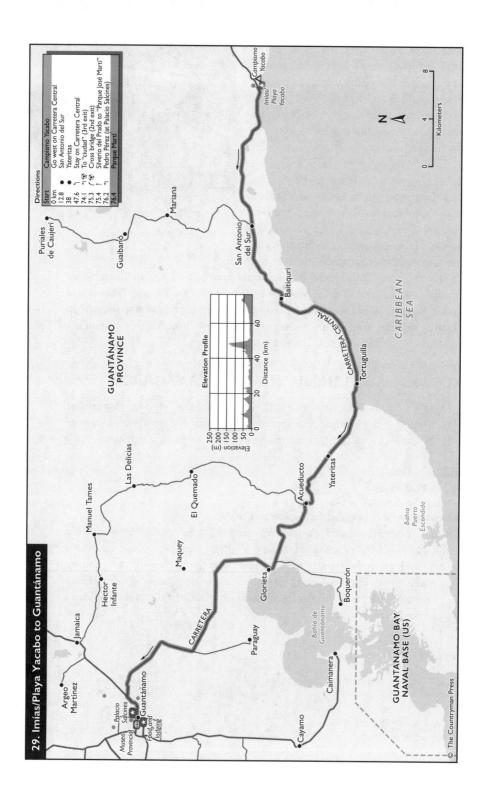

29. Imias/Playa Yacabo to Guantánamo

Directions

Start	
0 km	Campismo Yacabo Go west on Carretera Central
12.8	San Antonio del Sur
38	Yateritas
47.6	Stay on Carretera Central
74.1	To "ciudad" (3rd exit)
75.3	Cross bridge (2nd exit)
75.4	Silverio del Prado to "Parque José Martí"
76.2	Pedro Pérez (at Palacio Salcines)
76.4	Parque Martí

GUANTÁNAMO PROVINCE

CARIBBEAN SEA

GUANTÁNAMO BAY NAVAL BASE (US)

Bahía de Guantánamo

Bahía Puerto Escondido

CARRETERA CENTRAL

CARRETERA

Puriales de Caujeri

Mariana

Guaibanó

San Antonio del Sur

Baitiquri

Tortuguilla

Yateritas

Acueducto

Las Delicias

Manuel Tames

El Quemado

Maquey

Hector Infante

Jamaica

Argeo Martinez

Palacio Salcines

Museo Provincial

Guantánamo

Food and lodging

Paraguay

Glorieta

Boquerón

Caimanera

Cayamo

Imías

Playa Yacabo

Campismo Yacabo

N

0   4   8
Kilometers

Elevation Profile

Elevation (m): 250, 200, 150, 100, 50

Distance (km): 0, 20, 40, 60

© The Countryman Press

🚲 RIDE #29. IMÍAS/PLAYA YACABO TO GUANTÁNAMO

Distance: 47.5 miles/76.4 kilometers
Elevation: 1,690 feet/515 meters
Difficulty: Moderate to Difficult
Time: 5–7 hours

This ride starts from the Yacabo campground, but if you stayed in Cajobabo or Imías, just cycle a few extra miles to Yacabo and begin from there. For those short on time, consider catching a bus from Imías (across from the main park) halfway to Guantánamo, all the way to Guantánamo, or even to Santiago if you're really pressed. The road to Guantánamo is in good condition, and you'll have the sun on your back the entire way. The ride begins with a brief ocean view before creeping inland as the road meanders through hills and small villages. The surroundings turn a bit brown and dry but soon lead to bright green palms lining the road. Eventually the road peeks back out toward the ocean, offering some of the best scenery on the ride, before heading back inland through vast banana plantations.

Snacks are available in San Antonio del Sur (12.6k) and Yateritas (38k), where a particularly well-stocked stand sells high-quality produce, including bananas, papaya, pineapple, tomatoes, and cucumber that could be used to freshen up an egg or cheese sandwich you may have packed in the morning. Around 48k the bay peeks out in the distance. If you were to follow the bay south, you would reach the US Guantanamo Bay naval base. Obviously, this is not an optional day trip. Instead, follow the curve northwest and continue through sugarcane fields and dried-up fruit tree orchards on to Guantánamo City. Ride down Prado, pass the angel on the roof of Palacio Salcines, and arrive at the main park.

Guantánamo

Guantánamo is a small city with several worthwhile attractions that seem to be perpetually closed for repairs. Stop by the **Museo Provincial** (corner of José Martí and Prado), housed in an old jail and guarded by two cannons. The **Biblioteca Policarpo Pineda Rustán** (corner of Los Maceos and Emilio Giro) is a beautiful library that was the site of trials for Fulgencio Batista's thugs in 1959. **Palacio Salcines** (corner of Pedro Pérez and Prado) can be spotted by the Italian sculpture of an angel on top of the palace's turret. Inside is an art museum whose hours are sporadic.

Your best bet for entertainment in Guantánamo is live music at **Casa de la Trova** (corner of Pedro Pérez and Flor Crombet) and **Casa del Son** (corner of Serafin Sánchez and Prado), which attracts a younger crowd. Guantánamo's **Tumba Francesa Pompadour** (Serafin Sánchez #715) is one of Cuba's three remaining Haitian-style dance troupes, but they typically only perform for groups. Swing by to see if any special performances are scheduled during your visit. **Casa de Changüí** (Serafin Sánchez #710) is *the* place to experience

Guantánamo's indigenous music, changüí, and you can learn about music history in its small museum.

Tourist Information

Havanatur (8 a.m.–noon and 1:30–4:30 p.m. Monday–Friday) is on Aguilera between Calixto García and Los Maceos. **Infotur** (8:30 a.m.–5 p.m. Monday–Friday) is on Calixto García between Flor Crombet and Emilio Giro. WiFi is available in Parque Martí, and you can purchase Internet cards at **ETECSA** on the corner of Aguilera and Los Maceos.

The **Banco de Crédito y Comercio** (9 a.m.–3 p.m. Monday–Friday) is on Calixto García between Flor Crombet and Bartolomé Masó, and the **CaDeCa** (8 a.m.–4 p.m.) is on the corner of Calixto García and Martí.

ACCOMMODATIONS IN GUANTÁNAMO

Sr. Manuel Campos
Calixto García #718, between Jesús del Sol and Narciso López
2-1351759 or 5-2900847
mcamposcreme@yahoo.com
Manuel and his wife rent one large, comfortable room (CUC$15–$20) in the family home just a few blocks from the city center. Be sure to dine in the house, as the portions are large and the food is excellent.

Casa Maria Fauniel
Pedro Pérez #664 between Narciso López and Paseo Estudiantes
2-1326197
Maria rents four rooms (CUC$20–$25) of different sizes, so ask for the larger rooms when you arrive. The home has a large dining area, a beautiful patio, and loads of space for bicycles.

Casa Lisset Foster Lara
Pedro A Pérez #761 between Prado and Jesús del Sol
2-1325970
lisset128@gmail.com
lisset-arrendamiento.com
Lisset, who speaks perfect English, rents three rooms in a well-furnished family home that somehow resembles suburban America. Each room (CUC$20–$30) has two double beds, and the roof has a sunny patio. You may need to bring your bike upstairs.

RESTAURANTS IN GUANTÁNAMO

Most restaurants in Guantánamo are dark, blast reggaeton, and serve mediocre food. The best food you'll find is at your casa.

⬦ RIDE #30. GUANTÁNAMO TO SANTIAGO DE CUBA

Distance: 51.3 miles/82.6 kilometers
Elevation: 2,411 feet/735 meters
Difficulty: Difficult
Time: 7–9 hours

This ride begins at Parque Martí and guides you to Ahogados Street (13 de Junio on some maps), which isn't marked but is larger and busier than other streets. *Nacional*, the national highway, is mostly in good condition and wide enough to easily avoid bumps and holes without your having to swerve into (very light) traffic. Several moderate climbs are accompanied by the mountains peeking through the trees lining the roads. Note that while this route takes you along the Autopista and connects to the Carretera Central, you can also take the CC out of the city.

The scenery along the Autopista is nothing to write home about, but as you approach Santiago, a gorgeous backdrop of rolling hills and farmland awaits you, made even more majestic by the looming mountains in the background.

La Maya has several fruit vendors and cafeterias and is your best chance of finding food along the route. Continue on the CC as it curves left out of

CAMILO CIENFUEGOS MURAL IN GUANTÁNAMO

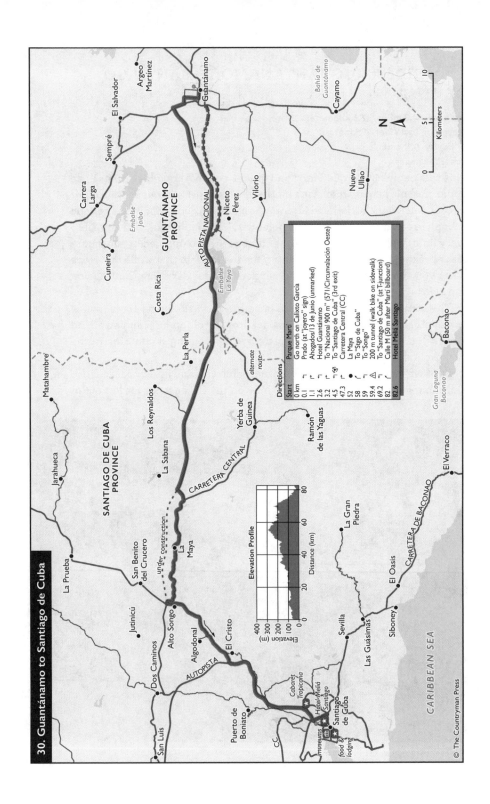

30. Guantánamo to Santiago de Cuba

Directions

Start	Parque Martí
0 km	Go north on Calixto García
0.1	Prado (at "Joyero" sign)
1.1	Ahogados/13 de Junio (unmarked)
2.6	Hotel Guantánamo
3.2	To "Nacional 900 m" (571/Circunvalación Oeste)
4.5	To "Santiago de Cuba" (3rd exit)
47.3	Carretera Central (CC)
52	La Maya
58	To "Sgo de Cuba"
59	To "Songo"
59.4	200 m tunnel (walk bike on sidewalk)
69.2	To "Santiago de Cuba" (at T-junction)
82	Calle M (50 m after Martí billboard)
82.6	Hotel Meliá Santiago

© The Countryman Press

La Maya, past pink and yellow flowers and a colorful mix of clothing hung to dry on clothes lines, cement gates, and corrugated metal roofs.

The ride ends at the Hotel Meliá Santiago de Cuba, formerly known as the Hotel Santiago. Several casas listed are a few blocks from here. If you prefer to stay closer to the city center, instead of turning right on Calle M, keep straight, then take the second exit at the next traffic circle and follow signs on Garzón to Plaza de Marte.

10

SANTIAGO DE CUBA

QUICK LOOK

Santiago de Cuba (usually referred to simply as "Santiago") is the second-largest city on the island and certainly the most Caribbean-influenced. Haitian, Jamaican, and African culture inspire art, dance, and everyday life, and this convergence of cultures comes alive at Santiago's wild summer carnival, said to be the largest in the Caribbean. July is a hot month in Santiago—literally and figuratively—where the streets burst with vibrant festivals but sweltering temperatures make cycling very uncomfortable.

There's no shortage of revolutionary history, culture, or entertainment, and the museums in particular stand out from others across the island. Instead of the usual array of military-themed museums dedicated to specific revolutionary battles and heroes, Santiago's museums explore art, music, dance, carnival, photography, and religion. A few military museums are thrown in for good measure, but they're much larger, detailed, and more well organized than museums in most cities.

Some of the best cycling in Cuba can be had in the mountainous eastern region, *El Oriente*, but hurricane damage and lack of road repairs have made some of the best routes unpleasant and nearly impossible to ride. The most beautiful stretch is the southern route from Santiago de Cuba to Chivirico, Uvero, and Pilón, before heading north to Manzanillo. At the time of research, much of the southern road was so badly battered by hurricanes that the only way to get a bike through many parts was to push it through several kilometers of large gravel (not to mention the gaping potholes). While this route is possible (mountain bikes are ideal), locals and tourists alike report heaps of flat tires, and some cyclists surveyed report that, despite the coastal beauty, it's not worth the time and energy output. As is the case elsewhere in the country, there's been talk of repairs and a new tunnel for many years, so it's worth asking to see if any progress has been made.

La Gran Piedra is another extremely challenging and rewarding route that local competitive cyclists use for training. The road is in disrepair, but those in search of an intense challenge can follow the Playa Siboney route to Las Guásmias, then take a left on the Carretera de la Gran Piedra. At 54 kilometers/1,430 meters of elevation (34 miles/4,700 feet), this trip would need to span across two days, so plan to stay at the Gran Piedra Hotel.

Highlights

- Santiago is a lively city with several not-to-miss **town squares and plazas** (Céspedes, Marte, Dolores), all buzzing with music, food, people, and fun.
- **Cuartel Moncada,** Santiago's famous military barracks, now houses a school and an elaborate museum dedicated to the historical battle that took place there. The museum's grisly and sometimes gruesome photographs detail the torture that captured revolutionaries suffered at the hands of Batista.
- **Museo de Municipial Emilio Bacardí** (corner of Pío Rosado and Aguilera) is a three-story neoclassical art gallery displaying antique weapons, colonial artifacts, and even an Egyptian mummy. It is one of Cuba's oldest museums, created in 1899 by Emilio Bacardí, founder of the Bacardí rum company and Santiago's first mayor.
- **Museo de la Imagen** (Calle 8 #106) is dedicated to camera, film, and photography and displays everything from vintage televisions and CIA espionage cameras to old photographs of Fidel Castro scuba diving.
- **Museo de la Lucha Clandestina** (General Jesús Rabí #1) is devoted to the clandestine struggle against Batista in the 1950s. Take a break from the bloody (and fascinating) displays to admire far-reaching views of the city from the upstairs balcony. The home Fidel Castro lived in while studying in Santiago (1931–33) is across the street but is not open to visitors.
- Live music can be found around every corner in Santiago, and the traditional music is especially good at **La Casa de la Trova** (Heredia #208) and **Casa de las Tradiciones** (General Jesús Rabí #154), which also hosts Sunday afternoon karaoke. For cabaret, head to **the Tropicana** 4 kilometers northeast of the city center, which puts on a show nearly as good as the one in Havana, but for half the price.
- Designed in 1587 and finished in the early 1700s, the **Castillo del Morro** fort is a UNESCO World Heritage Site offering dazzling ocean views.
- **Cementerio Santa Ifigenia** is second only to Havana's Necropolis Cristóbal Colón in importance and grandeur. It is the final

FIDEL CASTRO'S GRAVE AT CEMENTERIO IFIGENIA IN SANTIAGO

resting home of Fidel Castro and José Martí, the latter of whom is buried in an impressive mausoleum. The mausoleum, Fidel's grave, and a round-the-clock changing of the guard ceremony (every 30 minutes) can be viewed for free, while access to the rest of the cemetery requires admission. The best view of the changing of the guard is from Martí's tomb, so get there 10 minutes early or you'll be stuck watching from across the street.

Need-to-Know

- Santiago de Cuba is known for pickpockets and a higher amount of crime in general than other parts of Cuba. Keep an eye on your belongings.
- Motorcycles zipping through the maze of scraggly streets make Santiago's traffic seem worse than Havana's. Narrow and nonexistent sidewalks make walking more dangerous, and pedestrians forced into the street add an additional obstacle for cyclists.
- Some streets have two names (for example, José A Saco is also Enramadas, Av Juan Gualberto Gómez is also Patria), and the two names are not consistent across printed and digital maps.

Terrain

While the city ride is mostly flat, Santiago de Cuba is in the foothills of the Sierra Maestra mountain range, so get ready to climb!

Special Events

- Festival Internacional de Trova: March
- Festival Internacional Boleros de Oro: June
- Dia de la Rebeldía Nacional at Santiago's Moncada Barracks: July 26
- Carnaval de Santiago de Cuba: July
- Fiesta de Nuestra Señora de la Caridad: September
- International Chorus Festival: every other October

Tourist Information

Infotur (Felix Peña #562, 8 a.m.–8 p.m.) has knowledgeable staff and helpful maps. **Cubatur** (Heredia #701, 9 a.m.–noon and 1–4:30 p.m. Monday–Friday, 9 a.m.–noon Saturday) is across from Hotel Casa Granda on Parque Céspedes and is the best place to book Viazul tickets, flights, and hotels. **Ecotur** (9 a.m.–noon and 1–4:30 p.m. Monday–Friday, 9 a.m.–noon Saturday) is next to Cubatur and is the best place to make reservations at campismos. Ecotur would be especially important for anyone biking the Southeastern Circuit (page 201), as the *only* accommodation along one stretch is a campismo.

Internet is available at an increasing number of locations (including Parque Céspedes and Plaza de Marte), so ask your host for the nearest location. WiFi cards are available in some hotel lobbies and at the **ETECSA** in Parque Céspedes (corner of Heredia and Santo Tomás), where the line is typically out the door.

The **Banco de Crédito y Comercio** is at Felix Peña #614, and the **Banco Financiero Internacional** (which has an ATM) is on the corner of Av de las Americas and Calle I. Both are open 9 a.m. to 3 p.m. Monday through Friday. **Bandec** (José A. Saco and Mariano Corona) has an ATM and is open 8 a.m. to 3 p.m. Monday through Friday and 8 to 11 a.m. Saturday. There are **CaDeCas** at Aguilera #508 (8:30 a.m.–11:30 a.m. Saturday).

ACCOMMODATIONS IN SANTIAGO DE CUBA

Santiago is a huge city with casas just about everywhere. Travelers who enjoy exploring the city center on foot should stay downtown in the Centro, whereas those who want a more relaxed vibe may prefer Ampliación de Terrazas.

Casa Colonial 1893
Hechavarría #301, between General Lacret and Hartman (Centro)
2-2622470/5-3596213
casacolonial1893@gmail.com
This well-preserved colonial home has seven rooms (CUC$25–$30 each), a huge indoor patio, and a lovely, small roof terrace.

Casa 3 Ana
Lino Boza #17 between Padre Pico and San Basilio (Centro)
5-3147522 or 2-622192
anamo@nauta.cu
Large groups will appreciate that this home near Parque Céspedes rents six bedrooms (CUC$25–$30 each). Most rooms are on upper floors, but bikes can be stored on the ground floor. All rooms have double beds and AC, and most also have TV.

Casa de Edelio
Heredia #57b, between Padre Pico and Corono (Centro)
2-654928
Edelio and his elderly mother rent one comfortable upstairs room (CUC$20–$25) with two beds that comes with its own spacious patio and terrace. Bikes can be stored downstairs. Edelio's mother is an excellent cook and would be happy to show you her favorite produce markets nearby.

Hotel Rex
Intersection of Victoriano Garzón and Pérez Garbó, in front of Plaza de Marte (Centro)
2-2687032
History buffs can rent a room (CUC$90–$100) in the hotel that once served as a preraid base for revolutionaries in 1953. In fact, the hotel has preserved the room that the tortured and murdered revolutionary hero Abel Santamaría stayed in. Friendly staff are happy to show you to the room, which has been turned into a mini-museum.

Casa Mayda y Milton

Calle 1 #6, between Fourth (N on some maps) and Carretera del Caney (Ampliación de Terrazas)
2-2643441 or 5-2613532
maidamaria@nauta.cu

This charming home can be tough to find but is worth the hunt. It's on a small, dead-end street (that's unnamed on some digital maps and wrongly listed as Calle B on others) between B and C Streets, near the Meliá Santiago hotel. You'll spot it by the swing on the porch. Three rooms (CUC$25–$30 each) and a terrace are available on the second floor, and bikes can be safely stored in the ground-floor garage.

Anet Serret Lara

Calle B #6, between Fourth and M (Ampliación de Terrazas)
2-2644929 or 5-4691256
alara@uo.edu.cu or aserrettlara@gmail.com

Two upper rooms (CUC$25–$30) are available on this quiet street near the Meliá Santiago hotel. Relax in the downstairs patio, store your bikes on the ground floor, and take advantage of the in-home washing machine.

RESTAURANTS IN SANTIAGO DE CUBA

Rumba Café

Hartmann #455
Monday–Saturday 9:30 a.m.–10:30 p.m.
Sandwiches CUC$3–$7

This inviting space helps you escape from the downtown Santiago frenzy by serving up grilled vegetable or meat sandwiches, salads, and omelets in a calm, plant-filled patio. Happy hour is from 5 to 7 p.m.

Bendita Farándula

Monseñor Barnada #513, near Aguilera
Daily noon–11 p.m.
Meals CUC$5–$9

Not to be confused with the upstairs pizzeria of the same name (which also offers decent pizza in a more casual atmosphere), this cozy restaurant with a French bistro feel serves up pork steak, Baracoan coconut fish, and, in keeping with true Cuban fashion, pizza.

Restaurant Beijing

José A Saco (Enramadas) #606 between Barnada and Paraíso
Daily noon–midnight
Meals CUC$4–$7

Tucked behind an above-average pizzeria is Restaurant Beijing, which is more Cuban and international than Chinese but offers good food at a reasonable price. The menu offers the usual selection of pizza, pasta, and fried rice, but the food is of higher quality. You'll also find less common ingredients such as Gouda cheese, olives, octopus, and tuna. Perhaps the most interesting item on the menu is the spaghetti sundae/cocktail, or spaghetti served in an old-fashioned ice cream glass, topped with cheese and a tomato to mimic whipped cream and a cherry.

TOMATOES FOR SALE IN SANTIAGO

St. Pauli
José A Saco #605
Daily noon–11 p.m., until midnight Friday–Sunday
Meals CUC$5–$15

As soon as you step into the restaurant, which resembles a nightclub in the front (stay late and the bar turns into a club), you'll know this place is different. From the glass-walled kitchen to the blackboard menus, St. Pauli could be mistaken for a hip new restaurant in Havana. Try the vegetable lasagna, gazpacho, octopus with garlic, or the pineapple chicken fajitas.

Roy's Terrace Inn Roof Garden Restaurant
Santa Rita (Diego Palacios) #177, near Mariano Corona
2-2652292
roysterraceinn@gmail.com
Daily 7–9:30 p.m., until midnight Friday–Sunday
Meals CUC$10–$15

Come for the food, served on one of six candlelit rooftop tables, and stay for the gorgeous patio, overflowing with fresh flowers. A choice of a meat or vegetarian entrée is served with soup, salad, sautéed veggies, and a fried *vianda* (root vegetable or plantain). While the restaurant only officially serves dinner, breakfast and lunch could be arranged, depending on how busy the restaurant is, accommodating guests from its own three-bedroom casa particular (which is also quite nice).

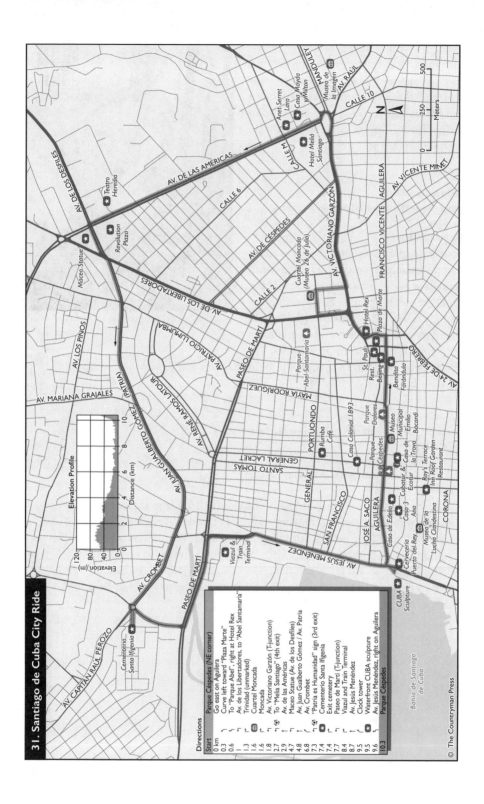

31. Santiago de Cuba City Ride

Elevation Profile

Directions		
Start		Parque Céspedes (NE corner)
0 km	←	Go east on Aguilera
0.3	←	Curve left toward "Plaza Marte"
0.6	←	To "Parque Abel", right at Hotel Rex
1		Av. de Los Libertadores, to "Abel Santamaría"
1.3	←	Trinidad (unmarked)
1.6		Cuartel Moncada
1.6		Moncada
1.8	←	Av. Victoriano Garzón (T-junction)
2.7	←	To "Melia Santiago" (4th exit)
2.9	←	Av. de las Américas
4.7		Maceo Statue (Av. de los Desfiles)
4.8	←	Av. Juan Gualberto Gómez / Av. Patria
6.8	←	Av. Crombet
7.3	←	"Patria es Humanidad" sign (3rd exit)
7.4		Cementerio Santa Ifigenia
7.4	←	Exit cemetery
8.4	←	Paseo de Martí (T-junction)
8.7		Viazul and Train Terminal
9.5	←	Av. Jesús Menéndez
9.5		Clock tower
9.6	←	Waterfront CUBA sculpture
10.3	←	Av. Jesús Menéndez, right on Aguilera
		Parque Céspedes

© The Countryman Press

RIDE #31. SANTIAGO DE CUBA CITY RIDE

Distance: 6.4 miles/10.4 kilometers
Elevation: 365 feet/111 meters
Difficulty: Easy
Time: 1 hour

Though Santiago de Cuba is surrounded by steep and punchy hills, the main attractions of the city can be explored on relatively flat streets. Get an early start to avoid the traffic. The ride starts at Parque Céspedes and takes you past the **Emilio Bacardí Museum, Parque Dolores, Plaza de Marte**, Hotel Rex, and **Parque Abel Santamaría** before reaching **Cuartel Moncada,** all within the first 2 kilometers!

Just before turning left toward Abel Santamaría (1k), look behind you for some nice propaganda billboards of Fidel Castro and his fellow revolutionary, Camilo Cienfuegos. After you turn, notice the statues of generals lining Av de Libertadores (Avenue of Liberators) as you approach Parque Abel Sanatamaría on the left. Across from Abel you will see a large, golden building. Follow this street for two blocks to get to the bullet-ridden walls of the Moncada barracks (also known as Museo 26 de Julio), which is well worth a visit (9 a.m.–2:30 p.m. Sunday–Monday, 9 a.m.–4:30 p.m. Tuesday–Saturday, CUC$2).

As you're enjoying a nice downhill ride down Garzón, you will see the blue and burgundy Meliá Santiago towering over all other buildings. You'll then

I WAS GREETED WARMLY IN SANTIAGO

follow Av de Americas to the **Teatro Heredia,** with the *Aqui no se rinde nadie* ("Nobody surrenders here") wall mural on the right and Antonio Maceo statue on the left inside **Revolution Plaza.** Turn left after the Maceo statue onto Av de Desfiles, which turns into Av Juan Gualberto Gómez (Patria). Once you cross Av de Los Libertadores, follow signs to Centro Histórico and Cementerio. When you arrive at **Cementerio Santa Ifigenia**, leave your bike with the parking attendant, along with a CUC$1 tip.

Toward the end, you'll ride along the malecón to Santiago's bright and welcoming waterfront *CUBA* **sculpture**. On the other side of Avenida Jesús Méndez is Cervecería Puerto del Rey, a huge beer hall that makes for an ending point that's just as nice as Parque Céspedes.

 RIDE #32. PLAYA SIBONEY

Distance: 20.8 miles/33.5 kilometers
Elevation: 1,161 feet/354 meters
Difficulty: Moderate
Time: 3–4 hours

After only a few turns out of Parque Abel Santamaría, you're on the Carretera de Siboney, which takes you all the way to the beach. **Granjita Siboney** (9 a.m.–5 p.m. Tuesday–Sunday, 9 a.m.–1 p.m. Monday; CUC$1) is 2 kilometers before the beach and is worth a stop. The farmhouse turned museum details how troops under Fidel Castro's command left this spot to attack the Moncada barracks in Santiago. The house retains many original details, including a room used by Melba Hernández and Haydée Santamaría, sister of Abel Santamaría.

Playa Siboney is close enough to Santiago to make it a day trip, but the vibe is relaxing enough that you may want to turn it into a two-day trip.

ACCOMMODATIONS IN PLAYA SIBONEY

Reggaeton plays day and night in Siboney, so while some of the rooms listed here may not be the fanciest in town, they're much quieter and offer fantastic views of the sea.

Casa Lucia
Ave Serrano #26A
5-8556695 or 5-2399352
Located a few blocks from the beach, this home (next to the police station) is one of the quietest in Siboney. One bedroom rents for CUC$20–$25, and there's a patio with a view of the water.

Sra. Violeta Babastro Maceo
El Barco #13
2-399256 or 5-5328212
The room (CUC$15–$20) is nothing to brag about and bikes will need to be

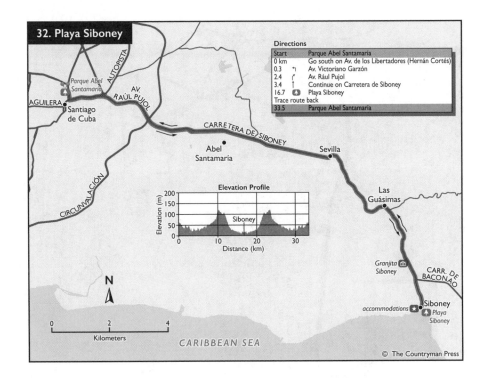

32. Playa Siboney

Directions

Start		Parque Abel Santamaría
0 km		Go south on Av. de los Libertadores (Hernán Cortés)
0.3	⌐	Av. Victoriano Garzón
2.4	⌐	Av. Rául Pujol
3.4	↑	Continue on Carretera de Siboney
16.7	🅰	Playa Siboney
Trace route back		
33.5		Parque Abel Santamaría

brought up to the third floor (the family will help with this), but the ocean and city view from the large, gorgeous terrace is enough reason to spend a couple days in Siboney.

Vilma Pellicier García
El Barco #15B (upstairs)
2-2399535 or 5-2468214
Two basic rooms (CUC$15–$20) rent on upper floors, and bikes can be stored safely on the first floor. Nice view of the water.

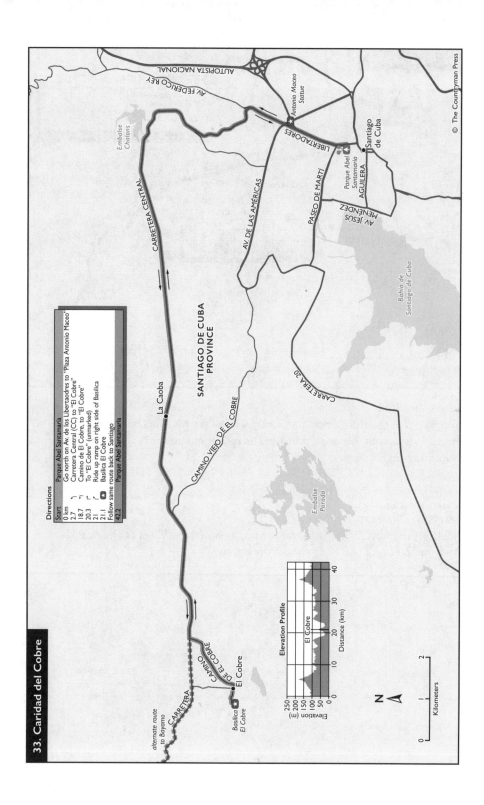

33. Caridad del Cobre

Directions

	Parque Abel Santamaría
Start	
0 km	Go north on Av. de los Libertaodres to "Plaza Antonio Maceo"
2.7	Carretera Central (CC) to "El Cobre"
18.7	Camino de El Cobre, to "El Cobre"
20.3	To "El Cobre" (unmarked)
2.1	Ride up ramp on right side of Basilica
21.1	Basilica El Cobre
	Follow same route back to Santiago
42.2	Parque Abel Santamaría

Elevation Profile

El Cobre

Elevation (m) — 250 / 200 / 150 / 100 / 50 / 0

Distance (km) — 0 / 10 / 20 / 30 / 40

N

Kilometers — 0 / 1 / 2

© The Countryman Press

AUTOPISTA NACIONAL

AV. FEDERICO REY

Antonio Maceo Statue

LIBERTADORES

Santiago de Cuba

Embalse Cholons

CARRETERA CENTRAL

Parque Abel Santamaría

AGUILERA

AV. JESÚS MENÉNDEZ

PASEO DE MARTÍ

AV. DE LAS AMÉRICAS

SANTIAGO DE CUBA PROVINCE

La Caoba

CAMINO VIEJO DE EL COBRE

Bahía de Santiago de Cuba

CARRETERA 20

Embalse Parada

CAMINO DE EL COBRE

El Cobre

Basílica El Cobre

CARRETERA DE EL COBRE

alternate route to Bayamo

RIDE #33. CARIDAD DEL COBRE

Distance: 26 miles/42.2 kilometers
Elevation: 1,701 feet/518 meters
Difficulty: Moderate to Difficult
Time: 3–4 hours

This ride begins at Parque Abel Santamaría. You'll head north on Liberta-dores, pass the Antonio Maceo statue (1.6k), and continue straight over a bridge, then merge onto the Carretera Central. The road is a bit bumpy, but there isn't much traffic to compete with. When you turn onto Camino de El Cobre, you'll pass vendors selling flowers that worshippers buy as offerings. The magnificent sanctuary will soon come into view, with gorgeous moun-tains behind it. Leave your bicycle with the parking attendant behind the church, along with CUC$1 as a tip.

The basilica is open seven days a week from 6 a.m. to 6 p.m. and has daily Mass at 8 a.m. Behind the church is a hotel with a bathroom (one peso nacional, about 5 cents). As usual, bring TP and hand sanitizer. I don't rec-ommend the hotel in terms of quality or practicality, but if interested, rooms can be rented for CUP$30 per night, less than CUC$2. Higher tourist prices are often introduced as demand increases.

"El Cobre" is short for *Basílica Santuario Nacional de Nuestra Señora de la Caridad del Cobre* (National Shrine Basilica of Our Lady of Charity). This is Cuba's most sacred pilgrimage site and the shrine to Cuba's patron virgin deity. One would normally expect silence and tranquility at such a sacred site, but reggaeton music blasting from the nearby homes finds its way into the church.

If this ride is being done as a day trip, just follow the same route back to Santiago. Cyclists getting an early start from Santiago could catch Mass on their way to Bayamo. If you wish to continue to Bayamo, head back to the Carretera Central and take a left. The CC is a straight shot to Palma Soriano (a good place to stop for lunch), and on to Contramaestre, then Bayamo. See the Santiago to Bayamo ride for details. The ride would be quite long (130k) and hot, but hearty cyclists have done it in one day. To break it up, Palma Soriano is your best bet for finding accommodations.

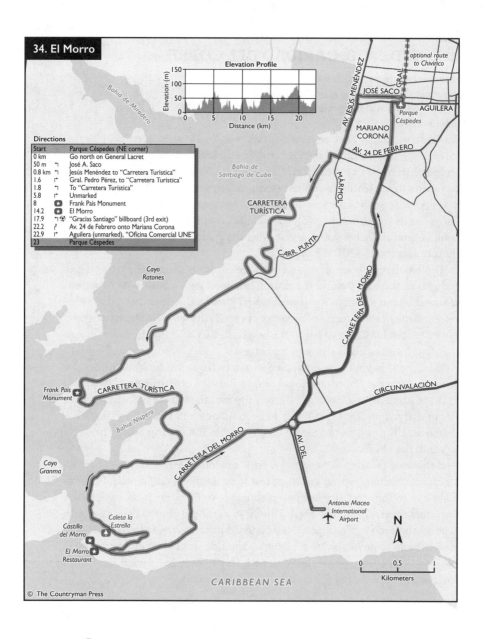

34. El Morro

Elevation Profile

Directions

Start		Parque Céspedes (NE corner)
0 km		Go north on General Lacret
50 m	⌐	José A. Saco
0.8 km	⌐	Jesús Menéndez to "Carretera Turística"
1.6	⌐	Gral. Pedro Pérez, to "Carretera Turística"
1.8	⌐	To "Carretera Turística"
5.8	⌐	Unmarked
8	★	Frank País Monument
14.2	★	El Morro
17.9	⌐	"Gracias Santiago" billboard (3rd exit)
22.2	⌐	Av. 24 de Febrero onto Mariana Corona
22.9	⌐	Aguilera (unmarked), "Oficina Comercial UNE"
23		Parque Céspedes

🚲 RIDE #34. EL MORRO

Distance: 14.3 miles/23 kilometers
Elevation: 1,773 feet/540 meters
Difficulty: Moderate
Time: 2 hours

This ride is short and hilly, beginning in Parque Céspedes, one of the city's three primary gathering grounds. Note that riding on José A. Saco (known as "Saco") during the early morning shouldn't be a problem, but later in the day, when it becomes a busy pedestrian path, you will be asked to dismount (and may be fined). The ride directions will have you continue straight on Jesús Méndez for simplicity, but feel free to curve right at the clock to ride closer to the water and back to Jesús Méndez when the smaller side street runs out.

The ride will take you along the oddly named *Carretera Turistica* (Tourist Highway), which meanders through miles of wasteland and past cement and animal feed factories. The Frank País monument (8k) isn't visible from the highway but can be reached by locking your bike and climbing up a long staircase. Frank País was a 22-year-old teacher who led a 1956 attack on the Santiago police headquarters to divert attention away from the *Granma* ship landing, bringing Fidel and his troops from Mexico. The attack failed because the *Granma* arrived several days late, but the murder of Frank País in the streets two months later sparked large protests and strikes that soon spread across the country.

Caleta la Estrella (12.8k) is a small beach where you'll likely see families swimming, though locals have reported leaving the water with black oil streaks on their legs as a result of the nearby petrol ships. Once you make it to El Morro, leave your bike with the parking attendant, along with CUC$1 for a tip. Forget to pack a lunch? Stop by El Morro, where the food was good enough for Sir Paul McCartney (his plate is framed on the wall) and the views are superb. After exploring the fort, you can either ride back the way you came or complete the circle by following the directions below.

THE SOUTHEASTERN CIRCUIT

The southern coastal road in Santiago de Cuba and Granma is one of the most beautiful in all of Cuba, but hurricane damage and the lack of road repairs (gaping potholes, kilometers upon kilometers of gravel, uneven roads, and cracked bridges) have made much of it unpleasant and nearly impossible to ride over. As a result, rides in this region are not included in this book. There's been talk of repairs for years, so ask around to see if progress has been made. Colectivo cars and crowded trucks shuffle passengers between Pilón and Uvero/Chivirico, and between Chivirico and Santiago several times per week. The schedule is unreliable and there is no guarantee your bike will fit, but it's an option should you begin a journey you'd prefer to end on four wheels.

Those interested in braving the rough roads could divide the ride into five days:

- Day 1: Santiago de Cuba to Chivirico (good road conditions); 74 kilometers/416 meters of elevation (46 miles/1,365 feet)

- Day 2: Chivirico to La Mula (bad road conditions); 40.2 kilometers/304 meters of elevation (25 miles/998 feet)
- Day 3: La Mula to Villa Punta de Piedra (bad road conditions); 61.6 kilometers/540 meters of elevation (38 miles/1,772 feet)
  - Villa Punta Piedra has a basic hotel and is the halfway point between casas in Marea del Portillo (which are nicer) and Pilón (which put you closer to Manzanillo).
- Day 4: Villa Punta Piedra to Manzanillo (decent road conditions); 96.6 kilometers/630 meters of elevation (60 miles/2,067 feet)
- Day 5: Manzanillo to Bayamo (good road conditions); 69.2 kilometers/349 meters of elevation (43 miles/1,144 feet)

Casas particulares operate in Chivirico, Marea del Portillo, Pilón, and Manzanillo. Each city has several, so you should have no trouble finding accommodations. Tabacal (just before Chivirico) also has a small hotel, Motel Guamá, with stunning ocean views and terrible service (rooms are CUC$15 but only one has AC; 2-2326124).

Between Chivirico and Marea del Portillo, there are no casas. The only accommodation is Campismo La Mula, with no frills (and no air-conditioning) but acceptable rooms. Large, semipermanent tents can be rented at the campsite (though the rooms would be more comfortable), but camping with personal tents is prohibited. The campismo may fill up on weekends during peak season and holidays, so make a reservation by calling 2-2326262 or in person at the Ecotur office in Santiago. A bus departs from the campsite Fridays at 5 a.m. to the base of Pico Turquino. The intense hike takes about 10 hours to complete, so don't plan to ride the next day.

THE ROUGH ROAD ALONG CUBA'S SOUTHEASTERN COAST

11

GRANMA

QUICK LOOK

Granma province retains a relatively low profile among travelers but is steeped in revolutionary history and natural beauty. Named after the boat that brought Fidel Castro and his fellow revolutionaries ashore to kick-start the war in 1956, Granma is a rural province with a fierce revolutionary spirit.

Trekking enthusiasts enjoy hiking to Pico Turquino, Cuba's highest peak, through mountains so dense that they hid fugitive Fidel Castro while he was on the run for two years in the late 1950s. Sun worshippers head to secluded hotels along the southern beachfront, where many never leave the grounds.

Bayamo and Manzanillo, the only two cities with populations above 100,000, receive the bulk of the tourism. The main attraction near the capital city, Bayamo, is the Comandancia de la Plata, the remote Sierra Maestra headquarters camp of Fidel Castro and his rebels. Visitors to the former HQ will find a small museum; the Radio Rebelde building where rebels aired their broadcasts; and *Casa de Fidel* (Fidel's House), including concealed escape routes, should the Revolution's leaders have been discovered.

Highlights

- **Fiesta de la Cubanía** is a weekly Saturday night street party when museums stay open late, streets close down, children on bicycles take over the town square, restaurants move their operations outside, and live bands perform in the streets. The main party is held along **Paseo Bayamés**, a pedestrian-only shopping "boulevard."
- **Casa Natal de Carlos Manuel de Céspedes** (Maceo #57; 9 a.m.–5 p.m. Tuesday–Friday, 10 a.m.–1 p.m. Saturday–Sunday) is the birth home (now museum) of the plantation owner turned revolutionary hero who freed his slaves and launched the 10-year Cuban War of Independence against Spain in 1868.
- If you've had your fill of Revolution-themed museums, head to the **Museo de Cera** (General García #261; 9 a.m.–5 p.m. Tuesday–Friday, 10 a.m.–1 p.m. Saturday–Sunday), to see Cuban heroes and international celebrities memorialized as wax statues.
- The **Fábrica de Coches** (Prolongación General García #530; 8 a.m.–3 p.m. Monday–Friday; CUC$1 donation) is Cuba's only horse carriage factory.

You'll see wooden horse carriages in various stages of assembly and repair, as well as miniature souvenir carriages being assembled and painted in a side room.

- **Plaza de la Patria** is the large square where Fidel Castro gave his final public speech in 2006 before becoming ill and stepping down as president. The plaza features a colorful new *CUBA VA* sculpture (similar to Santiago's waterfront *CUBA* sculpture) and a monument to Cuban heroes. It is the only monument in Cuba that features Fidel. Some maps refer to this as Plaza de la Revolución, but Bayamo's Plaza de la Revolución (also known as Parque Céspedes) is less of a plaza and more of a town square/park.

- Unlike climbing **Pico Turquino**, the **Comandancia de la Plata** is an exciting day trip that won't leave you too exhausted to bike the next day. Tours can be arranged in Bayamo, or just hire a taxi to take you there for a self-guided tour.

Need-to-Know

- Museums, nightclubs, churches, and other attractions tend to be closed without explanation more frequently in Bayamo than in other cities. Locals may tell you that the place *should* be open, but it's often impossible to ascertain why it's closed and when/if the regular schedule will resume. In some cases, a nightclub may close early or not open to begin with, if it's believed to be a slow night (for instance, if a large tourist group staying at a nearby hotel decides not to visit).

- Bayamo's grid of one-way streets, T-junctions, pedestrian-only boulevards, and bike-prohibited carreteras turns otherwise simple rides into more complex routes.

Terrain

Granma is Cuba's most mountainous province, so riders will face hills sooner or later. Those sticking to the Santiago–Bayamo–Holguín circuit will avoid the steepest hills.

Special Events

Incendio de Bayamo, which remembers the city's 1869 burning with live music, theatrical performances, and fireworks: January 12

Tourist Information

Cubanacán is located next to the Casa Natal de Carlos Manuel Céspedes, and **Ecotur** is inside the Hotel Sierra Maestra. Both organize hikes to Pico Turquino and elsewhere. **Infotur** (across from the Plaza del Himno Nacional) sells the same packages as the other two and also provides maps and good general travel information. Granma Travel has a Facebook page (in Spanish) promoting upcoming events in the province: www.facebook.com/GranmaTravel.

Parque Céspedes (Plaza de la Revolución) and the small park in front of Casa de la Trova have WiFi, and you can purchase Internet cards at the **ETECSA** office on General García, between Saco and Figueredo (8:30 a.m.–7 p.m.).

The **Banco de Crédito y Comercio** (8 a.m.–3 p.m. Monday–Friday, 8 a.m.–11 a.m. Saturday) has an ATM and is at the corner of General García and Saco. The **CaDeCa** (8:30 a.m.–4 p.m. Monday–Saturday) is at Saco #101.

ACCOMMODATIONS IN BAYAMO

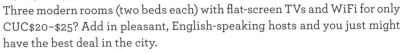

CHILDREN ON BIKES TAKE OVER THE PARQUE CESPEDES ON SUNDAYS

Villa La Paz

Coronel J. Estrada #32, between William Soler and Av Milanés
2-3423949 or 5-2773459
anyoleg2005@yahoo.es

Three modern rooms (two beds each) with flat-screen TVs and WiFi for only CUC$20–$25? Add in pleasant, English-speaking hosts and you just might have the best deal in the city.

Casa de la Amistad

Pío Rosado #60, between Ramírez and Narciso López
2-3425769
gabytellez2003@gmail.com

Two spacious, upper-floor apartments (CUC$25–$30 each) include their own kitchens, sitting area, bedroom, bathroom, and private entrance. The apartments have WiFi access, and bikes can be stored on the ground floor.

Casa Olga Korea

Padre Batista #73, between Eligia Estrada and Plaza del Himno
5-8259628

One room (CUC$25–$30) is available upstairs with a private bathroom and terrace. Bikes can be left downstairs on the patio.

RESTAURANTS IN BAYAMO

Restaurante San Salvador de Bayamo

Maceo #107
2-3426942
Daily noon–11 p.m.
Mains CUC$3–$9

Expect excellent service and great meals at this classic colonial restaurant. Meals are served on white linen tablecloths decorated with fresh flowers, but the mood remains unpretentious. Try the tortilla with cassava, which resembles a burrito, except the tortilla is made from cassava (yucca). The drink selection ranges from fresh grapefruit juice and guarapo to wine, cocktails, beer, and *pru* (a fermented, medicinal soft drink).

Meson La Cuchipapa

Parada between Marmol and Martí
5-2398905
lacuchipapa@gmail.com
Daily 11 a.m.–midnight
Mains CUC$6–$10

Grab a seat at one of the wooden picnic tables to sample traditional foods that hark back to when the Taíno roamed the island. The cassava bread stands out (and goes well with vegetable and bean soups), but for something really unique, try the *frutanga*, an intense, sugarcane-sweetened cocktail.

Restaurante Plaza

Maceo #53, inside the Royalton Hotel
2-3422246
Daily 7 a.m.–10 a.m., noon–5 p.m., 7 p.m.–10 p.m.

The restaurant in Bayamo's finest hotel offers standard Cuban fare that is just that, standard, but where the excellent service and ambiance make it worth a visit. Live guitars serenade diners, the luckiest of whom have snagged outdoor tables overlooking the town square. The restaurant fills up quickly when a tour group is in town, so be sure to make a reservation.

Restaurante Vegetariano

General García #173, corner of General Lora
Daily noon–2:30 p.m. and 6–9:30 p.m.
Meals CUC$1–$2

Don't let the locked front door and blacked-out windows fool you; this state-run restaurant is surely open for business. Simply knock on the front door and

HORSE CARRIAGES AND HORSE CARRIAGE ART IN BAYAMO

wait for unhurried (and sometimes unpleasant) staff to let you in. Don't be fooled by the restaurant name, either. Meat dishes are served, but this restaurant emphasizes plant-based sides and is the best place to find vegetable soups, pastas, and interesting salads using less common (in Cuba, at least) vegetables such as beets and okra. Prices are in moneda nacional and are astoundingly cheap, about 30 to 50 cents per small plate.

RIDE #35. SANTIAGO DE CUBA TO BAYAMO

Distance: 80 miles/128.9 kilometers
Elevation: 3,961 feet/1,207 meters
Difficulty: Very Difficult
Time: 8–10 hours

The ride from Santiago de Cuba is one of the longest and most challenging in the book in terms of distance and elevation. At the time of research, no casas particulares existed near the midway point of the ride, though riders preferring to break up the trip could likely find accommodations with a local in Palma Soriano or Contramaestre.

This ride begins at the familiar Abel Santamaría plaza. Once you loop under the bridge (3k), you're on the Autopista Nacional (Autopista A1 on some maps), which merges with the Carretera Central (CC) and takes you all the way to Bayamo. Remember that an alternate route to Bayamo can pass by the Cobre Basilica (page 199). The Autopista is busier than the Cobre route, but it is very wide, so there is more room to escape the fumes of big trucks. It's also a more direct route and will save time for those hoping to make the entire trip in a single day. The road is in good condition, and what small potholes exist are easily avoidable.

The landscape is green, with the occasional cornfield and banana plantation. Stunning views of valleys and mountains peek through here and there but are usually hidden by trees and small hills close to the road. Goats graze along the freeway and locals cycle between villages, carrying food in buckets.

Contramaestre is a medium-sized town with lots of food options, including food stalls, proper restaurants, and several very well stocked 24-hour fruit stands servicing locals and overnight bus and truck drivers. There's also WiFi in the main park. The casa particular and hotel in town only accommodate Cubans, but if you are too tired to continue, merely ask around and someone can likely help you find a solution. In general, it's not a good idea to stay in unlicensed casas, but it is sometimes the only option in small towns. As of this writing, no casa particular exists for tourists, but one may appear in the near future, making it a great spot to break the long trip into two parts.

Once you arrive at the Viazul bus station in Bayamo, you'll be forced to take a less direct route on side streets because bicycles are not allowed on that stretch of the CC. You'll ride parallel to the highway for 0.5k, then cross the CC as it curves right and you continue straight. Bayamo's messy street grid and one-way streets force you to zigzag your way to Parque Céspedes, also known as Plaza de la Revolución.

AT BAYAMO'S CUBA SCULPTURE IN PLAZA DE PATRIA

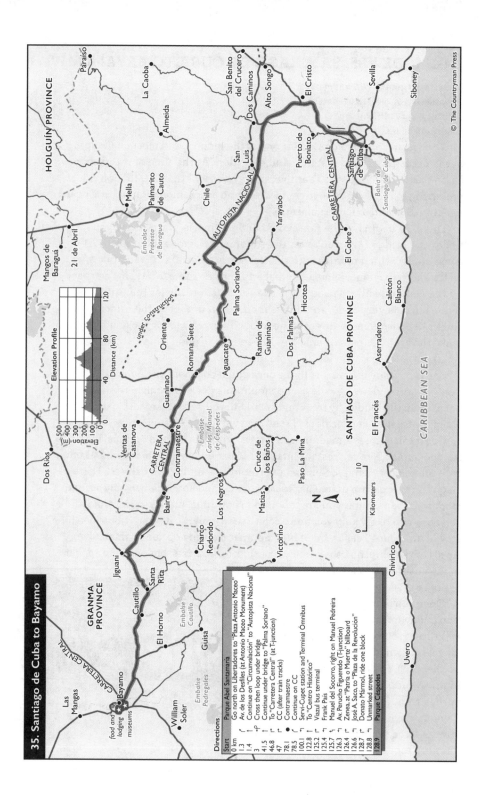

35. Santiago de Cuba to Bayamo

HOLGUÍN PROVINCE

Paraíso
La Caoba
San Benito del Crucero
Alto Songo
El Cristo
Sevilla
Siboney
Almeida
Dos Caminos
Mella
Palmarito de Cauto
Chile
San Luis
Puerto de Boniato
Santiago de Cuba
21 de Abril
Yarayabo
Mangos de Baraguá

Embalse Protesta de Baragua

AUTOPISTA NACIONAL
CARRETERA CENTRAL
El Cobre
Bahía de Santiago de Cuba

under construction

Ventas de Casanova
Dos Ríos
Guaninao
CARRETERA CENTRAL
Contramaestre
Embalse Carlos Manuel de Céspedes
Oriente
Romana Siete
Aguacate
Palma Soriano
Ramón de Guaninao
Dos Palmas
Hicotea
Caletón Blanco

SANTIAGO DE CUBA PROVINCE

Baire
Los Negros
Matías
Cruce de los Baños
Paso La Mina
Aserradero
El Francés

Charco Redondo
Victorino
Chivirico
Uvero

Jiguaní
Santa Rita
El Horno
Embalse Cautillo
Guisa

GRANMA PROVINCE

Las Mangas
Cautillo
Bayamo
Embalse Pedregales
William Soler

CARRETERA CENTRAL

food and lodging
museums

CARIBBEAN SEA

Elevation Profile

Elevation (m): 500 400 300 200 100 0
Distance (km): 0 40 80 120

N

Kilometers
0 5 10

© The Countryman Press

Directions

Start	Parque Abel Santamaría
0 km	Go north on Libertadores to "Plaza Antonio Maceo"
1.3	Av. de los Desfiles (at Antonio Maceo Monument)
1.4	Continue on "Circunvalación" to "Autopista Nacional"
3	Cross then loop under bridge
41.5	Continue under bridge to "Palma Soriano"
46.8	To "Carretera Central" (at T-junction)
47	CC (after train tracks)
78.1	Contramaestre
78.5	Continue on CC
100.1	Servi-Cupet station and Terminal Ómnibus
122.8	To "Centro Histórico"
125.2	Víazul bus terminal
125.4	Frank País
125.7	Manuel del Socorro, right on Manuel Pedreira
126.3	Av. Perucho Figueredo (T-junction)
126.4	Zenea, at "Patria a Muerte" billboard
126.6	José A. Saco, to "Plaza de la Revolución"
128.7	Donato Mármol, ride one block
128.8	Unmarked street
128.9	Parque Céspedes

RIDE #36. BAYAMO TO HOLGUÍN

Distance: 45.5 miles/73.2 kilometers
Elevation: 1,784 feet/544 meters
Difficulty: Moderate to Difficult
Time: 5–7 hours

This ride begins in Parque Céspedes, near the digital clock. You'll encounter quite a bit of traffic leaving the city, then enjoy a flat ride along the tree-lined

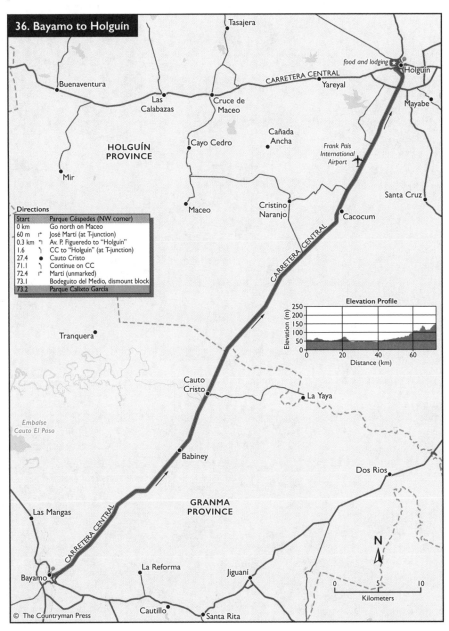

36. Bayamo to Holguín

Directions		
Start		Parque Céspedes (NW corner)
0 km		Go north on Maceo
60 m	⌐	José Martí (at T-junction)
0.3 km	⌐	Av. P. Figueredo to "Holguín"
1.6	⌐	CC to "Holguín" (at T-junction)
27.4	●	Cauto Cristo
71.1	⌐	Continue on CC
72.4	⌐	Marti (unmarked)
73.1		Bodeguito del Medio, dismount block
73.2		Parque Calixto García

Elevation Profile

Carretera Central through wide-open fields of corn, bananas, sugarcane, and grass. The incline doesn't come until the last 15 kilometers of the ride. The small town of Cauto Cristo (27.4) has a couple small snack shops, if you're hungry. This ride is a fairly straight shot with minimal turns. Note that you should walk your bike the final block of the ride, as Martí turns into a pedestrian-only boulevard just before Parque Calixto García.

Spanish Glossary for Cyclists

Can I put my bike on the bus/train/boat?
¿Puedo poner mi bicicleta en la guagua/el tren/la lancha?

I want to go to . . .
Quiero ir a . . .

How much is fare to . . .?
¿Cuánto cuesta hasta . . .?

How far is Baracoa?
¿A cuántos kilómetros queda Baracoa?

Turn left/right.
Doble a la izquierda/derecha.

Keep going straight.
Sigue derecho (or recto).

It is nearby/far.
Está cerca/lejos.

I'm looking for . . .
Estoy buscando . . .

North/south/east/west
Norte/sur/este/oeste

Wheel	*rueda*
Chain	*cadena*
Chainring	*plato*
Pedal	*pedal*
Brakes	*frenos*
Valve	*valvula*
Fork	*tenedor*
Cable	*cable*
Saddle	*asiento*
Tire	*goma*
Tube	*camara*
Handlebars	*manubrio*
Helmet	*casco*
Pump	*bomba*
Screwdriver	*destornillador*
Wrench	*llave*

Organized Cuba Bicycle Tours

Backroads
www.backroads.com
The Mercedes-Benz of bicycle tours

Bicycle Breeze
bicyclebreeze.net
Nine- to 18-day tours across Cuba, including mountain bike tours (stop by their bike-themed coffee shop in Havana at Línea 61, between M and N)

CicloCuba
www.ciclocuba.com
Bicycle and touring equipment rental and support for independent bike tour planning

Cubania
cubaniatravel.com
Cycling and "active travel" trips across Cuba with salsa, LGBT+, and other themes

EscapingNY
www.escapingny.com
Independent tour planning and bike-themed group trips that also include hiking, snorkeling, and walking tours

Experience Plus
www.experienceplus.com
Guided tours in central and western Cuba

Saddle Skedaddle
www.skedaddle.com/uk
Eight- to 15-day supported bike tours across Cuba

Wilderness Voyageurs
wilderness-voyageurs.com
Bike tours of western Cuba

Wow Cuba Bicycle Tours
www.wowcuba.com/cuba-bicycle-tours
Seven- and 14-day tours across Cuba

Index

About the Author

Cassandra grew up in the Midwest and moved to New York City in 2005, where she worked on food justice and community development issues before transitioning to travel writing. She fell in love with Cuba in 2013, when she began a series of multimonth hitchhiking, cycling, camping, scuba diving, and off-the-beaten-path solo adventures that would take her to every province on the island. Friends and family urged her to begin leading group trips to Cuba, and she soon launched EscapingNY. Cassandra now leads cycling and noncycling group trips to Cuba, Mexico, Peru, Israel, and Jordan, and helps individuals and groups from across the world plan their own travels. When she's not leading group tours abroad, you can find her in New York City, where she leads food and graffiti bike tours. If you'd like her to help review or create your itinerary and route, you can reach her through her website: www.escapingny.com.

Cassandra would like to thank every kind and generous Cuban person who contributed to this book; every driver who stopped to ask if she needed help when she looked confused on the side of the road; every farmer who let her hitch a ride on his tractor or trailer; every cyclist who let her borrow or buy precious, hard-to-find-in-Cuba basic bike tools and parts; and every adventurous soul who joined her first few group trips to Cuba, as it was those cycling day trips that inspired this book.